CAMP OUT!

THE ULTIMATE
Kids' Guide

From the Backyard to the Backwoods

Lynn Brunelle

Illustrations by Brian Biggs

Technical illustrations by Elara Tanguy

WORKMAN PUBLISHING · NEW YORK

Library of Congress Cataloging-in-Publication Data is available.

ISBN-13: 978-0-7611-4122-8

Cover design by Janet Parker
Cover illustration by Brian Biggs

Book design by Janet Parker and Kate Tomkinson

Photo Credits: page 145: (top left and center image) National Oceanic and Atmospheric Administration/Department of Commerce; page 148: (top) National Oceanic Atmospheric Administration/Department of Commerce; page 150: (top) National Oceanic Atmospheric Administration/Department of Commerce; page 260: Larry Ulrich/Larry Ulrich Stock; pages 272–273: Kristy Ramsammy; pages 335–357: Mark Elbroch; pages v, 162, 185, 188, 191, 192: Science Photo Library.

Workman books are available at special discounts when purchased in bulk for premiums and sales promotions as well as for fund-raising or educational use. Special editions or book excerpts can also be created to specification. For details, contact the Special Sales Director at the address below.

Workman Publishing Company
225 Varick Street
New York, NY 10014-4381

Printed in the United States of America

First printing May 2007
10 9 8 7 6 5 4 3 2 1

Dedication

For my wonderful dad, Jim Brunelle, who inspires me every day to see the wonder, joy, and delight in all things. And who also read every page of every version of this book and helped make it sing.

Acknowledgments

Because no one does a book like this alone, I would love to thank the following folks: First I thank my adorable husband, Keith, and my marvelous boys, Kai and Leo, who are my intrepid and joyful camping buddies these days. They are my tried-and-true in-the-field testers and my everyday cheerleaders. They make each day an adventure.

And thanks to Bill and Maura—my first tent sharers. I will never forget the countless games of freeze tag; the firefly hunts, burnt marshmallows, and atonal versions of old favorite songs; and the gripping ghost stories that filled my parents', aunts and uncles', and grandmother's backyards.

Thanks to Kate Renee, Pepper, and Jenna for their boundless energy.

Thanks to Meg, who knows the lyrics to *any* song ever sung!

Thanks to Robin, Randy, Alex, and Amanda for their creativity and enthusiasm in testing out my ideas in the wild.

Thanks to Kathleen Cullinan of the Girl Scouts of America and to Vanessa Farley for their invaluable camping expertise and advice. And thanks to J. B. Goessman for having stars in his eyes and checking my astronomy facts.

This book would still be a pile of ideas if not for my dedicated and talented editor, Kylie Foxx, and the hard-working and capable Randall Lotowycz and Eva Steele-Saccio, who put so much time and effort into crafting this book. Thanks to Brian Biggs and Elara Tanguy for their fabulous, fun, and informative illustrations. And thanks to Janet Parker, who, with help from Kate Tomkinson and Beverly McClain, breathed life into every page. Thank you, last but not least, Peter Workman.

Contents

CHAPTER 1

Gearing Up

CHAPTER 2

Home Away from Home

CHAPTER 3

Good Grub

CHAPTER 4

Camping Skills

CHAPTER 5

Something's in the Air

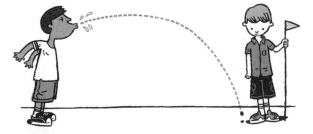

Introduction

"All who wander are not lost."
—WILLIAM SHAKESPEARE

Go on, get out! This book is your guide to everything camping, your companion in great adventures. I'll teach you the basics of preparing for a trip, packing, and setting up camp. You'll find tons of yummy recipes, fascinating projects, activities, and experiments, and really cool crafts to make and do while you're in the wilderness—or even in your own backyard. You'll learn essential camping skills like knot tying, compass reading, navigation, and weather forecasting. And you'll enjoy stargazing, stories, and songs around the campfire. Whether you're in the car, on the trail, or around the campfire, this book's got you covered. And there are awesome activities to teach you some interesting stuff about the natural world you'll encounter on your outdoor explorations.

There are a few different kinds of camping, and they're all lots of fun in their own way. Hopefully you'll have a chance to explore them all.

Your first camping trip might be heading in a car to a site in the woods, or it might be heading straight out the door and into your backyard! If you're going car camping, you and your grown-ups can pile a bunch of stuff in the backseat or the trunk, drive to a campsite, and set it all up like a home away from home. Car camping is cool because you can bring more with you. Obviously you won't be bringing your favorite recliner and a TV, but you *can* bring things like bikes, folding chairs, toys and games, and a cooler full of yummy food.

Backwoods camping is pretty much the

opposite of car camping—when you're camping somewhere that you have to get to on foot (or on bike or by boat), you can only bring the absolute, can't-live-without-it essentials. This includes a tent, sleeping bag, cooking gear, food that doesn't need to be refrigerated, and the least amount of clothing that'll keep you warm and dry. When you camp in the backwoods, you're really "roughing it"—it's a fantastic challenge and an amazing adventure.

No matter what kind of camping you do, it's all about connecting with nature. It's about opening your eyes, using your imagination, and discovering adventure all around. It's about practicing new skills, spending time with friends and family, seeing new things, having fun, and just being amazed by how lucky we are to find ourselves in the great outdoors, whether far from home or right beside it. So go on, get out!

—Lynn Brunelle

GEARING UP

How to Plan and What to Pack

> *"Be prepared..."*

ROBERT BADEN-POWELL,
Father of the Scouting Organizations

There are lots of different ways to camp. You can sleep out in Grandma's backyard, drive to a forest campground and spread out under the stars, or be like Daniel Boone in the backwoods. There are also all kinds of places to explore—from the desert and the woods, to fields and beaches, lakes and mountains. You can camp in national and state parks, in busy, crowded campgrounds, and in remote sites deep in the wilderness. Some campsites offer ponds for swimming and canoeing, trails for hiking, rocks to

SEARCH A SITE FOR YOUR SITE

If you want to go beyond the backyard, and your parents don't already have a campsite picked out, the Internet is a great place to start. Lots of websites let you search for campgrounds according to region, the activities offered there or nearby, and the type of setup you want (that is, will it be just one tent for you, your parents, and your annoying little brother, or will it be a tent village for your entire extended family, including Great-Aunt Cordelia). Get the game plan and then check sites like **www.gorp.com, www.reserveamerica.com,** and **www.gocampingamerica.com.**

scramble up, caves to explore, trees to climb, fields to wander through, or streams to fish in. The possibilities are endless.

No matter where you go and what kind of camping you choose, you'll need to do a little planning. Investigating with your family before you leave home will make your camping experience even more fun and fulfilling.

KNOW BEFORE YOU GO

Once you zero in on where you'll be camping, you can learn about the area's surrounding plants and wildlife. Go to your local library to find books about where you're headed, or look online. Knowing where you're going also helps you plan the kinds of games, activities, and projects you'll do, and—most important—what kinds of equipment and gear you need to bring.

YOU ARE HERE

WHERE TO GO?

The Five Big Before-You-Go Questions

Before you pack a thing, you need to get organized and put all your ducks in a row. Begin by asking yourself these questions:

1 **WHERE ARE WE GOING?** What's the landscape like, the weather, the temperature? You need to figure out whether you're headed for hot or cold, dry or wet, flat or rocky—or maybe some combination—and pack what you'll need accordingly.

2 **WHAT KIND OF CAMPING WILL WE BE DOING?** If you're in the yard out back, you'll need less gear and can be more flexible with what counts as "gear" than if you're sleeping in the woods. Same goes for other aspects of your intended campsite—if your campground has showers and bathrooms, you'll pack different stuff than if you'll be making your own.

3 **HOW WILL WE GET THERE?** Will you be hiking to your campsite or driving in a car? Obviously you can bring more if you're car-camping because you don't have to worry about carrying everything on your back.

4 **WHAT WILL WE BE DOING?** Hiking? Skiing? Swimming? Fishing? Hunting for animal tracks? Searching for bugs? Making crafts? You'll need special gear for these activities, so talk with your grown-ups and figure out what's planned for your trip.

5 **HOW LONG WILL WE BE THERE?** Knowing the length of your trip will help you figure out not only how many pairs of undies to bring, but also how much grub you'll need. You can wear clothes over and over, but when it comes to food, you have to plan what you'll eat for breakfast, lunch, dinner, and snacks each day. But don't get your sleeping bag in a bunch—all of this is covered in chapter 3.

tell your folks!

According to the U.S. Census, camping is the fourth most popular sport in America. With millions of people hauling gear and pitching tents in campgrounds all over the country, some places are bound to be crowded.

If you're going to a national or state park or campground, your family may need to make reservations months before your trip or you won't have a place to make your camp.

CHEW ON THIS

IN 1803, PRESIDENT Thomas Jefferson sent Meriwether Lewis and William Clark on an expedition to explore the West and find a water route through North America. Talk about a major trek! Here's part of the checklist for their cross-country trip: "Muskets, muzzle-loading flintlock rifles, small cannon . . . oiled linen, gunpowder, mosquito netting, liniment, medicines, one pair of low leather shoes, two pairs of socks, six kegs of brandy and 2,800 fishhooks."

After you answer all the key questions, you can get going on your lists. The Ultimate Packing List, on pages 5–18, will give you information on the basic gear you'll need to stay a happy camper (plus some would-be-nice-to-have-its, which aren't necessary but will make you an even happier camper). When you're ready to organize your stuff, turn to The Ultimate Checklist on page 19, and cross things off as you go.

ARE WE THERE YET?

Long car trip to the campsite? Do something fun to keep your brain busy.

Cow Counter:
Look out your window and count the cows you pass on your side of the car; have the folks on the other side count the cows they pass on theirs. See which side of the car can count more cows, the left or the right. If either team passes by a cemetery on their side of the car and someone on the other side notices and says, "Your cows are history," the team on the cemetery side loses all their cows. Try pointing out decoys along the way ("Hey, look, it's a pink hippo!") in order to make the other team miss cows on their side or a cemetery on yours. If you want, score bonus points for a white horse.

Critter Cam:
While you're watching the world whiz by, take a closer look at the side of the road—you may be amazed by the wildlife you see. Keep an eye out for raccoons, opossums, deer, rabbits, pheasants, even wild turkeys.

Hush, Hush:
Pick a word that's off-limits (e.g., road, Mom, hungry, clouds). If anyone says the word, they have to endure the "punishment" (e.g., sing a silly song, quack like a duck)—anything you choose before the game begins.

The Ultimate Packing List

Camping Gear

Backpack

You need one good backpack (or duffel bag) that isn't too heavy and is big enough to store all your stuff.

Tent

Sleeping under the stars is awesome, but when there are bugs and raindrops involved, you'll want a good tent—one that's waterproof, bug-proof, and big enough for you, your family, and your stuff (except your kitchen gear, of course, which goes outside the tent).

Doing an overnight in the backyard and want to make your own tent? Check out pages 32–35 for some fun ideas.

Tarp

A big sheet of durable plastic or plastic-coated canvas, a tarp is a camping essential. You'll need to spread a tarp underneath your tent to protect the tent floor. (A second tarp is handy inside the tent, to protect your stuff from moisture coming through the floor.) Tarps come in different sizes and can be purchased at hardware, home-and-garden, and outdoor-sports stores. Get the size that fits (or can be folded to) the floor size of your tent, or that is called for in the makeshift tent activities on pages 34–37.

Sleeping bag

Sleeping bags come in three different shapes: a mummy bag, a rectangular bag, and a semirectangular bag. A mummy bag is slim and tapered at the bottom, and comes with a sort of hood you can snuggle around your head. It is the most effective at keeping you warm in cold conditions—if you're going somewhere chilly, mummy's the word. A rectangular bag is nice and roomy—as

PILLOW TALK

Don't want to sleep pillow-less? Bring a pillowcase and stuff it with a fleece pullover at night. Voilà—a soft cushion for your cranium!

MUM'S THE WORD

Mummy bags take their name and shape from—you guessed it—ancient Egyptian mummies. Little did those old guys know the kooky, taper-toed, cloth-wrapped tomb-stuffers would be the inspiration for a great camping design. Luckily, today's version of sleeping like a mummy is a lot less claustrophobic!

far as sleeping bags go—and can be zipped together with another rectangular bag to make an even bigger bag. Semirectangular bags are sort of a compromise between the two—they offer more space than a mummy bag, so they're a bit more comfy, but they also taper at the bottom, making them better than the rectangle bags at retaining body heat.

Sleeping bags can be filled with synthetic fibers, cotton, or goose down. The synthetic bags are usually the best, because they stay warm even if they get wet. Different sleeping bags are designed to keep you comfortable in warm and cool temperatures, so make sure the bag you have is warm enough for where you'll be snoozing.

Camping out in the backyard or somewhere else close to home? You can make your own awesome sleeping sack—check out page 38.

Sleeping pad

A sleeping pad is a wonderful thing. Not only does it make the ground a little softer, it keeps you dry and insulated from the cold. The ground can actually draw heat away from your body if you sleep right on top of it—and who wants to sleep on a hard, chilly surface when you can curl up on a squishy pad instead? You can use a foam pad or an inflatable one (the inflatables tend to be cushier but heavier). In a pinch, you can even fold a wool or fleece blanket into a makeshift sleeping mat.

Day pack

Bring along a smaller backpack for carrying water, snacks, lunch, a rain poncho, and warm layers during short hikes and other excursions.

Toilet kit

In the event that your campsite doesn't have flush toilets, you'll need to provide your own privy. For more on making your own toilet, see page 47.

TOILET PAPER: This is a necessity if you're camping in the back-woods, but to be on the safe side, always pack a roll no matter where you're headed. Although some camping sites have toilets that are usually stocked with paper, you never know—don't get caught without a square to spare!

TROWEL: For digging a hole for a pit toilet (also handy for any other holes you might need to make).

TWO ZIP-TOP BAGS: One large bag to hold the trowel and clean toilet paper, one medium-size bag for the used toilet paper (seal this bag and store it in the large bag).

Flashlight or headlamp with batteries

It gets dark out there without street lights. We're talking D-A-R-K! But nothing that a little flashlight or headlamp can't fix. Plus, flashlights are always great for shadow puppets (page 322), flashlight tag (page 318), and making a midnight snack.

Plastic bags

Bring along about a dozen various size zip-top bags for keeping clothes dry, separating wet items from dry, and packing out garbage and other yucky stuff you come across or create while camping. You'll want some gallon-size bags for clothing and your wet towel, and some pint-size ones for toiletries and for stashing snacks in your day pack so you can nibble on the trail.

Bring two or three large heavy-duty garbage bags per person, too. These make great spur-of-the-

YOUR BOOTS OR sneakers will probably get pretty dirty and stinky during the day, so you won't want to snuggle up to them at night. Instead, stuff a sock in each shoe (so creepy-crawlies can't get in) and put them just outside the door of your tent, but still underneath the rain fly. That way they'll stay dry but nearby in case the bathroom calls your name in the middle of the night.

moment rain ponchos (just tear a large hole in one side of the sealed end for your head), and can also cover your stuff—backpack, rolled-up sleeping bag, and more—so it doesn't get soaked in a sudden downpour. Oh, and you can use them for garbage bags, too!

Lantern/candles

Your campfire will give off a lovely glow (if you're allowed to have one) wherever you set up camp, but it's also nice to have a little extra light to see by. Lanterns are terrific: Make sure your batteries are fresh before you leave. Candles are also a nice way to illuminate the darkness, but you have to be extra careful of open flames.

Repair kit

You can creatively solve most broken gear problems with a few Mr./Ms. Fix-It tricks and these trusty items:

DUCT TAPE: Use this miraculous mender to patch a tear in the tent, fix a hole in an air mattress, hang a lantern, lash together a broken fishing or tent pole, mend rips in clothes or boots, and secure a windshield for a camp stove—the possibilities go on and on. Instead of lugging around a whole roll of duct tape, make your own mini-roll: Pull off the amount you need and wind it around itself into a smaller, more compact roll (like a roll of toilet paper minus the cardboard core). Stash it in your pack, and you're ready to, um, roll. (Another idea: Wrap a foot or two of tape in a band around the middle of your water bottle—it looks cool, and keeps the tape handy.)

SUPERGLUE: Great for temporary but sturdy fixes.

GARBAGE BAGS: Include at least two at the top of your repair kit. Use one to wrap around a broken tent pole like a bandage before duct taping the pieces together; to line and waterproof your pack; to make a tarp by slicing it open along the seams (you can duct tape the seams together and make a decent emergency tent as well); to provide extra patching for holes in your tent, rain jacket, or tent fly.

DENTAL FLOSS AND A HEAVY-DUTY LEATHER NEEDLE: Makes a strong needle-and-thread team for repairing tears in clothing, webbed straps, backpacks, tents, and even window screens.

ADHESIVE-BACKED VELCRO STRIPS (one inch wide): A perfect stand-in for mashed-up jacket and sleeping bag zippers.

A MULTIPURPOSE TOOL: This fold-up contraption is similar to a Swiss Army knife and can have scissors, pliers, screwdrivers, a can opener, and sometimes even tweezers! Check with an adult before using one, because it may contain knife blades.

Kitchen Gear

These are just the basics to get you up and cooking in the wild. Your grown-ups should check with the campsite to figure out whether a fire pit or grill is provided, and if not, what kind of stove to bring.

Stove

Cooking over a campfire is fun, but sometimes it isn't practical or allowed. Thankfully there are a

DUCT TAPE

Out in the woods with a leak, a tear, or a broken something? Not to fear! Duct tape is here!

Fix a leaky water bottle

Write your name on your tent

Make a leash for your pet rock

Mend a broken marshmallow stick

Catch flies

Make suspenders for loose pants

Remove lint from your dressy camping clothing

Craft duct tape "minnows" for fish bait

Hang soggy clothes up to dry

wide variety of camp stoves available. They're easy to light and easy to use. If you're camping with your car, you can use a larger, heavier stove that has more than one burner (so you can have more pots going at once). If you have to carry your gear to the site, you'll need a lightweight backpack stove instead. And if you're camping in the backyard, ask a grown-up to help you use a barbecue.

Grill rack

You may need to bring your own grill rack if the fire pit at your campsite doesn't have one. Have your adults check with the campground manager.

Cooler

Obviously you won't be taking a huge cooler

chest if you're backpacking into the wilderness, but for car or boat camping, or even backyard camping, a cooler is nice to have along. Sometimes it makes more sense to use two small coolers instead of one big one: You can pack just as much food, but the smaller coolers are easier to carry. See page 53 for tips on packing a cooler.

Pots and pans

It's always a good idea to take along two cooking pots with lids, one big and one medium. This way you can cook two things at once, like noodles in one pot and sauce in the other. A Dutch oven, a large, heavy pot with a tight-fitting lid, is useful for cooking over a campfire. You can

use cooking pots as mixing bowls as well. A griddle or a skillet is also helpful if you want to make pancakes, pizza, or anything else that's cooked on a flat surface, like eggs and bacon. And as you've probably guessed, different kinds of camping call for different kinds of pots—bring lighter ones if you'll be lugging them on your back to the campsite.

Dishes and utensils

Each camper should have a durable, heavy-duty plastic plate, bowl, and cup of their own, plus a fork, knife, and spoon. You can keep your own set in a small carrying sack, or let everyone mark their name on their stuff with

a permanent marker and keep the whole lot in a bigger communal sack. Each person should be responsible for keeping his or her dishes and utensils clean and placing them back in the carry sack after every meal.

Cooking utensils

When you cook, chances are you'll be measuring, stirring, cutting, picking up, flipping, straining, and serving, so you'll need to have a good set of tools: A measuring cup and spoons, wooden spoon, pocketknife (see page 11), small lightweight cutting board, tongs, small spatula, strainer (for noodles), and a fastdrying kitchen towel will do the trick. To keep all your utensils together, you can pack them in an extra-large zip-top bag.

Oven mitts

For handling hot pots.

Matches

If you're going to cook anything, you'll need fire. To make fire, you need matches AND an adult—*never* light matches without a grown-up's permission and supervision. The last thing you want to do is hurt yourself or start a forest fire! Keep matches in a waterproof container. You can wrap a big box of safety matches in a zip-top bag, or tuck smaller matchbooks into a watertight container, like Tupperware or a film canister. Either way, you want to keep the matches dry, dry, dry. Damp matches won't light, and you'll be left in the cold.

tell your folks!

Before heading out, your grown-ups should check that there's enough fuel for the camp stove and give the stove a test run to make sure it's working properly.

If you're planning to cook the meals over the campsite's fire pit, your adults should check with the ranger/campground manager about rules for gathering firewood (at some campgrounds it's a no-no, which means you'll have to bring your own or purchase it at the campground supply store).

Water bottle

Each person should have a water bottle that's large enough for at least a pint of water but not so big that it weighs a ton. Heavy-duty plastic bottles are a great option.

Pocketknife

This is a camping necessity but should only be used if you have an adult's permission. Pocketknives are sharp and have a blade (often more than one) that folds out from a center piece. They're handy for camping because they can be folded up small and tucked away. But this fold-y-ness also means blades can easily nip fingers when folding back in. Have an adult teach you how to use a pocketknife properly— it's really easy to have an accident if you're not careful.

When used safely, a pocketknife is great for chopping vegetables and slicing fruit and cheese, smearing peanut butter, and even shaping sticks for weenie roasts and marshmallow toasts.

Roll of aluminum foil

Foil is perfect for wrapping up leftovers, but it's useful for cooking stuff, too. You can cut up food and put it in a foil pouch for cooking directly over the coals of your fire. Lots of the recipes in this book (see chapter 3) are cooked in foil pouches.

Food and Water

Food and water are beyond the creature comfort zone—we're

talking survival here. You can be in the most amazingly gorgeous place on the planet, and if you're hungry or thirsty, with nothing to munch or sip, you're outta luck. So make sure you organize well for this portion of your trip.

Food

You'll need breakfast, lunch, dinner, and snacks for as many days as you'll be camping, and enough portions for each camper. Some meals you can prepare at home ahead of time, wrap in foil and zip-top bags, and keep in a cooler to put on the fire when you set up camp. These meals are perishable, though, which means they can go bad—eat them within a day or two of getting to your campsite. Other meals you'll need to assemble right

before you eat. Look at chapter 3 for some tasty recipe ideas. Once you and your crew have figured out what to eat for each meal, see what ingredients you have on hand and make a shopping list for the ones you need to buy.

Also, be sure to bring along a spice kit to dazzle up any meals you

make. See page 69 for suggestions.

Water and water purifiers

Water, water everywhere, but not a drop to drink. Heard that one before? Well, it can be true: You can have lots of water around you—lakes, ponds, streams, the ocean— but that doesn't mean it's acceptable for drinking . . . or cooking . . . or cleaning up. Some water that looks really clean can actually have lots of gunk in it—like bacteria and animal poop—that can make you sick and send you skipping to the loo. If you're staying at a campsite that has bathrooms and taps or pumps with drinkable water, you're all set. But if you're heading into the remote wilderness, make sure you bring along the proper stuff to clean your water—that means a pump filter and/or water purification tablets.

Water filters are small, inexpensive hand-held devices that get rid of the microscopic stuff that can leave you longing for Pepto Bismol. Some water filters can

DIVIDE AND CONQUER

Carrying your food on your back instead of storing it in a cooler in the car? Try dividing the food up by meal so that one person carries breakfast, another carries lunch, and so on. This way, you'll only need to rummage through one person's pack at a time to grab the grub you need.

also remove chemicals and other impurities. If your group is going to use a water filter, you'll need one with a rating of 0.2, which will remove everything from parasites to bacteria to bug babies. Before heading out, have your grown-ups make sure there are enough clean filters to last you the whole trip. Give the filter a dry run (well, really a wet run!) at home to make sure you know how it works.

Water purification tablets will knock out any pests too small for your filter to catch. Some types can make the water taste a little funny, but funny water is a heck of a lot better than the alternative.

If you're going somewhere that doesn't have lots of water, like the desert, you'll need to bring enough for each person in your group: a

YOU MIGHT SEE the words "potable water" posted around your campsite. That doesn't mean that the water should be put in a pot. It means the water's drinkable. "Potable" comes from the Latin word *potare*, which means "to drink."

minimum of one gallon of water per person per day just for drinking, and more for cooking and cleaning. It's probably safe to say two gallons per person per day to be comfortable. That's 32 cups of water, or 1,536 teaspoons. Gulp.

Safety Gear

First-aid kit

Always keep a kit on hand to treat any blisters, bumps, and aches: Band-Aids (a bunch of different sizes); antibacterial spray or cream; antibacterial hand cleanser; gauze pads and adhesive tape; small scissors; tweezers (for pulling out thorns or splinters); an old credit card or playing card (to scrape across and remove insect stingers—tweezers can actually push more venom into you!); instant cold pack; elastic bandage; safety pins; moleskin (for blisters); alcohol wipes (for cleaning wounds); pain

relief/fever-reducing medicine; anti-itch cream (for bug bites or stinging plants); antacid; antidiarrheal medicine; baking soda (about one tablespoon in a small plastic canister—add water to make a paste for treating bee stings); antihistamines (for treating allergic reactions); and a first-aid booklet (available through the American Red Cross or at a local bookstore).

Matches (waterproof)

You'll already have a set for cooking, but you should keep a set (stored in a waterproof container or zip-top bag) with your safety gear. Although you should never light them without an adult present, they are useful to have in the unlikely event that you're lost and need to build a fire for warmth. (See page 42 for information on how to build a fire safely.)

Map(s)

Always get a map of the area where you'll be camping and exploring (unless, of course, it's your backyard—then you can make a map if you like). Surprises like sighting a rare bird or spotting a deer are fun. Surprises like "Hey, where the heck are we?" are not. Topographic maps, which show changes in elevation, are especially useful for hiking.

Compass

This handy little instrument always tells you which direction you're headed. With a compass

and a map and a few landmarks, you'll never be lost. See page 120 for details on using a compass and a map.

Spare batteries

Pack a few fresh batteries in a waterproof bag and tuck them into your pack. There's nothing worse than running out of flashlight juice in the woods.

Whistle

Always carry a whistle with you when you go adventuring. You can wear it on a cord around your neck, under your shirt. If you're lost, making noise is a good thing. You can also blow your whistle on the trail to keep bears and other animals aware of your presence. Most animals

are shy, and if they know you're around, they'll clear out.

List of emergency contacts

When you're going off into the wilderness, it's smart to let people know where you're headed and how long you'll be away. It's also smart to keep a list of contact names and numbers in a safe place in your pack just in case something happens.

Rope

Bring along a 15-foot cotton clothesline-type rope (found in hardware stores). You can use it to tie down gear around camp, hang laundry to dry, string up food away from hungry critters, or dangle lanterns from branches.

Tarp or painter's plastic

Keep a six- to eight-foot square tarp for use as an emergency shelter.

Clothing

The great outdoors can be pretty unpredictable. Temperatures can change quickly, bugs wake up and look for their next meal, rain showers appear out of nowhere, and when the sun goes down, the air can get really chilly, even in the summer. Layering your clothes is the only way to stay comfortable and dry.

The following clothing list covers all the basic camper needs, but you'll notice it's short—you want to pack smart, which also means packing light. This isn't the time to break out the steamer trunk in the attic! A good guideline is to bring at least one full change of clothing, so that if you get wet or sweaty, you'll have something dry to change into.

Walking shoes or hiking boots

These should be snug, well worn-in, and sturdy.

Comfy camp shoes

Bring along a pair of old sneakers or sandals to wear around camp so you can change out of your wet or muddy walking shoes. Closed-toe shoes are best to help avoid stubbed toes and wayward splinters.

Socks

Thin wool or synthetic socks made specifically for hiking are great, though athletic socks work, too (remember, wool and synthetics stay warm when wet; cotton doesn't).

Undies

A pair for each day.

T-shirt or tank top

These can be made of cotton, but ones that "wick" sweat away from your body are better (see box, right). These are great first layers.

Long-sleeve button-up shirt

Excellent for keeping bugs and sun off your skin and easy to tie around your waist if you get too warm.

Long pants

Protect you against sun, bugs, and cold. Try fleece pants if you want something that'll

WICK IT, WICK IT GOOD!

Wicking fabrics whisk sweat away from your skin and keep you dry even when you're really active. They're perfect for camping and tromping around outdoors, when a sudden cool spell can really chill you to the bone if you're damp. Wool is a natural wicking fiber, and synthetic fabrics like polypropylene do a great job, too. Lots of different types of clothes come in wicking fabrics—from underwear to T-shirts to turtlenecks and long johns.

protect your legs during the day but is comfortable at night. Otherwise, khakis with lots of pockets work well.

Fleece jacket or wool sweater

No matter what the time of year, you always want to have some warm clothing. Weather can change unexpectedly.

Long johns

It's important to change out of the day's sweaty clothes before hopping into the

When to Go

Summer

Camping is fun in every season of the year, but summer is probably the most popular time to go. And why not? You're out of school. It's warm. You can swim, hike, boat, bike, and wear shorts and T-shirts! The trees and flowers are in full bloom, and you have a good chance of seeing wild animals collecting food, wandering, and raising their young.

Autumn

Camping in autumn is a treat. There are fewer crowds in state and national parks. If you're lucky, you can see the bright colors of turning leaves. The smell of fall air is exhilarating. The days are still warm and the nights are chilly—but cozy as can be by the fire or in your tent. You might see lots of wildlife getting ready for winter.

Winter

Winter camping is full of adventure and challenge. You need lots of planning for a winter trip. Imagine cross-country skiing or snowshoeing to your campground with your tent, sleeping bag, and supplies on your back. You can dig snow forts and set up your tent inside for extra protection from the elements. The landscape is stark and beautiful, and you'll probably be the only folks for miles. The campfire is so welcoming, and you can imagine what it was like for early pioneers to live on the move. Camp food prepared over the fire is even more delicious after a long day in the snow. Plus, the night sky is so clear; it seems like you can see forever.

Spring

In the spring, buds are popping up and life is stirring in the wilderness once again. State and national parks are less crowded and bursting with spring colors. Birdsong fills the air, and many animals are having babies. In some places, like the Alpine meadows of the Cascade Mountains in Washington, fields are filled with the pinks, purples, and yellows of wildflowers.

sack, so pack long johns (top and bottom) for PJs. They're warm and cozy and if you need an extra layer during the day, you can use them again.

Rain jacket or poncho

Breathable rain gear is more comfortable than the plastic-coated "slicker" kind, but either one will do.

Waterproof windbreaker

A great light layer if you're working up a sweat but want to stay dry.

Warm hat

Most of your heat escapes from the top of your head, so keep it covered and warm. A hat will come in especially handy when huddling around the campfire at night.

Brimmed hat or baseball cap

Sunblock and sunglasses are great, but you might want a little more protection for your noggin.

Sunglasses

It's a good idea to protect your eyes, no matter what the season.

Bandannas

Bandannas are really useful little items—they can be used to hold your hair back, as a napkin, to shield your neck from the sun—and much more. Pack a few.

Toiletries

You're not going to have all the comforts of home with you when you're roughing it outdoors, but you'll want a few things to keep you from feeling and smelling like a Neanderthal. The list of essentials (see page 20) is probably the same for everyone, but any extras are your call. Make sure you pack all the "wet" stuff in one zip-top bag and all the "dry" stuff in another—you don't want your toothpaste squishing out all over your hairbrush or your dental floss coated with sunscreen. Yuck!

Fun Stuff

What you pack for fun depends on the activities you've got planned. You may want to bring your camera, a book or two, a journal, and some pens or colored pencils. A deck of cards is a lifesaver on rainy days in the tent. Look through the following chapters to find some projects or activities you want to try. Each project calls for specific items; make your own lists so you'll have everything you need.

Warm Weather Add-Ons

Here are a couple of extras to consider if you're camping in warm weather or will be in a place where you can swim.

Shorts

Bring a pair of quickdry shorts that won't stay wet for long if you splash around in them.

Bathing suit

Store in a zip-top bag to keep your other clothes dry when your swimsuit is wet.

Towel

Pack it in a big zip-top bag (again, to protect your other stuff when your towel is damp).

Water sandals

These are awesome for walking or playing in the water. It's nice not to worry about sharp objects or biting bugs.

Cool Weather Add-Ons

In cold weather, layers are your best friend.

Warm socks

Pack several pairs of heavy wool or synthetic socks so you can change into fresh ones after hiking or playing in the snow.

Long johns

Look for long underwear—bottom and top—made from "wicking" fabrics (see page 15) like wool, which will keep you warm when wet. Bring two sets—one for daytime and one for bed.

Fleece pants and snow pants

To keep you warm and dry in the snow.

Turtleneck

The high neck keeps body heat from escaping.

Extra wool sweater or fleece pullover

A nice heavy layer that'll stay toasty even when wet.

Fleece vest (optional)

A great extra layer.

Warm, waterproof parka

This gives you added weather protection.

Scarf or neck warmer

A neck warmer that pulls on over your head is compact, while a scarf is versatile (it can be worn like a shawl or wrapped around your neck).

Mittens or gloves

Pack waterproof ones if you plan on playing in the snow.

Collapsible shovel

In the event of a blizzard, to dig away the snow.

The Ultimate Checklist

In these checklists there is one blank box and one blank line before each item, one labeled "Got it?" and the other labeled "How many?" After taking a look at The Ultimate Packing List (pages 5–18) to figure out exactly what you'll need, make a photocopy of the checklists on this page and pages 20–21. Fill in your "How many?" blanks (how many you need of each item), and check off what you've gathered in the "Got it?" boxes as you go. This way you can use the lists over and over again, adapting them to the trip you're taking each time.

Camping Gear

Got it?	How many?	Item description
☐	_____	Bag
☐	_____	Tent
☐	_____	Tarp
☐	_____	Sleeping bag
☐	_____	Sleeping pad
☐	_____	Day pack
☐	_____	Toilet kit
☐	_____	Flashlight or headlamp with batteries
☐	_____	Zip-top bags
☐	_____	Garbage bags
☐	_____	Lantern/candles
☐	_____	Repair kit

Kitchen Gear

Got it?	How many?	Item description	Got it?	How many?	Item description
☐	_____	Stove or grill rack*	☐	_____	Tongs
☐	_____	Cooler (for car camping)	☐	_____	Small spatula
☐	_____	Pots	☐	_____	Strainer
☐	_____	Pans	☐	_____	Fast-drying kitchen towel
☐	_____	Plate, cup, and bowl (per person)	☐	_____	Oven mitts
☐	_____	Knife, fork, and spoon (per person)	☐	_____	Matches
☐	_____	Measuring cup and spoons	☐	_____	Water bottle
☐	_____	Wooden spoon	☐	_____	Aluminum foil
☐	_____	Pocket knife			
☐	_____	Small, lightweight cutting board			

*A stove may not be necessary if there's a fire pit at the campsite. A grill rack may not be necessary if the fire pit has a grill.

Clothing

Got it?	How many?	Item description
☐	_____	Walking shoes or hiking boots
☐	_____	Comfy camp shoes
☐	_____	Socks
☐	_____	Undies
☐	_____	T-shirt/tank top
☐	_____	Long-sleeve button-up shirt
☐	_____	Long pants
☐	_____	Fleece/wool sweater
☐	_____	Long johns
☐	_____	Rain jacket/ poncho
☐	_____	Waterproof windbreaker
☐	_____	Warm hat
☐	_____	Brimmed hat or baseball cap
☐	_____	Sunglasses
☐	_____	Bandannas

Warm Weather Add-Ons

Got it?	How many?	Item description
☐	_____	Shorts

Got it?	How many?	Item description
☐	_____	Bathing suit (in a zip-top bag)
☐	_____	Towel (in a zip-top bag)
☐	_____	Water sandals

Cool Weather Add-Ons

Got it?	How many?	Item description
☐	_____	Warm socks
☐	_____	Long johns (2 pairs)
☐	_____	Fleece pants
☐	_____	Snow pants
☐	_____	Turtleneck
☐	_____	Extra wool sweater/fleece pullover
☐	_____	Fleece vest (optional)
☐	_____	Warm, waterproof parka
☐	_____	Scarf/neck warmer
☐	_____	Mittens/gloves
☐	_____	Collapsible shovel

Toiletries

Got it?	How many?	Item description
☐	_____	Toothbrush and toothpaste
☐	_____	Hairbrush/ comb
☐	_____	Medicines
☐	_____	Glasses/ contacts
☐	_____	Sunscreen
☐	_____	Small towel (in a zip-top bag)
☐	_____	Lip balm with sunscreen
☐	_____	Bug repellant
☐	_____	Biodegradable soap/shampoo

Safety Gear

Got it?	How many?	Item description
☐	_____	First-aid kit (see right)
☐	_____	Matches (waterproof)
☐	_____	Map(s)
☐	_____	Compass
☐	_____	Spare batteries
☐	_____	Whistle
☐	_____	List of emergency contacts
☐	_____	Rope
☐	_____	Tarp or painter's plastic

First-aid Kit

Got it?	How many?	Item description
☐	____	Band-Aids
☐	____	Antibacterial spray/cream
☐	____	Antibacterial hand cleanser
☐	____	Gauze pads and adhesive tape
☐	____	Small scissors
☐	____	Tweezers
☐	____	Instant cold pack
☐	____	Elastic bandage
☐	____	Safety pins
☐	____	Moleskin
☐	____	Alcohol wipes
☐	____	Pain reliever/fever-reducer
☐	____	Anti-itch cream
☐	____	Antacid
☐	____	Antidiarrheal medicine
☐	____	Baking soda
☐	____	Antihistamines
☐	____	First-aid booklet

Food and Water

Got it?	How many?	Item description
☐	____	Breakfast, lunch, dinner, and snacks (per person/day)
☐	____	Spice kit
☐	____	2 gallons of clean water (per person/day)*
☐	____	Water filter (with extra filters)
☐	____	Water purification tablets

*Only necessary if there won't be water sources at your site.

Fun Stuff

Got it?	How many?	Item description
☐	____	Camera
☐	____	Paperback book(s)
☐	____	Journal and pens/markers
☐	____	Playing cards
☐	____	Travel board games
☐	____	Binoculars
☐	____	Bird-watching book
☐	____	Nature guide
☐	____	_____
☐	____	_____
☐	____	_____

"Simplicity, simplicity, simplicity!"

—Henry David Thoreau

Living out of a bag is easiest when you pack smart. Here are a few tips:

Play favorites. Pack on top or in side pockets the things that you'll use a lot or want to keep nearby, like a rain jacket, sunscreen, camera, whistle, flashlight, and first-aid kit. This way you can get to them easily and will always know where to find them.

Line your sleeping bag stuff sack with a plastic garbage bag and then stuff the sleeping bag inside. Squeeze the air out to make it small, twist and loosely knot the garbage bag and tighten the stuff sack's drawstring, then put another garbage bag around the sack. This way your "bed" will remain dry (plus you'll have an extra garbage bag if you need it). If there's room, put your sleeping bag in the bottom of your pack to cushion the rest of your stuff.

Pack It In

You've made your lists. Now gather everything together and check each item off the list. Next round up your grown-ups and check the equipment. Does everything that runs on a battery have fresh batteries? Are all the tent stakes there? Is there fuel in the camp stove? Do you have film? Do your boots still fit? This is the time to make sure everything is in working order.

Once you have everything double-checked and in one place, organize it. Separate the group gear (like tents and pots and pans) into one pile, your gear (sleeping bag, sleeping pad, etc.) into another, and your clothes and toiletries into a third. An adult will be in charge of packing up the group gear and probably your non-clothing items, too, but you can help out with your clothing and toiletries. Divide your clothes into smaller piles, putting similar items in the same pile (for example, socks and underpants go together) and put each pile into a medium or large zip-top bag according to its size. Bag all your toiletries, too—especially runny or gooey ones, like shampoo and toothpaste (you won't want to spend the night in a shampoo-coated sleeping bag!). Squeeze all the air out of each bag before you close it. Bagging your clothes and toiletries makes it easier to find specific items when you need them and keeps everything safely separate.

Put the smaller bags into your backpack or duffel bag. This is the moment of truth—if you can't fit everything, you might need to leave out some of the nonessentials. Check with an adult to see if there's any room elsewhere for some of your extras, or if you need to leave something behind.

HOME AWAY FROM HOME

Setting Up Camp

You've arrived! You've planned, packed, and traveled to your site, be it backyard or backwoods, and now it's time to make camp. Think of your campsite as an outdoor house. It has a bedroom, kitchen, dining room, family room, and bathroom. You just have to figure out where the "rooms" should go and then set everything up.

Where's the best place to pitch your tent? Where do you build your campfire? And where do you set up the kitchen? Whether you are in the backyard, a campground with fire pits and running water, or out in the wilderness, there are a few guidelines to follow to ensure you'll be happy campers.

THE BEDROOM

When you're going to spend the night outside, you need shelter. Here's the nitty-gritty on everything from where to pitch camp to how to set up a tent, and even how to put together a couple makeshift tents on your own.

YOU'LL WANT TO PITCH YOUR TENT on "high ground," but that doesn't mean the top of a mountain, or even the top of a hill. It just means any area that's slightly elevated—even by just a few inches—and not at the bottom of an incline.

Location, Location, Location

Tents come in all sorts of shapes and sizes: big, round, small, and pointy. Some are high-tech, pop-up, designed for cliffs, built for families, or created just for one. But no matter what type of tent you have, before you put it anywhere, think about the location in terms of water, sun, slope (is it on a hill or in a ditch?), ground surface, and wind. Tents are incredible contraptions, but they work best when smartly placed. After all, the tent *is* your outdoor bedroom; in some ways, it's the most important room in the "house"!

TENTS ARE NOT A NEW idea. Throughout history, humans who traveled great distances to hunt, gather food, or discover new territory needed a way to carry their home with them. The earliest tents were fashioned from the natural materials that were available, such as wood, bone, and animal skins. In some cases, travelers carried the hides along with

STAY DRY The first thing to look for is water. Though it may seem ideal to pitch your tent on the banks of a pretty lake or near that pond in your yard, you should always be at least 200 feet from any kind of water. First of all, you want to stay dry. Being next to water can mean you'll wake up drenched in dew. Water evaporates from the body of water and forms a cloud as the night air cools. Land around a body of water gets a bigger share of the moisture or dew. Also, water is where mosquitoes and other biting insects live, which means that if you're near water when the sun goes down—insect feeding time—you'll be on the menu for dinner.

them and made frames from found objects like branches or trees. In other cases, people set up tent or tepee villages and stayed in one location for an entire season while the hunting there was plentiful. On the Great Plains, tribespeople brought their tent poles with them, since there weren't enough trees from which to make wood beams. These poles not only held up the tents, but were used to drag them from place to place. Tents sure have come a long way since then, don't you think?

Leave No Trace

One day, when you're older and grayer, you might have kids of your own. Wouldn't it be great to take them camping? If you want the wilderness to be as splendid and fun tomorrow, then it's a good idea to help take care of it today. In 1994, concerned citizens founded the Leave No Trace program, which offers guidelines to help us reduce our impact on the Earth's beautiful wild places. Here's what you can do to pitch in:

- **Stay on marked trails** and choose campsites that are made of tough materials like rock, gravel, dry grasses, or snow. Leave pretty untouched areas untouched and take care not to mash plants or break twigs off trees when you hike or set up camp.

- **Use a fire ring** or grill if provided; and if you're setting up a camp stove, place it on a large, flat rock.

- **Take care** of your trash (including leftover food and used toilet paper)—pack it in and pack it out. Check your campsite and rest stop spots for trash or spilled foods (if you find *other people's* garbage, put it in the trash, too).

- **Leave rocks,** plants, and other natural objects as you find them.

- **Treat water well.** Don't use the lake or stream as a toilet, or bath, or for washing dishes—soap and human wastes can really damage fragile ecosystems.

- **Respect wildlife.** Observe critters from afar, and don't follow or approach them. Animals like being followed and chased about as much as you do!

- **Be considerate** of other visitors— remember, you're not the only one on vacation!

Instead, pitch your tent away from water. Find a well-drained spot that is on high ground and avoid dips and depressions—if you pitch your tent on low ground or in a dip and it rains, you'll be snoozing in a puddle.

MADE IN THE SHADE It's usually best to put your tent in a shady spot, if possible, especially if you'll be staying for more than one night. If the sun bears down on your tent all day, it will feel like an oven when you get back from frolicking in the woods. (Plus, as with your skin, too much sun exposure isn't so great for the tent; it can weaken the fabric, making it more susceptible to tears and leaks.) If there are no trees around, try finding a natural feature that can block the sun, like a boulder.

BE GROUNDED Seek out a smooth, flat patch that will fit your tent comfortably. If the ground slopes everywhere you look, you can still pitch your tent, but make sure you arrange it so your head will be uphill. Move away any rocks, large pebbles, sticks, or debris so you won't be lying on top of them. But remember that this stuff isn't garbage, it's part of the environment—leave it nearby so you can replace it after you've taken down your tent. You always want to leave a campground nicer than you found it, so the next family that comes by can enjoy it, too.

FRESH AIR If you're going to a car camping site with bathrooms, check to see where the camp toilets are and which way the wind is blowing. You want to be close enough to use the bathroom easily, but not so close you can smell it—after all, you want fresh air! If you're in a remote area where you have to dig your own pit toilet (see page 48), make sure you set it up at least 200 feet away from water, trails, and camp, and downwind (the wind direction might change, of course, but at least you gave it a shot).

TARPS AND BLANKETS are useful items at any campsite. If you don't have a tarp, you can make one in a pinch by joining together heavy-duty garbage bags with duct tape.

The best blankets to use outdoors are made of wool or polar fleece. Both fabrics wick moisture away and will keep you warm even if they get wet.

Tent Full o' Fun

So you're stuck in the tent—it's pouring out, and you've got nowhere to go. No worries. There are a lot of fun things to do:

- **Play cards**—Old Maid, Crazy 8s, Go Fish, Rummy, Solitaire, Hearts, War, and more.

- **Tired of card games?** Try building structures out of the cards. See who can build the highest card house without it toppling over.

- **Play charades** or one of the Car Games in chapter 9.

- **Tell secrets**—it's a great way to get to know your fellow campers. Each person writes a secret about himself (the more outrageous the better!) on a piece of paper and then someone reads each of the secrets aloud. Players have to guess which secret belongs to which player.

- **Sing!** Check out the campfire songs in the Extras, pages

358–366. If you happen to have a harmonica, provide some musical accompaniment. No harmonica? Those pots and pans would make some fine drums.

- **Create your own stories.** Someone starts with a sentence or two then the next person goes and so on, until you have woven a whole twisty story. Make 'em scary, make 'em funny, just as long as you keep 'em going.

- **Write** down your ideas and thoughts in a journal.

- **Sketch.**

- **Sock puppet theater.** Those extra pairs of socks might as well be put to good use. Decorate them with duct tape, stickers, markers, or whatever else you have.

- **Read a book**, but skip the spooky stories unless you're going to read them aloud.

DON'T GET WINDED Fresh air is wonderful, but too much too fast can really blow you over. When you're looking for the perfect spot, choose a place that will be protected from the wind should it kick up. You don't want your rain fly to flap around too much or blow away.

FLEE FROM FIRE Pitch your tent a good distance from your fire pit and kitchen area. Why? It's simple: Fires make sparks, sparks can land on tents, and sparks on tents can equal fire. And as you can imagine, tents on fire equal bad news. You also want to steer clear of pitching a tent near your kitchen or dishwashing area, because animals are attracted to the scent of food. If critters come looking for leftovers in the middle of the night, they'll be sniffing around your kitchen but also your sleeping bag.

Setting Up Your Tent

When you've chosen where to put your tent, get pitching. Here are the basics:

Spread out a tarp to act as a ground cloth. This sheet of plastic should be ¼ inch smaller than the size of your tent floor. If the tarp is larger than your tent, fold the edges under to make it slightly smaller than your tent floor. (If you don't and it rains, water will collect in the ground tarp, pool up under your tent, and you'll get wet.)

Set up your tent according to the directions. (It's a good idea to practice in the living room or yard before you leave home, just to make sure you have all the pieces and everything is in working order.) Put all the stakes and poles in separate piles. Put together all the poles before threading them through the tent. When the tent is assembled, toss the rain fly over the top, make sure it's lined up properly with the door, and secure the corners with the

CHEW ON THIS

FOR THOUSANDS OF years, Plains Indian tribes such as the Lakota, Blackfeet, Arapaho, and Crow built and lived in tents called tepees. They made these tepees by positioning long straight wooden poles in a circle, joining them at the top and draping them with a cover made of sewn-together animal skins. These shelters protected the people from the weather. They were also easy to construct and easy to take down and move—ideal homes for these American Indians who so often moved from place to place.

A RAIN FLY DEFLECTS moisture and protects your tent (and you) from too much sun, rain, and even wind.

tent stakes. You want to pull the corners pretty tight—a loose rain fly can flap around in a storm and let rain into the tent. Put the stakes into the ground at a slight angle (the tops of the stakes should point *away* from the tent) and gently hammer them in with a rock or push them in with your foot (be careful not to bend or break them!). If you hit a rock, move the stake over a bit and try to find a softer spot.

Use another tarp on the inside of the tent to prevent wear and tear on the floor. (It's optional, but it's a good idea!)

Settling In

Once your tent is set up, go on in and make yourself at home. Claim your spot inside and unpack your stuff. Roll out your sleeping pad and sleeping bag and let them sit while you explore your site. Sleeping bags are made with materials that work best when there is air inside, so unrolling them early gives them time to fluff up. And it's nice to have everything ready for bed so you can crawl in and not have to fuss in the dark.

Next, air out your tent, which can get a bit stuffy and funky-smelling: Open the windows, keep the screens closed, and let the air (not the bugs) flow through.

If weather permits, leave your backpack or duffel bag outside the tent to maximize space inside. Cover it with a garbage bag so it doesn't get soaked by morning dew.

Anatomy of a Tent

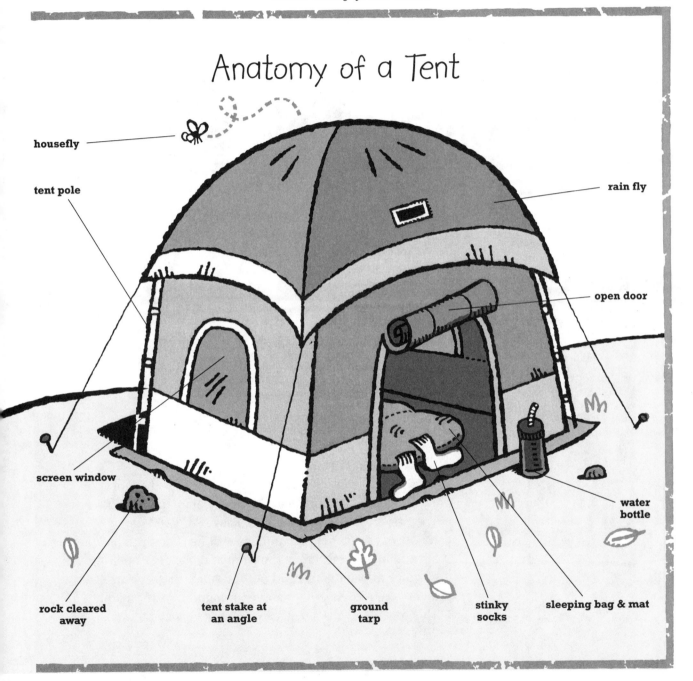

housefly

tent pole

screen window

rock cleared away

tent stake at an angle

ground tarp

stinky socks

sleeping bag & mat

water bottle

open door

rain fly

Camping Activity

The Two-Tree Tent

What You Need

About 20 feet of rope

2 sturdy trees about 10 to 15 feet apart

2 waterproof tarps (at least 8 x 10 feet)

About 10 softball-size (or bigger) rocks (see Note)

1 blanket (any size will do)

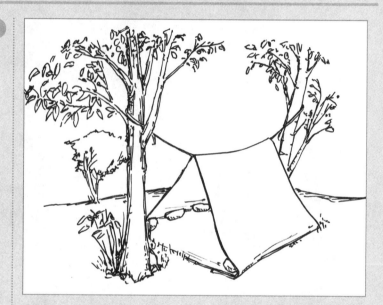

Even if you already have a tent, it can be fun to make one from scratch and camp out in your backyard. This quick and easy tent will keep you cozy for a night out under the stars (but try to pick a warm night!). Although the front and back are open—so you can peek your head out for stargazing—you will be covered in case it rains in the middle of the night. This tent also works well as an emergency shelter.

What You Do

1 With a grown-up's help, tie one end of the rope around one of the trees about 4 to 5 feet up using a clove-hitch knot (page 112). Pull the rope very tight, then tie the free end around the other tree, also 4 to 5 feet up. Tie the knots above a branch if possible.

2 Clear the ground between the trees of any rocks or lumpy debris.

3 Lay 1 tarp on the ground with the short end parallel to the rope. Fold it in half by lining up both short ends. Center the folded tarp on the ground directly under the rope. This will be the floor of your tent.

4 Anchor the floor tarp:

- Place 5 rocks along one edge of the floor tarp, parallel to the center rope—1 at each corner, and then the other 3 equally spaced in between. Repeat with the other side of the tarp and the remaining 5 rocks.

- If you think you want more rocks, go ahead and add them along the parallel edges—avoid placing rocks at the openings of your tent (unless you're fond of stubbing your toes!).

5 Line up the second tarp (this is the roof tarp) on the ground so the short end is parallel to the rope. Place one short end of the roof tarp over the rope and tug on it until it is divided equally over the rope.

6 Pull out the sides of the roof tarp and anchor the edges by tucking them under the rocks you put down.

7 Adjust the roof tarp until it is taut. Spread the blanket inside the tent to cushion the floor (you may need to fold it, depending on its size).

Note: *If you don't have rocks nearby, be creative and ask your grown-ups for suggestions (and permission)—you want fairly heavy, weather-resistant objects that will anchor your tent, such as croquet balls, potted plants, or buckets filled with sand.*

Camping Activity

The One-Tree Tent

What You Need

About 20 feet of rope

A sturdy tree

1 large rock approximately the size of your head

2 tarps (at least 8 x 10 feet)

About 12 softball-size (or bigger) rocks (see Note)

A roll of duct tape

1 blanket (any size will do)

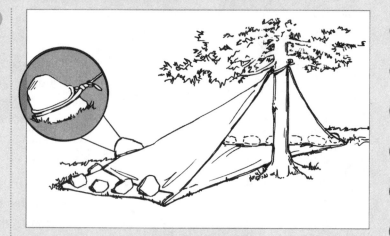

A tent made with one tree offers a little more protection from the elements. It only has one open side, which means less room for unwanted weather to sneak in. When you're putting together this tent, try to imagine what life was like back when a tent was a necessity and when, in order to pitch one, you'd have to gather, prepare, or carry all the necessary items—animal skins, ropes, wooden poles—before you could set up camp.

Like the two-tree tent, this is fun to build and sleep in, but best for a backyard overnight.

What You Do

1 With an adult's help, tie one end of the rope around the tree about 4 to 5 feet up using a clove-hitch knot (page 112) or 2 half hitches (page 110).

2 Clear the ground around the tree so it won't be lumpy, rocky, or covered with debris.

3 Place the large rock about 8 to 10 feet away from the tree. Stretch the rope out and attach it to the rock using a rolling hitch (page 111). Pull the rope tight so it doesn't sag.

4 Spread 1 tarp on the ground and fold it in half so the short edges meet. Center the tarp lengthwise under the rope. Place the 12 smaller rocks, equally spaced, along the tarp's side edges, making sure there's a rock at each corner. This tarp will be the floor of your tent.

5 Toss a short end of the second tarp over the rope. Pull the tarp over the rope until each side dangles down the same amount. This tarp will be the roof of the tent.

6 Pull the top edge of the roof tarp up the rope so it's as close to the tree as possible; secure it to the rope using duct tape. (You can use duct tape all along the inside length of the rope to keep the tarp from slipping off the rope.)

7 Pull the sides of the roof tarp away from the center and anchor the roof tarp on three sides (left, right, and bottom) with the rocks you have placed on the ground tarp. Make sure there is enough room for you to lie down inside the tent.

8 Crawl into your tent on the tree side. Spread the blanket on the floor for cushion and warmth (you may need to fold it, depending on its size).

Note: *If you don't have rocks nearby, be creative and ask your grown-ups for suggestions (and permission)—you want fairly heavy, weather-resistant objects that will anchor your tent, such as croquet balls, potted plants, or buckets filled with sand.*

Camping Activity

A Tepee to Call Your Own

What You Need

4 two-inch-wide, six-foot-long wooden dowels (use broom handles in a pinch—just get permission first)

2 large blankets

A roll of duct tape

When there's a hole in your roof, you usually want to fix it. But not so with tepees. Traditionally, these sturdy tent-houses always have a hole in the top. The hole acts as a chimney, so the people inside the tent can cook and stay toasty around a fire without getting smoked out.

P ut together this cool, modern makeshift tepee inside or outside and experience a part of Great Plains culture!

What You Do

1 Line up the dowels on the floor. Bundle them together and loosely wrap the duct tape around them about 6 to 10 inches from one end (as you would if you were taping together one end of a bunch of sticks—see Figure 1).

2 Lift the dowels upright and spread out the bottoms to form a tepee shape.

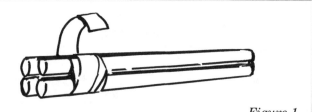

Figure 1.

3 Hold up the short edge of 1 blanket so it is parallel to 1 pole. (You'll need a grown-up or a tall friend for this part.) Wrap it gently around the pole and use duct tape to secure it all along the length of the pole (see Figure 2).

4 Gently wrap the blanket around the tepee structure, using strips of tape to tape it in place (on the inside) to each dowel as you wrap.

5 When you get to the last pole, tape the blanket only to the top half of the pole so you will have a door. Be sure to tape the top half well, so the weight of the blanket doesn't pull it off the dowel (see Figure 3).

6 Use the second blanket to pad the floor inside your tepee—you may need to fold it to fit.

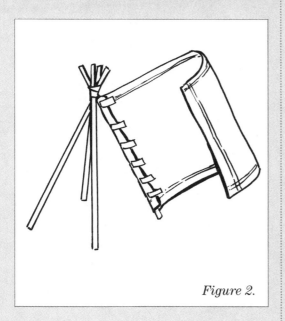

Figure 2.

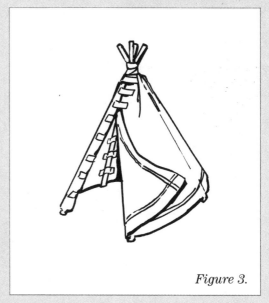

Figure 3.

No-Sew Sleep Sack

What You Need

2 fleece or wool blankets, plus 1 to use as a mat

A roll of duct tape

While it may not be the best solution for camping in Antarctica, making your own sleeping bag out of a couple of blankets is a great solution for backyard (or living room) fun.

In order to get into the sleep sack, you have to wriggle in from the top. Once inside, it feels like you're sleeping in a big burrito!

Figure 1.

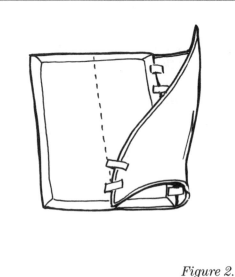

Figure 2.

What You Do

1 Spread 1 blanket on the ground and find the center line lengthwise.

2 Place the right half of the second blanket over the left half of the blanket on the ground. Duct-tape the seam (see Figure 1).

3 Fold the right side of the ground blanket over and duct-tape the side seam (see Figure 2). Fold the remaining left side of the second blanket over and duct-tape the side and bottom seams, leaving the top open (see Figure 3).

4 Fold the third blanket in half lengthwise and place it underneath your bag as a mat (see Figure 4). Snuggle in and snooze away—toasty warm.

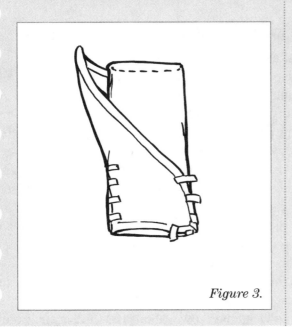

Figure 3.

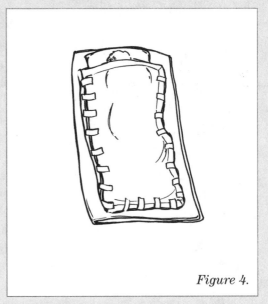

Figure 4.

THE KITCHEN AREA can be small, but it should have enough room for prepping food and cooking, with space dedicated to each. If your site doesn't have a picnic table, find a nice flat rock (or a few flat rocks) that will be a good perch for your cutting board and mixing bowls. It's amazing how you can transform "just a rock" into a kitchen counter.

THE KITCHEN AND FAMILY ROOM

When you're not off exploring or catching some Zs, chances are you'll be spending most of your time around the campfire. The campfire is like a kitchen, dining room, and family room all in one—it is *the* hangout hotspot. Same thing goes if you don't have a fire but are cooking over a camp stove. The kitchen area is a toasty, comfortable place to gather, make food, sing songs, and tell stories.

Many campgrounds have fire pits or grills to cook over and relax by, and also picnic tables where you can prep your food and eat it. If your campsite is in a remote place, you may need to bring a grill rack and make your own fire pit (if fires are allowed) or else use a stove. But before you can do any of this, you'll need to set up your kitchen area.

Kitchen Confidential

Some campsites have a loosey-goosey setup—they're all open spaces and no predetermined places for tent, bathroom, or kitchen. If you're camping in one of these (most likely in the backwoods), you get to choose where to set up your kitchen and campfire.

In choosing a site for your stove or fire pit, pick a place that is at least ten feet away from your tent so that smoke or sparks won't travel from the fire to the tent. Make sure your kitchen area is located in sand or gravel or on flat rocks. Flat surfaces are especially important for camp stoves, since a stove that wobbles is a stove that tends to spill dinner—a major bummer! And if you'll have a campfire, make sure you choose an open place—free of dried grasses, bushes, or dangling tree branches that could catch fire.

When it's time to do the dishes (yup, you still have to clean up in the outdoors), take some biodegradable soap, a bucket (or pot) of hot water, and a kitchen towel about 100 yards away from camp and any water source. Wash everything, then filter food particles from dirty water and toss the food scraps in the trash. Scatter the dirty gray water so you don't have one big, soapy wet spot in the dirt. Drip soapy water on gravel or rock. (It's important to spread out this dirty, soapy water to reduce its impact on the environment.)

Camping Activity

How to Build a Fire Pit

ADULT SUPERVISION

What You Do

1 Ask your grown-up to help you select an area that has bare sand or soil with no grasses, plants, or dangling branches or vines nearby—these can easily catch fire.

2 Dig a hole about 2 feet wide and 6 inches deep.

3 Circle the pit with rocks, leaving no bare spots.

4 Now you're ready to build a fire! (See Get Your Flame On, page 43.)

What You Need

A trowel

About 20 rocks (from softball- to bowling ball–size)

No fire pit at your campsite? No worries! Building one is pretty easy—just make sure that it's allowed where you're camping.

Make sure you have permission. Check to see if campfires are allowed before building one. Your grown-up may need to get a written permit.

Let the grown-up start the fire.

Always make sure you have enough wood—and then some—*before* you start your campfire. Campfires can be unpredictable, and you don't want to run out of wood just as the fire gets going.

The old saying goes that "Where there's smoke, there's fire," but that's not always true. You'll get lots of smoke if you try to burn wood that is wet with rain or green (alive), but the wood won't really catch. Instead, use dry, dead wood for campfires, and always pick it up from the ground instead of cutting or pulling branches off a tree.

Never build a fire under overhanging branches.

Fire

is beautiful, warm, and fun to watch, but it can also be dangerous . . . and tough to control. Follow these guidelines to keep your fire strong *and* safe.

Never leave a fire unattended.

Always have water available to douse the fire if you need to.

Always build a fire inside a fire pit. Make your own fire pit if necessary (see page 41).

Gather only dead wood around the campsite. Make sure you are allowed to gather firewood. In some places you have to bring your own or purchase it at the camp store or ranger station.

Keep the fire contained. If your fire starts to spark and flame too wildly, douse it quickly with water, then cover it with a layer of dirt. Sparks and high flames can set nearby trees aflame and cause a forest fire.

When you break up camp, be sure to douse the fire pit thoroughly with water— even if you think it is completely burned out. Stir the fire pit with a hardy stick and re-wet it as you go to make sure there are no glowing embers or smoking ashes. Wet the area around the pit as well. Sometimes there can be hot embers hidden under the rocks or dead ashes, and these can be blown from the pit and spark a fire elsewhere or ignite roots under the pit.

Get Your Flame On

uilding a fire takes some practice, but once you have the bare bones down, it's not too tough. Before you get started . . . and you know where this is going . . . you *must* grab a grown-up and ask for his or her permission and supervision. Fire is an amazing and wonderful force of nature, but it can be dangerous and difficult to control. That's why you ALWAYS must have an adult present when flames are involved.

Now that we've got that down, here's how to make a campfire.

What You Do

1 Make a ball of dried grass, pine needles, and/or pinecones. Put it in the center of the fire pit.

2 Place 1 handful of tiny twigs on top of the ball. Make a tepee around the tiny twigs with some pencil-size twigs. Leave a small opening for a match.

3 Make a larger tepee around the small tepee with some of the thumb-size sticks. Make sure there are spaces about a finger's width in between the sticks.

continued on next page

What You Need

A big handful of dried grass, pine needles, or pinecones

A fire pit—see page 41

A few big handfuls of dry tiny twigs

A few big handfuls of pencil-size twigs

Matches

A few big handfuls of thumb-thickness sticks about 1 foot long

A few armloads of wrist-thickness logs about 1 foot long

A few armloads of leg-thickness logs up to 2 feet long

A bucket of water and a long, sturdy stick

Get Your Flame On, contd.

4 Take some of the wrist-size logs and make a tepee around the twig tepee.

5 Get an adult to strike a match and place the flame to the ball of grass or needles within the tepees. Blow gently to ignite the flame. Let the tepees catch fire and burn. Practice patience—you'll need to nurse the fire, adding more twigs, blowing on it, making sure it doesn't topple, until you're certain it's okay on its own.

6 Get a grown-up to carefully add bigger logs to the fire by gently placing the logs in a tepee shape around the flame. As the logs burn and then start to turn to glowing embers, you may want to add more logs to keep the fire burning.

7 Keep the bucket of water handy in case you need to douse the fire in a hurry. When the fire dies naturally, make sure it's out all the way by pouring water on it and stirring it with the stick.

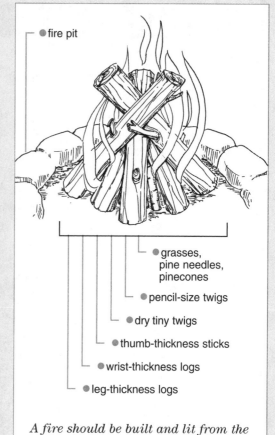

fire pit

grasses, pine needles, pinecones

pencil-size twigs

dry tiny twigs

thumb-thickness sticks

wrist-thickness logs

leg-thickness logs

A fire should be built and lit from the inside out, beginning with the very tiniest twigs and ending with thick, sturdy logs.

Cooking with Coals

The traditional tepee campfire is fun to lounge around and toast marshmallows over, but it's not great for cooking because it burns so hot (which means it'll probably burn your food). If you plan to cook in the campfire on either a grill or in foil packets over the coals (see pages 60–93 for some great campfire recipes), make this log cabin–style fire instead.

What You Do

1. Make a ball of dried grass, pine needles, and/or pine cones. Put it in the center of the fire pit.

2. Place 1 handful of tiny twigs on top. Take some of the pencil-size twigs and make a tepee around the tiny twigs, leaving a small opening for a match.

3. Make a larger tepee around the small tepee with some of the thumb-size sticks. Make sure there are spaces about a finger's width in between the sticks.

4. Take the wrist-size logs and build a log cabin–like structure around the tepee: Lay 2 logs parallel to each other outside the tepee and then 2 across the ends of these logs to make a square. Keep building up the

What You Need

A big handful of dried grass, pine needles, or pinecones

A fire pit—see page 41

A few big handfuls of dry tiny twigs

A few big handfuls of pencil-size twigs

Matches

A few big handfuls of thumb-thickness sticks about 1 foot long

A few armloads of wrist-thickness logs about 1 foot long

A few armloads of leg-thickness logs up to 2 feet long

A grill rack (optional)

A bucket of water and a long, sturdy stick

Cooking With Coals, contd.

logs in a crisscross pattern until they near the top of the tepee.

5 Get an adult to strike a match and place the flame to the ball of grass or needles within the tepee. Blow gently to ignite the flame. Let the tepee catch fire and burn. This is the time to be patient and hardworking—you'll need to nurse the fire, adding more twigs to the tepee, blowing on it, making sure it doesn't topple, until the fire is burning steadily.

6 Place the grill rack, if using, on the fire pit and get your food ready to cook while the fire is burning. In about 20 to 30 minutes, the wood will have burned down to glowing embers. Have a grown-up test the heat of the embers and place the food on the grill, over the coals, or on the metal rim of the fire pit. Now you're cookin'!

7 Keep the bucket of water handy in case you need to douse the fire in a hurry. When the fire dies naturally, make sure to put it out completely by pouring water over it and stirring it with the stick.

Living Room Campfire

Sometimes an actual campfire isn't practical or even allowed. But that doesn't mean you can't enjoy one. As the saying goes, "If you can't make it, fake it"—set up a "kinda campfire" wherever you camp.

If you're out in the backyard, ask your folks to set up a barbecue for toasting marshmallows and roasting hot dogs. Or create your own "fire pit" indoors or out by making a circle of "rocks" from balled-up newspaper. Build a "fire" from orange, yellow, and red construction paper cut into flame shapes, crunched up, and placed inside the rock fire pit. Light the "fire" by putting flashlights around the rock ring and pointing the beams at the "flames." You won't be able to cook anything over this fire, obviously, but s'mores (page 88) made on the stove or in the microwave are still a sweet treat.

And if the campout is in your living room and you're lucky enough to have a fireplace, ask your adults to help you build a crackling fire and then roast some 'mallows around it.

THE BATHROOM

If you're at a site with facilities, you can skip this whole section because there are showers and sinks and hopefully you know how to use them! But if your site is a little more rustic and doesn't have restrooms, read on. The secrets of pit toilets, wilderness showers, and spraying toothpaste await.

Pack Out the Yucky Stuff

As unpleasant as it sounds, if you're digging your own pit toilet (see page 48), you'll have to take all the toilet paper you use (and the paper you don't use) out of the wilderness with you. In your Toilet Kit (page 7) you'll have a trowel for digging and filling the toilet hole, a roll of clean toilet paper, and a zip-top bag for the dirty paper. After you use toilet tissue, put it in the appropriate zip-top bag (make sure to zip it!) and keep it in the big zip-top bag with the clean TP. (You can leave the trowel near the hole or stash it in the big bag if you plan to go on a long hike and will need to make a "pit stop" on the way.) Once the bag of dirty TP is full, put it with the rest of your trash and replace it with a fresh bag.

Can You Dig It?

What You Need

A Toilet Kit (trowel, toilet paper, and zip-top bag—see page 7)

D igging a toilet pit may sound gross, but it's kinda fun and not so bad when you really do it.

What You Do

1 Pick your spot. This should be at least 200 steps from water, DOWNwind of your campsite (so you won't have any foul-smelling breezes blowing your way), and nicely hidden by trees or large boulders—you do want privacy in your privy, after all.

2 Use the trowel to dig a hole about 2 feet wide and 1 foot deep. Leave the trowel and the rest of the Toilet Kit by the hole so people can use the trowel to sprinkle the hole with dirt after each use (a layer of dirt encourages the decomposition of waste material). You already know what to do with the clean toilet paper; for what to do with the used toilet paper, see Pack Out the Yucky Stuff, page 47.

3 When you leave camp, make sure the hole is completely filled with dirt and covered over with fallen leaves and branches.

Brushing Your Teeth

Just because you're camping in the wild doesn't mean your teeth should be green. Brush twice a day, as the dentist says, but only use a small amount of toothpaste. Do your brushing business then take a swig of clean water and rinse. Here's the fun part—SPRAY the water out of your mouth to spread the foamy stuff around. (This reduces the environmental impact because you're spreading a little bit of toothpaste across a wider area instead of leaving a big gooey clump in just one spot.) Rinse and spray again. Ta-da! Clean mouth and minimally impacted wilderness.

Washing Up

When you're camping in the backyard, staying clean isn't an issue—just pop inside for a shower or bath whenever you get too grimy. And in many campgrounds there are showers available, so the big stink never really catches up to you.

But camping in the backwoods is a whole different ballgame. Part of the fun of being in the wild is that you don't have to take a bath every night! Wahoo! But a few active days and bathless nights can make for a pretty fragrant bunch of campers. The problem is that most soaps can really harm nature and its inhabitants. Not to worry, though: There are ways to stay clean and keep the environment safe.

If you're going to use soap outside, make sure you use special biodegradable soaps made specifically for camping. And always wash at least 100 yards from any water source. As when washing dishes (page 40), scatter your dirty gray water and drip soapy water on hardy surfaces like rock and gravel.

IT'S GOOD TO BE clean when you're camping, but choose your soap products wisely. Most soaps contain harmful chemicals that can upset the balance of nature, killing plants and insects and making animals sick. And all soaps contain something called "surfactants," which break up the surface of water and make it hard for floating insects to float. To be on the safe side, use soaps that are labeled all-natural, biodegradable, and hypo-allergenic.

Camping Activity

Wilderness Shower

What You Need

2 to 3 large zip-top bags

A dark piece of cloth (like a black T-shirt)

A sunny spot

Biodegradable soap

A friend to hold the bags (or some rope to tie them to a sturdy branch)

Something to poke small holes: a pocketknife (with grown-up supervision), a small nail, or even a pen or a pencil

There are portable showers available at camping stores but it's more fun to make your own. The shower doesn't last long, but it certainly gets the crust off!

What You Do

1 Fill the bags with clean water and zip them closed.

2 Place the full bags on top of the dark cloth in a sunny spot for a couple of hours. The cloth will soak up more heat and speed up the heating process. (For a cold shower, skip this step.)

3 When the water is warm, get your biodegradable soap ready and find a place at least 100 yards away from camp or a body of water—you will be producing waste water that you don't want nearby.

4 Have a friend hold up 1 bag over your head. Quickly poke a few holes in the bottom. Get wet and lather up. Do this quickly—the water runs out fast!

5 Poke holes in the second and third bag to rinse.

GOOD GRUB

Fun Food for Hungry Campfolk

*"Food is good,
food is great.
Pile it higher
on my plate!"*

—OLD SUMMER CAMP CHANT

There's just something about being outdoors that makes food taste better. Maybe it's the fresh air. Maybe it's playing in the woods that works up the appetite—riding bikes, hiking, canoeing, and horsing around.

When you cook outdoors you may not have the same comforts of your home kitchen—no sink, no counters, no oven. But with some planning and improvisation, you can whip up delicious, satisfying meals without a hitch.

MAPPING OUT YOUR MEALS

If you're camping in the backyard or by car, you'll have more food options than if you have to carry all your food (and maybe even water) to a backcountry site. With car or backyard camping, you will be able to enjoy a variety of fresh foods that can safely be kept in a cooler. If you're embarking on a backcountry trip, you'll have to plan a little differently—carrying a heavy cooler isn't really an option. You *can* bring some fresh foods, but you'll eat those early on and then rely on foods that will keep at room temperature.

Either way, it's smart to be organized. Take these steps at home before taking one step out the door.

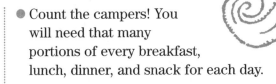

- Count the campers! You will need that many portions of every breakfast, lunch, dinner, and snack for each day.

- Design daily menus. (You don't have to stick to them exactly, but it'll help ensure all the meals are covered.) For some examples, see pages 55 and 57. Choose recipes that seem tasty and doable—deep-fried mozzarella sticks may sound delish, but they're not really campfire-friendly.

- Make lists of the ingredients you will need for each meal and snack (keeping in mind the number of portions for each).

- Here's the fun part: You can start to prepare the meals before you leave. If you're using recipes from this book, simply follow the

"Before You Leave Home" directions. Put each partially prepared meal into a foil pouch and/or a zip-top bag as directed. You can bag other foods, like biscuit and brownie mix, as well. Using a permanent marker, label each bag with the day and meal you plan to eat it (for example, "Day 2, Breakfast") and any directions necessary to finish the meal (e.g., "Add ½ cup water"). If it's an individual portion, write the name of the person it belongs to.

● Pack your meals in order—backward. Put the last day's meals on the bottom. Stack the remaining meals in the order that you'll eat them. The last meal you stack will be for the first day so you can reach it easily. If you're packing a cooler, put a few inches of ice on the bottom and layer ice between each day's layer of food. Cover the top layer with ice, too.

IN ORDER TO STAY cool, coolers need ice . . . and ice melts. Restock your cooler's ice supply every day (fresh food should be kept at 40°F or colder), or else plan to switch to nonperishable food (that is, food that doesn't go bad) after the first or second day. Eating rotten food can really spoil a good trip!

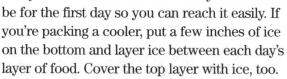

Campground Comfort Cafe

Use this menu as a guide as you plan your meals—you'll probably want to tweak it to fit each day's activities. For example, if you're planning a sunrise hike one day, you might want to have a quick breakfast and then linger over a cooked lunch; if the next day calls for a morning-to-afternoon canoe paddle, a speedy breakfast and lunch might be in order. Mix up the menu as you see fit.

You'll notice that we've included fresh fruit, meat, and dairy in this menu, thinking that you'll probably have a cooler handy. Just be sure to restock the cooler with ice *every day*, or else eat these items within the first or second day of your trip—they don't call them perishables for nothing! (You could also ask a grown-up to make a midweek supermarket run if you expect to hanker after a hunk of meat later in the week.)

Backyard or Car Camping

	Breakfast	Lunch	Dinner	Snacks
Day 1	Flapjacks (page 61); with butter and syrup; fresh fruit; juice; cocoa	Solar Oven Pizza (page 85); carrot sticks; apples; juice or water	Chow Down Chili (page 74), corn bread*; s'mores (page 90); juice	GORP (page 67); fresh fruit; cheese sticks; water
Day 2	Hearty Oatmeal (page 62); toast with jam; juice; cocoa	Salami-and-cheese roll-ups; cucumber slices; celery sticks; fresh fruit; juice	Coconutty Curry Chicken (page 79); couscous; salad; Kick-the-Can Ice Cream (page 90)	Energy bars; water; chocolate milk
Day 3	Foil Breakfast (page 64); toasted bagels with peanut butter and jam; juice; cocoa	Cheese and crackers; fresh fruit; hummus; hard-boiled eggs; chocolate milk	Stew for a Crew (page 73); biscuits*; Banana Boats (page 87); water or milk	Fruit leather; animal crackers; water
Day 4	Cold cereal with milk; dried fruits; seeds; and nuts; juice; cocoa	Boxed macaroni and cheese with dehydrated peas; crackers; avocado slices; juice	Spider Dog (page 70); Bannock (page 71); brownies*; iced tea	Jerky; dried fruit; chocolate; water
Day 5	Bacon and Eggs in a Bag (page 63); toast with margarine; honey; and jam; hot cocoa	PB&J sandwiches; dried apricots and apples; leftover brownies; water	Tuna Wiggle (page 81); instant vanilla pudding; canned peaches; powdered lemonade	Chocolate; fresh fruit; water
Day 6	Granola and milk; fresh fruit; juice; cocoa	Instant noodles with broccoli and cheese; fresh fruit; cookies; juice	Baked beans with sliced hot dogs; Apple Crisp (page 93); iced tea	Yogurt-covered pretzels; nuts; water
Day 7	Bannock (page 71); with margarine and jam; hard-boiled eggs; juice	Instant soup; bread; cheese; apples; cookies; water	Eat on the way home!	GORP (page 67); jerky; water

* For tips on baking biscuits, corn bread, brownies, and other goodies, see "An Easy Campfire Oven," page 92.

No-Frills Noshery

Take a gander at the menu on the right. You'll see that fresh ingredients are used at the beginning of the trip and dried foods play a key role toward the end of the week. While you're probably used to eating lots of fresh fruits and veggies at home, you'll be amazed by the yummy meals you can put together with some dry, no-spoil ingredients and a bit of imagination.

It's easy to pack light *and eat well*—everything tastes better outdoors.

Backcountry Camping

	Breakfast	**Lunch**	**Dinner**	**Snacks**
Day 1	Eat before you head out on your trip.	Salami-and-cheese roll-ups; cucumber slices; celery sticks; fresh fruit; juice	Stew for a Crew (page 73); biscuits*; Banana Boats (page 87); juice	GORP (page 67); fresh fruit; cheese sticks; water
Day 2	Hearty Oatmeal (page 62); toast with jam; powdered juice; cocoa	PB&J sandwiches; dried apricots and apples; cookies	Boxed macaroni and cheese with dehydrated peas; fried slices of canned ham; water	Energy bars; water; powdered chocolate milk
Day 3	Toasted bagels with peanut butter and jam; powdered juice; cocoa	Leftover sliced ham; bread; hard cheese; dried fruit; water; powdered juice	Noodles with dehydrated spaghetti sauce; Bannock (page 71) with jam and honey; powdered fruit punch	Fruit leather; GORP (page 67)
Day 4	Powdered eggs* (see page 82) in tortillas; powdered juice; cocoa	Instant soup; leftover Bannock with hard cheese; apples; cookies; water	Dehydrated chili; vanilla or chocolate instant pudding; powdered lemonade	Jerky; dried fruit; chocolate; water
Day 5	Granola with powdered milk* (see page 82); dried fruit; powdered juice; cocoa	Instant noodles with sauce; dried fruit; jerky; crackers; cookies; powdered juice	Dehydrated stew; Bannock (page 71); s'mores (page 88); water	Chocolate; pretzels; water
Day 6	Kid Power Cold Cereal (page 60); powdered juice; cocoa	Crackers with peanut butter and honey; apples; carrot sticks; hard cheese; banana chips; powdered juice	Dehydrated curry vegetables; couscous; Sloppy Berry Cake (page 92); water	Dried fruit; cookies; nuts; water
Day 7	Hearty Oatmeal (page 62); toast with jam; powdered juice; cocoa	Crackers with hard cheese and dehydrated hummus; apples; jerky; powdered chocolate milk	Eat on the way home!	Yogurt-covered raisins; jerky; water

If you're backpacking and a recipe or packaged food calls for milk or eggs, you can use powdered instead—you'll just need to add water. Check the package directions for the correct amount of water needed, and also see "Take a Powder," page 82, for helpful hints.

Get Fresh

Fresh foods are healthy, delicious, and a welcome addition to any camping meal, but they are heavy and can go bad. If you won't have access to a fridge or a cooler, you'll want to use fruits, veggies, and some dairy sparingly, and no fresh meats. (Some hardier fruits and veggies, like apples and carrots, can last a few days without refrigeration; so can hard cheese, such as Cheddar.) Here's the basic breakdown of what stays fresh and for how long.

Meat and Dairy

Meat, poultry, and fish:

Always keep these on ice—they should stay at a temperature of at least 40°F, or they will spoil. Ground meat should be eaten on the first day; poultry, fish, and whole meat (like steak) should be eaten in a day or two. Don't bother with fresh meat, poultry, or fish if you don't have a cooler—unless you buy it (or catch it) an hour or so before you cook it.

Bacon, hot dogs, cold cuts, and processed meats:

These meats are specially prepared or treated so that they last longer, but most of them still need to be kept cool. Eat cold cuts within three to four days. Bacon and hot dogs will keep for about a week in a cold cooler. Dried meats like jerky will last a good long time; hard salami should last about a week, but keep it well wrapped and cool. And canned meats, such as ham, Spam, Vienna sausages, chicken, or tuna, will last for a long time as long as the can is sealed. Once you pop that bad boy open, though, eat it immediately.

Milk, eggs, and cheese:

Milk should be kept cold and used within five days (it'll start to smell sour if it's going bad). Eggs should last for about a week, but they need to be chilled, too. Hard cheese, like Cheddar and Swiss, will last for at least a week (even at room temperature), and longer if it's kept in a block (instead of presliced). Individual prewrapped slices of American cheese are a good bet for the cooler, since they're processed and take longer to spoil.

Vegetables and Fruit

Lettuce:

If you don't have a cooler, eat lettuce the first day. Otherwise, it will keep about three days if wrapped in plastic and stored in a cold place.

Tomatoes, cucumbers, peppers:

Pack these in a hard plastic container—they get squished pretty easily. Eat them in about three days if you don't have a cooler; they should last longer on ice (but if you cut one open, finish it there and then).

Green beans, cauliflower, and broccoli:

Prep these first by cleaning them, snapping off the ends of the beans, and cutting broccoli and cauliflower into bite-size pieces. Pack them in zip-top bags. Eat them on day one or two, or keep them in the cooler for about four days (toss them if they start to smell funky).

Carrots, celery, cabbage, potatoes, onions, turnips, beets, and almost ripe avocados:

These are a camper's best veggie friends. They can take a beating in a pack and still come out fresh as a daisy. (Leave the avocado whole until you're ready to eat it.) If you cut these veggies beforehand and pack them into zip-top bags, they're a snap to store and easy to add to soups and stews.

Kiwis, mango, melon, berries, peaches, and plums:

Cut up the kiwis, mango, and melon and put them in zip-top bags or plastic containers on ice. Peaches, plums, and berries should be kept whole, wrapped in plastic, and stored on ice. Eat these fruits within the first few days.

Apples, oranges, and pears:

These guys can go the distance, with or without a cooler. Just keep them whole and they should last the entire time you're camping (provided you're not going away for more than a week and you don't leave them baking in the sun).

IT MAY SOUND gross (and look even grosser), but a little mold on your hard cheese isn't the end of the world. Molds are tiny microscopic creatures that have threadlike roots that can burrow into the foods they grow on. Most of them are harmless, and some are even used in the cheese-making process. You can still eat hard cheeses (like Cheddar or Parmesan) even if they have mold on them. Just have a grown-up remove it with a knife—the cheese underneath will still be good!

ENERGY- BOOSTER BREAKFASTS

I t's nice to have a delicious and filling breakfast after a night in camp and before a day spent tromping around. You've probably already heard it before, and it's true—breakfast is the most important meal of the day! If you don't start the day with a full tank, you may just peter out before you reach the top of that mountain or the end of that bike ride, or finish whatever fun you and your fellow campers have in store. The last thing you want to do is run out of energy and miss something great along the way, so be sure to fuel up on breakfast every day.

Kid Power Cold Cereal

Cold cereal really packs a power punch when you charge it up with delicious treats like nuts and dried fruits.

What You Need

✔ **1 cup of your favorite cereal**

✔ **3 tablespoons powdered milk**

✔ **¼ cup dried fruits (such as cranberries, blueberries, raisins, or chopped apricots or dates)**

✔ **¼ cup nuts and seeds (such as peanuts, cashews, walnuts, almonds, or sunflower seeds)**

✔ **1 quart-size zip-top bag**

✔ **A permanent marker**

Before You Leave Home

1. Place all ingredients in the zip-top bag.

2. Write: "Add ½ cup water" on the outside of the bag with a permanent marker.

3. Toss the bag in your pack.

At the Campsite

1. Open the bag, add ½ cup water, zip the bag closed, and shake, shake, shake until all the ingredients are mixed. (The powdered milk will turn into liquid milk in the bag.)

2. Open the bag and use it as a bowl. Grab your spoon and start munching.

1 serving

Flapjacks

These tasty pancakes help you greet the day with gusto.

What You Need

- ✔ ²⁄₃ **cup unbleached white flour**
- ✔ ¹⁄₃ **cup whole wheat flour**
- ✔ **1 tablespoon sugar**
- ✔ **2 teaspoons baking powder**
- ✔ ¹⁄₂ **teaspoon salt**
- ✔ **Dash of nutmeg**
- ✔ ¹⁄₃ **cup powdered milk (or 1 cup regular milk, to be added at the campsite)**
- ✔ **1¹⁄₂ tablespoons powdered egg (or 1 fresh egg, to be added at the campsite)**
- ✔ ¹⁄₂ **cup chopped fruit, fresh or canned (optional)**

- ✔ **4 teaspoons oil**
- ✔ **Butter and maple syrup, for serving**

- ✔ **1 gallon-size zip-top freezer bag**
- ✔ **Permanent marker**

Before You Leave Home

1. Place the flours, sugar, baking powder, salt, and nutmeg in a zip-top bag. If you are using powdered milk and eggs, add those as well. Seal the bag and shake it to mix the contents.

2. If you used powdered milk and eggs, write: "Add 1 cup plus 1¹⁄₂ tablespoons of water, 3 teaspoons of oil, and fruit" on the bag with a permanent marker. If you didn't use powdered milk and eggs, write: "Add 1 cup milk, 1 egg, 3 teaspoons oil, and ¹⁄₂ cup chopped fruit" on the bag.

3. Toss the bag in your pack. Store the butter and fruit (and fresh milk and eggs, if using) in your cooler (canned fruit and maple syrup can be stored in your pack).

At the Campsite

1. Follow the directions that you wrote on the bag for adding the liquid ingredients. Seal the bag and massage it with your fingers to mix.

2. Open the bag and add the fruit. If you use canned fruit, drain it first.

3. Seal the bag and massage it again.

4. Get a grown-up to help you heat a griddle over a low fire.

5. Put the remaining teaspoon of oil in the griddle.

6. Pour about ½ cup batter per flapjack on the griddle.

7. Cook until the center of the flapjacks start to bubble and the edges look cooked, about 3 minutes. Turn the flapjacks and cook a few minutes more on the second side.

8. Serve with butter and maple syrup.

4 servings

Hearty Oatmeal

Oatmeal, only better—packed with sweet and crunchy surprises.

What You Need

- **2 individual serving–size packets plain instant oatmeal**
- **¼ cup chopped walnuts or peanuts**
- **¼ cup chopped almonds**
- **¼ cup raisins**
- **¼ cup chopped apricots**
- **2 tablespoons brown sugar**
- **½ cup powdered milk (optional)**
- **Fresh berries (optional)**

- **2 quart-size zip-top bags**
- **Permanent marker**

Before You Leave Home

1. Place the oatmeal, walnuts, almonds, raisins, apricots, brown sugar, and powdered milk in a zip-top bag.

2. Write: "Oatmeal—add 1½ cups boiling water and fresh berries" on the bag with a permanent marker.

3. Toss the bag in your pack. Put the fresh berries in a zip-top bag and store them in the cooler.

At the Campsite

1. Pour your oatmeal into a bowl.

2. Boil water and add 1½ cups to your bowl.

3. Mix it well and add the fresh berries if you like.

4. Let it cool a bit and enjoy.

1 serving

Breakfast in a Bag

ADULT SUPERVISION

This nifty breakfast cooks in a paper bag over hot coals, so try not to let the bag get too close to the fire or it will ignite. This recipe is better for the backyard or campsite than for the backwoods.

What You Need

✔ **3 to 4 thick slices of bacon**
✔ **2 fresh eggs**
✔ **Salt and pepper, to taste**

✔ **A brown paper lunch bag**
✔ **A Good Stick (see page 71)**

What You Do

1. Open the paper lunch bag and place it on a flat surface with the opening facing up.

2. Lay the bacon on the bottom of the bag to cover it completely.

3. Crack the eggs into the bag on top of the bacon.

4. Pinch the top of the bag closed, fold it down 3 or 4 times, and run your fingers across the fold until it is secure.

5. Get an adult to help you poke 2 holes for your stick through the folded-closed top of the bag. Thread the end of your stick through both holes. Make sure this is secure, because you will be dangling the bag over the fire.

6. Using the stick, hold the bag over hot coals for about 10 to 15 minutes—don't let it touch the coals, or it could catch fire! You'll hear sizzling and popping sounds—that means the food is cooking.

7. Peek into the bag and check to see if your breakfast is cooked. When the eggs are set and the bacon is browned and crispy, it's ready.

8. Place the bag on a plate. Open the bag and roll down or tear off the top to make a dish.

9. Add salt and pepper, if you like, and eat!

1 serving

Foil Breakfast

ADULT SUPERVISION

What You Need

- ✔ 1 small potato, grated
- ✔ 1 precooked sausage, chopped
- ✔ 2 fresh eggs (or powdered eggs if you're backcountry camping; see page 82)

- ✔ Salt and pepper to taste
- ✔ 2 sheets (12 x 12 inches each) of heavy-duty aluminum foil
- ✔ 1 quart-size zip-top bag

Figure 1.

Before You Leave Home

1. Lay 1 sheet of foil on your countertop. Fold up the corners (so the egg won't run off the foil when you add it).

2. Put the grated potato and chopped sausage on the foil (see Figure 1).

3. Scramble the eggs and pour them over the potato and sausage.

4. Fold the food-topped foil sheet into a packet (see Figures 2 and 3): Bring together 2 opposite ends of the foil and fold them down a few times to seal the edge. Roll up the open ends a few times. Make sure all the food is inside the foil—no leaks—and that there is about an inch of breathing room all around (food expands when it cooks, so the pouch will burst if it's too tight). Wrap the second sheet of foil around the packet to make sure it's sealed.

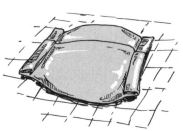

Figure 2.

Figure 3.

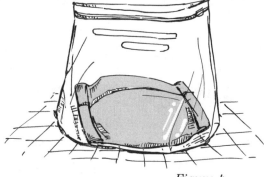

Figure 4.

5. Place the packet in the zip-top bag (see Figure 4), gently press out the air, and seal it. Label the bag "Foil Breakfast—cook on embers or on grill for 20 minutes." Store on ice in a cooler for up to 4 days.

At the Campsite

1. Remove the foil packet from the plastic bag and cook:

> **Over a campfire**—when the campfire has burned long enough to make embers, have an adult move aside some of the burning wood and settle the foil pouches in the embers (see Figure 5). Place some embers on top of the packet. The breakfast should cook in 15 to 20 minutes.

> **On a grill**—when the fire is hot, have a grown-up place the packet of foil on a grill directly over the heat. Cook for about 15 to 20 minutes.

(If you can't make a campfire for cooking, place the contents of the foil pouch in a pan over medium heat on your camp stove, and cook until the eggs are set and the potato is soft. Not as much fun, but still mighty tasty.)

2. Remove the packet from the fire. Have a grown-up open the foil carefully (watch out for steam escaping from the foil pouch). Check to see if the eggs are cooked through and the potato is soft. If they aren't, rewrap the packet and place it back on the fire for a few more minutes.

3. When the packet is done, place it on a plate. Open it carefully and eat the breakfast directly out of the pouch.

1 serving

Figure 5.

LUNCH IN A FLASH

These quick-and-easy lunch ideas are perfect for when you're mid-hike, mid-ride, or mid-exploration and a speedy meal is in order. Just prep 'em, bag 'em, and put 'em in your pack.

As for snacks, stash some small snack baggies in your pocket or pack so you can stop for a quick munch if your hunger pangs hit before or after lunch.

Sandwiches

- ✔ Turkey, roast beef, ham, or salami and cheese
- ✔ Peanut butter and jelly
- ✔ Almond or peanut butter and chocolate chips
- ✔ Honey and fresh fruits such as banana, peach, or apple
- ✔ Hummus, shredded carrots, and cucumber slices
- ✔ Cream cheese and jam
- ✔ Tuna salad

Finger Foods

- ✔ Beef or turkey jerky
- ✔ Hard-boiled eggs
- ✔ String-cheese sticks or mini cheese rounds
- ✔ Fresh fruit (apples, pears, and oranges are good bets)
- ✔ Dried fruit or fruit leather
- ✔ Nuts and seeds
- ✔ Granola bars
- ✔ Fresh cut-up veggies like carrots, celery, and broccoli florets, with dip such as hummus or peanut butter
- ✔ Crackers, pretzels, or chips

Quick, Hot, and Filling

- ✔ Instant soups—just add hot water.
- ✔ Instant noodles. Bring your bowl, spoon, and a Thermos of boiling water with you on the trail.

Drinks

✓ Water—it's delicious after a long hike— see page 94 for safe drinking water tips.

✓ Juice, milk, or chocolate milk boxes. Get the ones that keep without refrigeration.

✓ Instant powdered juice drinks—just pour some powder into your full water bottle.

✓ At night (or even at breakfast), warm up with a hot drink such as cocoa, fruity herbal tea, or hot Tang with a bit of cinnamon (it's actually really tasty). Bottoms up!

Something Sweet

✓ Chocolate bars

✓ Cookies

✓ Red or black licorice

✓ Instant pudding or packaged pudding cups

✓ Toaster tarts or breakfast bars

✓ Energy bars

✓ Yogurt-covered raisins or pretzels

✓ GORP (see below)

GOOD OL' GORP

GORP stands for Good Old Raisins and Peanuts, but you can make it with anything you like. Just grab a plastic bag, toss in a handful of nuts, a handful of raisins, and whatever else you want. (You can also try Friendship GORP, where everyone adds their favorite ingredient to the bag.) Some "add-on" ideas:

✓ Peanuts, cashews, walnuts, pecans, and/or almonds

✓ Chocolate chips and/or M&M's

✓ Banana chips

✓ Goldfish crackers

✓ Tiny graham crackers

✓ Mini pretzels

✓ Mini marshmallows

✓ Crunchy cereal such as Golden Grahams, Kix, or Chex

✓ Pumpkin and/or sunflower seeds

✓ Coconut flakes

✓ Granola clusters

✓ Dried cranberries, apricots, apples, and/or cherries

✓ Gummy candies

WHAT'S FOR DINNER

After a day of activity, it's fun to gather together and make dinner at the campsite. You'll find lots of delicious, easy-to-make recipes here, but you and your grown-ups can also adapt your favorite recipes to outdoor cooking. And if you want to get really funky and experiment while outdoors, check out The Dinner Pantry, right, and see what sorts of delicious creations you can come up with.

Pigs in Blankets

Use the Bannock dough from page 71 to make this old campout favorite.

What You Need

✔ 4 hot dogs
✔ 1 recipe Bannock dough (page 71)

✔ Ketchup, relish, or mustard

✔ 4 Good Sticks, (see page 71)

What You Do

1. Poke each stick about 3 inches into one end of each hot dog.

2. Divide the dough into four small balls. Flatten each ball between your hands into a pancake about ½- to ¼-inch thick.

3. Wrap each pancake around a hot dog and pinch it closed along the edge.

4. Roast the dogs over the fire. Make sure to hold them close to the embers but not touching.

5. When the dough is puffy and brown and the hot dogs are sizzling, they're done, about 10 to 15 minutes.

6. Let them cool, slather on the condiments, and gobble 'em up!

4 servings

The Dinner Pantry

These foods and flavorings stay fresh for a long time and are great to have on hand for adding to recipes or for whipping up amazing meals on the fly when fresh food is running a bit low.

Proteins

- ✔ Canned tuna and meats: for sandwiches, or to mix with a prepared package of mac and cheese

- ✔ Beans (dehydrated or canned): lentils, black beans, pinto beans, or chickpeas. These are great for chili, soups, dips, and burritos. You can also use instant hummus or black bean dip—just add water.

- ✔ Nuts: whole nuts for snacking, or adding to pancakes and GORP; peanut butter for slathering on crackers and breads

- ✔ Chicken, beef, or vegetable bouillon cubes: Add these "square soups" to stews and chilis, or put one in a cup of boiling water for a quick sip of broth.

Fruits and veggies

- ✔ Dried veggies: add to soups, sauces, or casseroles

- ✔ Dried fruits: add to pancakes, GORP, biscuits, and other baked goods

- ✔ Canned fruits: a delicious, sweet treat

Grains / starches

- ✔ Instant rice
- ✔ Instant potatoes
- ✔ Pasta and couscous
- ✔ Bisquick: great for making biscuits, dumplings, and quickie bread
- ✔ Bread and crackers
- ✔ Corn bread and brownie mixes

Dairy

- ✔ Dried eggs: Use them in baking or to make scrambled eggs for egg burritos.

- ✔ Dried milk: Add to cereal, oatmeal, packaged macaroni and cheese, cocoa, and baked goods.

Basics / spices

- ✔ Cooking oil and vinegar
- ✔ Sugar (white sugar, brown sugar, and honey)
- ✔ Powdered eggs and nonfat milk
- ✔ Coffee, tea, and cocoa mix
- ✔ Condiments (mustard, ketchup, soy sauce, jam, and hot sauce)
- ✔ Salt and pepper
- ✔ Spices: Depends on what you're making, but cinnamon, nutmeg, chili powder, curry, garlic salt, and Italian spices are always useful.

Spider Dog

ADULT SUPERVISION

For campout deliciousness pure and simple, you can't beat a fire-roasted hot dog on a stick. But give that dog a slice here and there, and you'll have a leggy-looking spider dog. YUM!

What You Need

✔ **A hot dog**

✔ **A knife—and a grown-up to help use it**

✔ **A Good Stick (see page 71)**

What You Do

1. Poke the stick into one end of the dog. Go about halfway in to be sure the hot dog stays on the stick and doesn't do any fancy dives into the fire.

2. Get a grown-up to help you make 2 lengthwise slices in an ✕ on the other end of your hot dog. The slices should end about ½ inch from the end of the stick.

3. Roast your hot dog over a campfire, barbecue, or stove until the ends sizzle and curl up.

4. Let it sit for a few minutes until it's cool enough to touch, then take it off the stick.

Poke the stick into the hot dog's other end (where the ends are curled back).

5. Make 2 lengthwise slices in an ✕ in the hot dog's free end, to about ½ inch from the end of the stick.

6. Roast this end until it sizzles and the "legs" curl back.

7. Let the spider dog cool a bit, then chomp it right off the stick.

1 serving

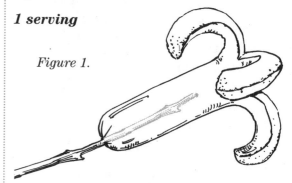

Figure 1.

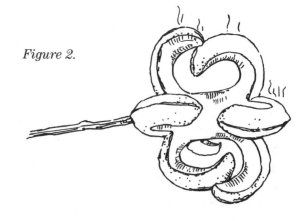

Figure 2.

Bannock: Bread on a Stick

ADULT SUPERVISION

Bannock is an old word meaning "wilderness bread." The cool thing about bannock is that you start it in the kitchen at home, bring the dry ingredients in a bag to camp, add water, put it on a stick, and bake it over a fire. It smells amazing, and when it's done it's the most delicious hot trail bread you can imagine!

Bannock is great as a snack with butter and jam, or with a meal of chili, stew, or soup.

What You Need

- 2 cups all-purpose flour
- 4 teaspoons baking powder
- ½ stick (4 tablespoons) butter, plus extra if cooking in a skillet
- 2 teaspoons white sugar
- ½ teaspoon salt
- ½ cup cold water
- 1 gallon-size zip-top bag
- Permanent marker
- 2 Good Sticks (below)

A Good Stick

You can cook almost anything on a stick—from bread to hot dogs to dessert—but you need to have a good one first. Here are a few tips:

- Look for a young stick (it should be flexible and greenish on the inside). Older sticks will catch fire.

- Find a stick that's straight, strong, and about the width of your index finger and the length of your arm.

- Have a grown-up remove all the bark and branches and sharpen the end of the stick with a knife. The point makes it easier to insert the stick into food—think hot dogs or marshmallows—and stripping the bark makes the stick a little cleaner and less likely to spark up.

Before You Leave Home

1. Place the flour, baking powder, butter, sugar, and salt in the zip-top bag.

2. Seal the bag and massage it until you end up with a crumbly mixture.

3. Write "Add ½ cup cold water" on the bag with a permanent marker.

4. Toss the bag in the cooler (the butter in the bread mixture will spoil if it's not kept cold.

At the Campsite

1. Add ½ cup of water to the bag. Seal it and massage the bag well until a dough forms.

2. Open the bag and pull out the dough. Divide it into 4 balls.

3. Roll each ball between your hands to make a snake about the width of a hot dog.

4. Wind each snake around a stick.

5. Roast the bread sticks over hot embers. Hold the bread close to but not touching any ember or flame.

6. When the bread is puffy and golden brown, you know it's done—10 to 20 minutes, depending on how hot the fire is.

7. Let it cool, then dig in.

4 servings

Dough Diversity

Try these variations with a ball (¼ recipe) of bannock:

Cheeseburger Pie: Roll out the dough and top half with cooked hamburger meat, salt, pepper, and slices of cheese. Fold the dough over the filling and pinch the edges closed. Prick the top of the pie with a fork, and fry it in a greased skillet until the dough browns and the cheese melts.

Pizza on a Pole: Roll out the dough, top it with tomato sauce and grated mozzarella cheese, and roll it into a snake (with the filling inside). Wrap the snake around a sturdy stick and roast it until the dough is golden brown.

Cinnamon Roll-ups: Dot the top of a rolled-out bannock with butter, then sprinkle it with brown sugar and cinnamon. Roll up the dough, (with the filling inside) wind it around a sturdy stick, and roast until the dough is golden brown.

Apple Pie on a Stick: Place some diced apples, cinnamon, and sugar on a flat piece of bannock, roll it into a snake (with the filling inside), wind it around a sturdy stick, and roast it until golden.

Stew for a Crew

Yummy, filling, and healthy, too! Ask an adult to help you cut up the meat and veggies. See the illustrations on pages 64–65 for help with preparing and cooking in foil packets.

What You Need

- About 1 pound of stew beef, cut into 1-inch cubes
- 1 tablespoon cornstarch
- 3 cloves garlic, minced
- 2 big carrots, sliced into rounds about ½-inch thick
- 2 potatoes, cut into ½-inch cubes
- 1 large onion, diced
- 1 cup frozen peas
- 1 cup frozen corn
- 1 teaspoon dried thyme
- 1 teaspoon garlic salt
- Pepper, to taste
- 1 gallon-size zip-top bag
- 8 to 12 sheets (12 x 12 inches each) heavy-duty aluminum foil (2 to 3 sheets per serving)
- 4 quart-size zip-top bags
- Permanent marker

Before You Leave Home

1. Put the beef and the cornstarch in the gallon-size zip-top bag. Seal the bag and shake it until the beef is coated with the cornstarch.

2. Empty the bag into a large bowl.

3. Place the garlic, carrots, potatoes, onion, peas, corn, thyme, garlic salt, and pepper in the bowl and stir everything together with a spoon.

4. For each serving, place a 12 x 12-inch piece of foil on the counter, turning up the edges a bit (so the food doesn't run when you add it). Divide the stew mixture evenly among the foil squares (see Figure 1, page 64).

5. Fold each food-topped foil sheet into a packet (see Figures 2 and 3, page 64): Bring together 2 opposite ends of the foil and fold them down a few times to seal the edge. Roll up the open ends a few times. Make sure all the food is inside the foil—no leaks—and that there is about an inch of breathing room all around (food expands when it cooks, so the pouch will burst if it's too tight).

6. Wrap a second sheet of foil around each packet to make sure it's sealed (you may need to add a third sheet, if the mixture is drippy).

7. Place each packet in a quart-size zip-top bag (see Figure 4, page 64). Seal each bag and label it with a permanent marker: "Stew for a Crew. Cook over hot coals for 30 to 40 minutes until done." Store the packets in a cooler for up to 2 days.

At the Campsite

1. Remove the foil packets from the plastic bags and cook:

Over a campfire—when the campfire has burned long enough to make embers, have an adult move aside some of the burning wood and settle the foil pouches in the embers (see Figure 5, page 65). Place some embers on top of each packet. The stew should cook in 30 to 40 minutes.

On a grill—when an adult says the fire is ready, place the packet of foil on a grill directly over the heat. Cook for 30 to 40 minutes.

2. Have a grown-up remove the packets from the fire and open the foil carefully (watch out for steam escaping from the foil pouch). Check to see if the meat is cooked through. If it isn't, rewrap the packets and place them back on the fire for a while.

3. When the packets are done, place each on a plate. Open the foil carefully and eat the stew directly out of the pouch.

4 servings

Chow Down Chili

This make-ahead meal is so easy— just pop the pouches on the coals, and in a half hour you'll have a delicious supper. See the illustrations on pages 64–65 for help with preparing and cooking in foil packets.

What You Need

- ✔ 1 can of black beans, rinsed and drained
- ✔ 1 can of kidney beans, rinsed and drained
- ✔ 1 large can of chopped tomatoes with liquid
- ✔ 1 large onion, chopped
- ✔ 1 pound ground beef or turkey
- ✔ 1 tablespoon chili powder
- ✔ Salt and pepper, to taste
- ✔ 1 gallon-size zip-top bag
- ✔ 8 sheets (12 x 12 inches each) heavy-duty aluminum foil
- ✔ 4 quart-size zip-top bags
- ✔ Permanent marker
- ✔ Shredded cheese and sour cream, for garnish

Before You Leave Home

1. Put the beans, tomatoes, onion, ground beef or turkey, chili powder, and salt and pepper in the gallon-size zip-top bag and seal it. Massage the bag until the ingredients are mixed well.

2. Lay 4 sheets of foil on the countertop, turning up the edges a bit (so the food doesn't run when you add it). Divide the chili among the squares of foil—approximately 2 cups of chili per foil sheet (see Figure 1, page 64).

3. Fold each food-topped foil sheet into a packet (see Figures 2 and 3, page 64): Bring together 2 opposite ends of the foil and fold them down a few times to seal the edge. Roll up the open ends a few times. Make sure all the food is inside the foil—no leaks—and that it has about an inch of breathing room all around (food expands when it cooks, so the pouch will burst if it's too tight).

4. Wrap a second sheet of foil around each packet to make sure it's sealed. Place each packet in a quart-size zip-top bag (see Figure 4, page 64). Seal each bag and label it with a permanent marker: "Chili—cook over hot coals for 20 to 30 minutes until done." Store the bags in a cooler for up to 1 day.

At the Campsite

1. Remove the foil packets from the plastic bags and cook:

> **Over a campfire**—when the campfire has burned long enough to make embers, have an adult move aside some of the burning wood and settle the foil pouches in the embers (see Figure 5, page 65). Place some embers on top of each packet. The contents of the pouches should be cooked in 20 to 30 minutes.

> **On a grill**—when the coals are hot, place the packet of foil on a grill over the heat. Cook for 20 to 30 minutes.

2. Have a grown-up remove the packets from the fire and open the foil carefully (watch out for steam escaping from the foil pouch).

Check to see if the ground beef or turkey is cooked through. If it isn't, rewrap the packet and place it back on the fire for a while.

3. When the packets are done, place each on a plate. Open the foil carefully and eat directly out of the foil pouch.

4 servings

IF YOUR CLOTHES smell like dinner, change out of them before going to bed. You don't want them advertising any "all-night dining" messages to animals that happen to pass by.

Rigging Up a Bear Bag

ADULT SUPERVISION

What You Need

Gallon-size zip-top bags

Tall garbage bags

3 heavy-duty industrial-strength garbage bags

A tall, sturdy tree about 100 yards downwind from camp, with a wrist-thickness branch about 15 feet up

50 feet of rope

A "rock sock" (an old sock filled with a few rocks and knotted close to the rocks)

Bears aren't picky eaters. They like food, garbage, dirty pots and pans, even tempting toiletries like toothpaste and mouthwash.

If you're camping in bear country and your site doesn't have designated food storage bins, you'll want to tightly bag all of your food and trash and put it out of reach of hungry bears. Here's how.

What You Do

1 Using the gallon-size zip-top bags and the tall garbage bags, double-bag all your food items, garbage, and anything else that a hungry animal might smell and come searching after.

2 Place all these bagged items in a plastic garbage bag. Squeeze out all the air and tie a knot in the top.

3 Repeat step 2 with each of the remaining garbage bags. This is your "bear bag."

4 Tie one end of the rope to the rock sock. With a grown-up's help, toss it over the branch (this may take a few tries). Watch out when you do this—you don't want to conk anyone on the head.

5 Grab hold of the rock sock once it's over the branch, and use it to move the rope out along the branch about 10 to 15 feet from the tree trunk.

6 Tie the free end of the rope to the bear bag using a timber hitch (see page 111).

7 Pull the rock-sock end of the rope until the bear bag hangs down a good 4 feet from the branch. (This makes it hard for the bear to reach the bag from the ground, and also tough to reach it from the tree.)

8 Have a grown-up wrap the rock-sock end of the rope around the tree trunk about 3 times at head height. Tie off the rope using the figure-eight knot (see page 104).

Be UnBearable

Old candy wrappers and rotten lunch meat may not sound so appealing to you, but to bears, it's a feast! If you're camping in bear country, you'll want to take some precautions, or you might have an uninvited guest rummaging through your camp. Bears may seem cute and cuddly, but they're wild animals and they have not-so-cute-or-cuddly teeth and six-inch claws. These guys can be dangerous—you definitely don't want them nosing around your camp. Here are some tips to remember:

● If your campground has a bear locker, use it to store your food and garbage overnight. Include unexpected items like an empty ketchup bottle or the pants you spilled supper on (bears and other scavenging animals have a very strong sense of smell and don't mind eating stuff that we think of as inedible or gross).

● If you're car camping, keep all food double-bagged in a cooler in the trunk. Put garbage bags in the trunk, too.

● NEVER keep food, food wrappers, garbage, or scented toiletries in your tent.

● NEVER leave food— trail snacks, fruit, nuts, even juice—in your pack overnight.

● After every meal, always wash the dishes—don't leave them dirty. Store your clean dishes in the plastic bag you packed them in.

● If you're in the backcountry, have an adult rig up a bear bag (see page 76) at least 100 yards downwind of your campground. Make sure it's not near the path to the toilet area—you don't want to bump into a bear on your midnight bathroom run!

Coconutty Curry Chicken

ADULT SUPERVISION

This tasty, hearty meal refuels you after a day on the trail. See the illustrations on pages 64–65 for help with preparing and cooking in foil packets.

What You Need

- ✓ **4 tablespoons canola oil**
- ✓ **4 cups couscous, uncooked**
- ✓ **1 cup thinly sliced carrots**
- ✓ **1 cup thinly sliced zucchini**
- ✓ **2 cups thinly sliced potatoes**
- ✓ **2 cups frozen peas**
- ✓ **1 cup shredded coconut**
- ✓ **1 cup raisins (optional)**
- ✓ **4 skinless boneless chicken breasts**

- ✓ **2 cups mango chutney (or apricot preserves)**
- ✓ **4 teaspoons (or more) curry powder**
- ✓ **½ teaspoon salt**
- ✓ **2 cups water or chicken broth**

- ✓ **8 to 12 sheets (12 x 16 inches each) heavy-duty aluminum foil**
- ✓ **1 gallon-size zip-top bag**
- ✓ **4 quart-size zip-top bags**
- ✓ **Permanent marker**

Before You Leave Home

1. Lay out 4 sheets of foil on the countertop, turning up the edges a bit (so the food doesn't run when you add it).

2. Drizzle 1 teaspoon of oil on each sheet.

3. Place 1 cup of uncooked couscous in the center of each sheet.

4. Place the carrots, zucchini, potatoes, peas, coconut, and raisins in the gallon-size zip-top bag. Seal the bag and massage it with your fingers to mix the ingredients.

5. Divide the vegetable mixture evenly among the foil sheets. Place a chicken breast on each vegetable mound. (See Figure 1, page 64.)

6. Place the remaining oil, curry powder, salt, chutney, and water in the same bag you used to mix the vegetables. Seal the bag and massage it with your fingers to combine the ingredients.

7. Divide the curry mixture by pouring it evenly and carefully over the contents of each foil sheet.

8. Fold each food-topped foil sheet into a packet (see Figures 2 and 3, page 64): Bring together 2 opposite ends of the foil and fold them down a few times to seal the edge. Roll up the open ends a few times. Make sure all the food is inside the foil—no leaks—and that there is about an inch of breathing room all around. (Food expands when it cooks, so the pouch will burst if it's too tight.)

9. Wrap a second sheet of foil around each packet to make sure it's sealed (you may need to wrap a third sheet around each if the mixture is runny). Place each packet in a zip-top bag (see

Figure 4, page 64). Seal each bag and label it with a permanent marker: "Coconutty Curry Chicken—cook over hot coals for 45 minutes to 1 hour." Store the bags in a cooler for 1 to 2 days.

At the Campsite

1. Remove the foil packets from the plastic bags and cook:

> **Over a campfire**—when the campfire has burned long enough to make embers, have an adult move aside some of the burning wood and settle the foil pouches in the embers (see Figure 5, page 65). Place some embers on top of each packet. The contents of the pouch cook in 45 minutes to 1 hour.

On a grill—when the coals are hot but no longer flaming, place the foil packets on a grill over the heat. Cook for 45 minutes to 1 hour.

2. After 45 minutes have a grown-up remove the packets from the fire and open the foil carefully (watch out for steam escaping from the foil pouch). Check to see if the chicken is cooked through (the juices should run clear when the chicken is cut with a knife). If it isn't, rewrap the packet and place it back on the fire for a while.

3. When the packets are done, slide each onto a plate, unwrap the foil, and eat the curry chicken right from the pouch.

4 servings

Simple Foil Veggie Roasts

Even vegetables taste great when you cook them over a fire. You can roast almost anything in foil over a fire's embers or on a grill.

Clean and prep veggies first (with a grown-up's help), cutting them into bite-size pieces (except for corn on the cob, which you should husk and leave whole). You can cook vegetables separately on sheets of foil or mix them together (just check with your adult to make sure the veggies have similar cooking times, or some will be raw and others mush).

Put a tablespoon of butter or oil on top of the veggies, add salt and pepper (garlic salt tastes wonderful), and fold together the edges of the foil to create a packet. Set the packet on the embers or on the grill, and let the goodies cook. Potatoes, carrots, onions, and squash will take about an hour; corn, peppers, tomatoes, and green beans will take 20 to 30 minutes. Open the packets toward the end of the cooking time to check that the vegetables are cooked through.

Tuna Wiggle

This camp dinner treat is so tasty, you'll want to make it at home, too. See the illustrations on pages 64–65 for help with preparing and cooking in foil packets.

What You Need

- ✔ **4 baking potatoes**
- ✔ **2 cans light tuna packed in water, drained**
- ✔ **2 cans cream of mushroom soup**
- ✔ **2 cups frozen peas**
- ✔ **2 cups frozen corn**
- ✔ **Salt and pepper, to taste**

- ✔ **8 sheets (12 x 12 inches each) heavy-duty aluminum foil**
- ✔ **1 gallon-size zip-top bag**
- ✔ **4 quart-size zip-top bags**
- ✔ **Permanent marker**

Before You Leave Home

1. Lay 4 sheets of foil on your countertop, turning up the edges a bit (so the food doesn't run when you add it).

2. Get a grown-up to help you slice the potatoes in half lengthwise. Place 2 potato halves face up on each foil sheet.

3. Put the tuna, mushroom soup, peas, corn, and salt and pepper in the gallon-size zip-top bag. Seal it and mix the ingredients by massaging the bag with your fingers.

4. Pour the mixture on top of the potatoes on each foil sheet, dividing it evenly (see Figure 1, page 64).

5. Fold each food-topped foil sheet into a packet (see Figures 2 and 3, page 64): Bring together 2 opposite ends of the foil and fold them down a few times to seal the edge. Roll up the open ends a few times. Make sure all the food is inside the foil—no leaks—and that there is about an inch of breathing room all around. (Food expands when it cooks, so the pouch will burst if it's too tight.)

6. Wrap a second sheet of foil around each packet to make sure it's sealed. Place each packet in a quart-size zip-top bag (see Figure 4, page 64) and label each bag with a permanent marker: "Tuna Wiggle. Cook over hot coals for 1 hour." Place the bags in a cooler and store for up to 3 days.

At the Campsite

1. Remove the packets from the plastic bags and cook:

> **Over a campfire**—when the campfire has burned long enough to make embers, have an adult move aside some of the burning wood and settle the foil pouches in the embers (see Figure 5, page 65). Place some embers on top of each packet. The contents of the pouches should cook in about 1 hour.

On a grill—when the fire is hot, place the foil packets on a grill over the heat. Cook for about 1 hour.

2. Have a grown-up remove the packets from the heat and open the foil carefully (watch out for steam escaping from the foil pouch). Check to see if the potato is cooked through (you should be able to pierce it easily with a fork). If it isn't, rewrap the packet and place it back on the fire for a while.

3. When the potatoes are done, slide each packet onto a plate. Carefully open the foil and eat the Wiggle right from the pouch.

4 servings

Take a Powder

Got Dry Milk?

Use the chart below to figure out how much dry milk and water to substitute for regular milk.

A smart cereal tip: If you're having cereal with dry milk, pour the cereal into the bowl, sprinkle 1½ tablespoons of dry milk on top, pour ¼ cup water over that, and stir it all to mix.

To equal this amount of liquid milk	Use this much water	And this much non-fat dry milk powder
¼ cup	¼ cup	1½ tablespoons
½ cup	½ cup	3 tablespoons
1 cup	1 cup	⅓ cup

The Incredible Edible Dried Egg

To make the equivalent of one egg: Add ¼ cup water to 2 tablespoons powdered egg.

KEEP A CONDIMENT and spice bag handy. You'll probably use it at every meal. Fill it with little bottles of salt, pepper, and other spices; honey, sugar, coffee, tea, cocoa; powdered juice, iced tea, and lemonade; jam, ketchup, mustard, oil, and vinegar; extra powdered milk and powdered eggs.

Pizza Box Solar Oven

N eed an oven? Grab a pizza box, some aluminum foil and plastic wrap, and get cooking.

Take a look at the illustrations on page 84 for help making your oven.

To Make the Oven

1 Open up the pizza box and glue aluminum foil, shiny side up, to all the inside surfaces of the box except the top. Close the box.

2 On the outside of the top of the box, measure one inch from the edge on all sides and draw a square.

3 Have a grown-up help you cut along three lines of the square, leaving the fourth line along the box's hinge uncut. Fold open this newly cut flap, making a crease along the fourth line.

4 Open the box lid and glue aluminum foil to the inside surface of the new flap. Smooth any wrinkles in the foil as you go.

5 Tape the black construction paper to the inside bottom of the box.

What You Need

1 large pizza box

White glue

Several feet of aluminum foil

Ruler

Permanent marker

Sturdy scissors

1 sheet black construction paper

2½ feet clear plastic wrap

4 feet masking tape

2 feet string

A sunny day (peak hours are best—from 9:00 A.M. to 3:00 P.M.)

Pizza Box Solar Oven, contd.

6 Carefully stretch the plastic wrap over the opening of the box created by the new flap. Tape all around the edges of the plastic to seal it to the box.

7 Cover any cracks or tears around the box edges with tape to prevent air leaks. Make sure you can still open the box.

To Cook Stuff

1 Place the oven on a flat, level surface in the sunlight. The solar oven works best on sunny days from 9:00 A.M. to 3:00 P.M.

2 Place the food inside the oven. Close the top of the box.

3 Tape a piece of string to the outside of the foil-covered flap (be sure to tape it on well). Pull the string back so that the flap reflects sunlight onto the food in the oven (tape the string down or tie it to a rock).

4 Let the food cook, adjusting the angle of the flap occasionally to make sure it still reflects the sunlight into the oven.

5 Peek through the window to check on your food. It's done when it's melty and hot.

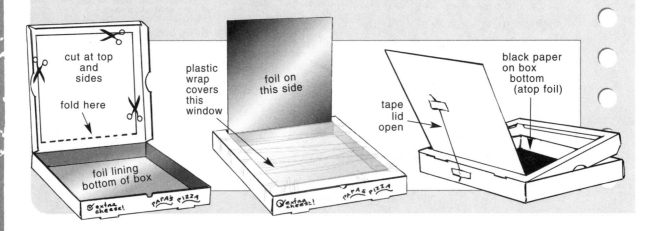

cut at top and sides

fold here

foil lining bottom of box

plastic wrap covers this window

foil on this side

black paper on box bottom (atop foil)

tape lid open

Solar Oven Pizza

Pizza in the woods? Well, is the sun shining? If the answer is yes, then the answer is yes!

What You Need

- ✔ 1 pita bread
- ✔ ¼ cup tomato sauce
- ✔ ¼ cup shredded mozzarella cheese
- ✔ Pepperoni slices (optional)

- ✔ Pizza Box Solar Oven (see page 83)
- ✔ About 2 feet heavy-duty aluminum foil

What You Do

1. Set the oven in a sunny, unshaded spot (preferably during peak sunshine hours— 9:00 A.M. to 3:00 P.M.).

2. Fold the foil in half and bend up the edges to make a little tray.

3. Place the pita bread on the tray.

4. Spread the tomato sauce on the pita.

5. Sprinkle the cheese over the sauce.

6. Place the pepperoni on the pizza if you like.

7. Place the tray in the oven and close the lid. Adjust the reflector flap so the sunshine hits the

Sunny Day Gourmet

You can use the power of the sun to cook almost anything. The trick is to keep an eye on your food through the oven window: You'll see signs of doneness like melting, browning, or sizzling (in some cases this could take an hour or so, but remember—good things come to those who wait!). Try these camp favorites (cook them on a tray made from heavy-duty aluminum foil):

● **Solar s'mores** (see page 89 for filling ideas)

● **Sun-baked apples** (core small apples and fill the holes with brown sugar and cinnamon)

● **Hot dogs** (pierce them with a fork a few times before baking)

● **Cheesy-spicy potato skins** (top halved baked potatoes with cheese and pepperoni slices and cook until the cheese melts and the 'roni sizzles)

● **Cookies, muffins, biscuits** (with an adult's help, bake until the treats are cooked through)

pizza. Bake the pizza until the cheese bubbles, about 30 minutes.

8. Remove the pizza from the oven—careful, it's hot.

9. Let it cool slightly and cut it into wedges before eating.

1 serving

Sun-Power Nachos

Put the sun to work and make some yummy nachos!

What You Need

- ✔ **A few handfuls tortilla chips**
- ✔ **1 cup shredded cheese (try Monterey Jack or Cheddar)**
- ✔ **Salsa, for dipping**
- ✔ **Pizza Box Solar Oven (see page 83)**
- ✔ **About 2 feet heavy-duty aluminum foil**

What You Do

1. Set the oven in a sunny, unshaded spot during peak hours (9:00 A.M. to 3:00 P.M.).

2. Fold the foil in half and bend up the edges to make a little tray. Place it inside the solar oven.

3. Place the tortilla chips on the tray in a single layer.

4. Sprinkle the cheese over the chips.

5. Close the lid of the oven and adjust the reflector flap so the sunshine hits the nachos. Bake the nachos until the cheese gets bubbly, about 30 minutes.

6. Remove the tray from the oven and eat the nachos straight off the tray, dipping them in salsa. ¡Olé!

About 2 servings

ON THE MENU: MOON FOOD

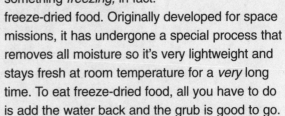

Astronauts and backpackers have something cool in common, something *freezing,* in fact: freeze-dried food. Originally developed for space missions, it has undergone a special process that removes all moisture so it's very lightweight and stays fresh at room temperature for a *very* long time. To eat freeze-dried food, all you have to do is add the water back and the grub is good to go.

It comes in lots of different flavors, from chicken gumbo to spaghetti and tomato sauce—even dessert! Check out the selection at your local sporting goods store. One word of advice: Give freeze-dried food a test-run at home before you go. Some dishes taste pretty good, but others may leave you, er, cold.

SWEETS

Dinner's not over until you share something deliciously sweet around the campfire. From s'mores to fire-baked fruit crisp to ice cream you make yourself, here's a collection of campground favorites.

Banana Boats

This boat's a-rockin' with the flavors of warm banana, melted chocolate, nuts, raisins, and sweet, gooey marshmallows. Just the ticket when you're sitting around the fire.

What You Need

- ✔ 1 banana
- ✔ ¼ cup chocolate chips
- ✔ ¼ cup chopped nuts
- ✔ ¼ cup raisins
- ✔ ½ cup mini marshmallows
- ✔ 1 sheet (12 x 12 inches) heavy-duty aluminum foil

What You Do

1. Slice the whole banana—skin and all—down the middle from tip to tip, but only cut partway through. Place it cut-side up on the aluminum foil.

2. Spread open the banana slightly so it looks like a canoe. Stuff it with the chocolate chips, nuts, raisins, and mini marshmallows.

3. Squeeze the sides back together and gently wrap the whole thing in the foil.

4. Place the foil-wrapped banana boat atop the burning embers of your campfire or on a hot grill. Cook for about 10 minutes.

5. Have a grown-up remove the banana boat from the fire and open the foil carefully (watch out for steam escaping from the foil pouch). Check to see if the chocolate and marshmallows are melted. If they aren't, rewrap the packet and place it back on the fire for a little while.

6. When the chocolate and marshmallow are melted, slide the packet onto a plate and eat the banana boat right from the foil pouch.

1 serving

s'mores!

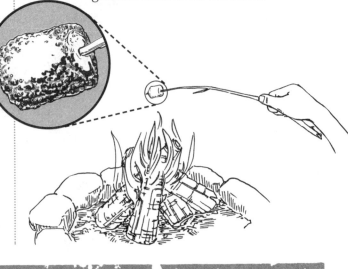

The word s'more means "some more," because that's what everyone says after they eat one. This recipe shows you how to make just a single traditional s'more. You'll want to have extra goodies on hand so you can have s'more and s'more.

What You Need

✔ **3 rectangles of a Hershey's chocolate bar (experiment with your perfect ratio)**

✔ **1 graham cracker rectangle, broken into two squares along the dotted line**

✔ **A marshmallow**

✔ **A Good Stick (see page 71)**

✔ **A buddy**

What You Do

1. Put the chocolate on 1 square of the graham cracker. Keep the other graham cracker square ready for the top.

2. Place the marshmallow on one end of your Good Stick.

3. With a grown-up's supervision, carefully roast your marshmallow over the fire: either hold the marshmallow about 2 inches above the fire, rotating it until it's golden brown, or let it burn to a crisp on the outside.

4. Get a buddy to hold your chocolate-topped graham cracker in one hand and the empty graham cracker in the other.

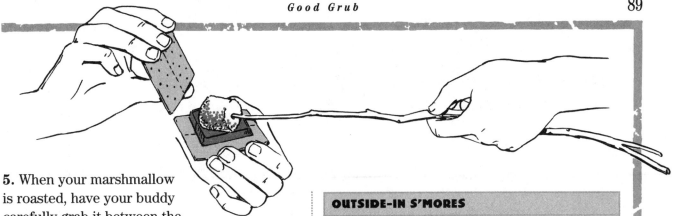

5. When your marshmallow is roasted, have your buddy carefully grab it between the 2 graham crackers and slide it off the stick.

6. Grasp the 2 crackers and gently squish the marshmallow until it oozes over the chocolate (the chocolate should melt a little). Careful—it will be hot!

7. Let the whole s'more cool slightly, then take a bite.

1 serving

OUTSIDE-IN S'MORES

Flip your s'mores outside-in by stuffing chocolate pieces into the marshmallow before you roast it. When the marshmallow is done, skip the chocolate on the bottom graham cracker and simply squeeze the stuffed marshmallow between two plain graham crackers—the chocolate will already be inside the marshmallow, all gooey and delish!

S'MORE S'MORES

- Sliced bananas and a roasted marshmallow between coconut cookies

- Peanut butter, jelly, and a roasted marshmallow between graham crackers

- Apple slices, peanut butter, chocolate, and a roasted marshmallow between graham crackers

- Strawberry slices and a roasted marshmallow between shortbread cookies

- Mint-flavored chocolate and a roasted marshmallow between graham crackers

- Raspberry jam, dark chocolate, and a roasted marshmallow between shortbread cookies

- Pineapple slices and a roasted marshmallow between coconut cookies

- A peanut butter cup and a roasted marshmallow between graham crackers

Kick-the-Can Ice Cream

This ice cream is as much fun to make as it is to eat. Take turns kicking the can around, and in no time you'll have a sweet and creamy delight. It's great on its own, but serve it alongside the Campfire Apple Crisp (page 93) or Sloppy Berry Cake (page 92) for a little piece of heaven.

What You Need

Ice cream mix:
- ✔ **1 pint half-and-half**
- ✔ **½ cup sugar**
- ✔ **1 teaspoon vanilla extract or 2 tablespoons chocolate syrup**

Ice cream maker:
- ✔ **A 1-pound coffee can**

with a tight-fitting plastic lid
- ✔ **Duct tape**
- ✔ **Crushed ice**
- ✔ **A 3-pound coffee can with a tight-fitting plastic lid**
- ✔ **9 tablespoons rock salt**

What You Do

1. Place the ice cream ingredients into the small coffee can.

2. Put the lid snugly on the coffee can and tape it closed with duct tape for security: Wrap the duct tape once around the outside of the can and lid, overlapping both, then take 2 long pieces of tape and make an X over the top of the lid and down the sides of the can.

3. Pour crushed ice into the large coffee can to come one inch up the sides. Place the small coffee can on top of the ice inside the large coffee can.

4. Pour more crushed ice into the large can until it comes one inch up the sides of the small can.

5. Sprinkle the ice with about 3 tablespoons of rock salt.

6. Add another inch of ice and another 3 tablespoons of rock salt.

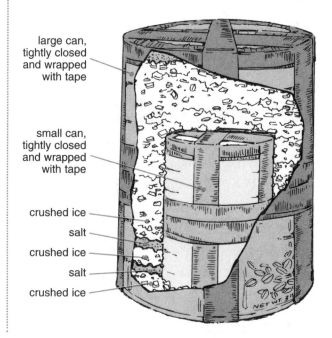

large can, tightly closed and wrapped with tape

small can, tightly closed and wrapped with tape

crushed ice

salt

crushed ice

salt

crushed ice

CHEW ON THIS

HOW IS IT THAT ICE cream, which is sweet, is made with salt, which is . . . well . . . salty. In fact, you can't even *make* ice cream without salt. The trick is that the salt doesn't go *in* the ice cream, it goes *around* it—it's combined with ice in the cooling chamber of the ice cream maker.

Ice cream isn't ice cream unless it's chilled to a crisp 27°F or colder. Anything warmer won't result in ice cream—more like ice cream slush. But ice itself is only 32°F, which means it's not cold enough on its own to do the job. That's where the salt comes in. When you sprinkle rock salt onto the ice in the cooling chamber around the ice cream mixture, you make a briny bath that is colder than the ice on its own. This low temperature allows the ice cream mixture to freeze into the scoopable stuff we all know and love.

7. Fill the rest of the large can with crushed ice and sprinkle the remaining salt over it.

8. Place the lid on the large can and secure it with tape as you did the small can.

9. Now the fun begins! Find a partner or partners and roll the can. You can gently kick the can back and forth, sit on the ground and gently roll it back and forth, or roll it between 2 sticks.

10. Roll the can consistently for about 10 minutes, then check to see if the ice cream is hardening up (don't take the small can out of the large can; instead, simply remove its lid). The ice cream won't be as hard as the stuff you get in the freezer section of the grocery, but it should be thick and frosty—like soft ice cream. If it's too runny, replace the lid on the small can and add more ice to the large can. Tape the cans back up and roll them for another 8 minutes.

11. When the ice cream is the right consistency, scoop it out and serve.

AN EASY CAMPFIRE OVEN

Think you can't bake a cake on the trail? Think again. You can bake a cake, corn bread, biscuits, brownies, or even cookies with the campfire and a few simple tools.

You'll need a large pot with a tight-fitting lid (Dutch ovens work best), three round golf-ball-size rocks, and a small cake pan that fits inside the pot. First, place your batter or dough in the pan. Arrange the rocks in a triangle shape on the bottom of the pot (near the sides) and balance the full cake pan on top of the rocks. Cover the whole shebang with the lid and voilà!—a camp oven.

To cook, have a grown-up settle the "oven" on top of the red and glowy coals of an almost burnt-out campfire.

Place a few coals on top of the lid to help create true "oven" heat inside the pot. For cookies, check the oven after 15 minutes; for cakes, biscuits, and corn bread, check after 30 minutes; and for brownies, after 45 minutes.

large pot with lid

cake pan

three rocks

Sloppy Berry Cake

ADULT SUPERVISION

This cake is warm and gooey (and healthy . . . shh)—it really hits the spot any old time. It's even great for breakfast!

What You Need

- ✔ **2 cups Bisquick mix**
- ✔ **¼ cup powdered milk**
- ✔ **2 tablespoons sugar, more to taste**
- ✔ **¼ teaspoon cinnamon**

- ✔ **3 to 4 cups fresh (or frozen) berries**
- ✔ **2 quart-size zip-top bags**
- ✔ **Permanent marker**
- ✔ **A skillet with a tight-fitting lid (cast-iron works best)**

Before You Leave Home

1. Place the Bisquick, powdered milk, 2 tablespoons sugar, and cinnamon in 1 of the zip-top bags. Seal the bag and shake it well to combine the ingredients. Label the bag with the permanent marker: "Sloppy Berry Cake—add ⅔ cup water and cook for 20 minutes." Store this bag in your pack.

2. Place the berries in the other zip-top bag, label it "Sloppy Berry Cake," and zip it closed. Store this bag in the cooler for up to a week.

At the Campsite

1. Pour 2 tablespoons of water into the skillet, place the skillet over a stove or fire, and bring the water to a boil.

2. Add the berries and simmer until they become runny and start to make their own sauce, about 15 minutes. Add a bit of sugar if you like your berries sweeter.

3. Add ⅔ cup water to the bag of dry ingredients. Seal the bag and massage it to make a batter. Drop large spoonfuls of the batter over the berries in the skillet.

4. Cover the skillet and let it cook over low heat (move it away from a direct flame if cooking over a campfire or grill).

5. After about 20 minutes, lift the lid and check to see if the dough is cooked through and light brown. If not, replace the lid and let the cake cook a little longer.

6. When the dough is cooked, remove the cake from the heat and divide it between 4 dishes.

4 servings

Campfire Apple Crisp

This recipe is great with apples (that's why it's called Apple Crisp!), but it's also yummy with berries, pears, peaches, apricots, cherries, or even a combination.

See the illustrations on pages 64–65 for help with preparing and cooking in foil packets.

What You Need

Filling
✔ **6 apples, cored, peeled, and chopped**
✔ **½ cup sugar**
✔ **1 teaspoon cinnamon**
✔ **1 tablespoon flour**
Topping
✔ **1 cup quick-cook oats**
✔ **⅓ cup flour**

✔ **4 tablespoons butter**
✔ **¼ cup brown sugar**

✔ **4 sheets (12 x 12 inches each) heavy-duty aluminum foil**
✔ **1 gallon-size zip-top bag**
✔ **4 quart-size zip-top bags**
✔ **Permanent marker**

Before You Leave Home

1. Lay the 4 sheets of foil on the countertop, turning up the edges a bit (so the food doesn't run when you add it).

2. Place all the filling ingredients in the large zip-top bag. Seal the bag.

3. Massage the bag with your fingers to combine all the ingredients. Divide the mixture among the 4 sheets of foil (see Figure 1, page 64).

4. Place all the topping ingredients in the same zip-top bag (which is now empty) and seal it.

5. Massage the outside of the bag with your fingers until you get a crumbly mixture.

6. Open the bag and sprinkle the crumbs on top of the apples on each foil sheet.

7. Fold each foil sheet into a packet (see Figures 2 and 3, page 64): Bring together two opposite ends of the foil and fold them down a few times to seal the edge. Roll up the open ends a few times. Make sure all the food is inside the foil—no leaks—and that there is about an inch of breathing room all around. (Food expands when it cooks, so the pouch will burst if it's too tight.)

8. Wrap a second sheet of foil around each packet to make sure it's sealed. Put each packet in a zip-top bag (see Figure 4, page 64). Seal the bag and label it with a permanent marker: "Apple Crisp. Bake over hot coals 45 minutes." Store the packets in a cooler for up to 3 days.

At the Campsite

1. Remove the packets from the plastic zip-top bags and cook:

> **Over a campfire**—when the campfire has burned long enough to make embers, have an adult move aside some of the burning wood and settle the foil pouches in the embers (see Figure 5, page 65). Place some embers on top of the packets. The crisps should cook in about 45 minutes.

> **On a grill**—when the fire is hot, place the foil packets on a grill over the heat. Cook for about 45 minutes.

2. Have a grown-up remove the packets from the fire and open the foil carefully (watch out for steam escaping from the foil pouch). The crisps are done when the apples are soft. If the apples are still a bit raw, rewrap the foil and cook them for a while longer.

3. When the apples are soft, slide each packet onto a plate. Open the packet, and eat the crisp directly out of the foil.

4 servings

WATER WISDOM

If you're camping deep in the woods or in a place where clean tap water isn't available or reliable, be sure to think before you drink. Really—just because water looks clean doesn't mean it *is* clean. That crystal-clear stream water could be packed with bug larvae, raccoon poop, and a host of unseen microbes that can *really* hit you below the belt.

When you're collecting drinking water for filtering from natural sources, you should choose running water like rivers or streams over standing water such as lakes or ponds. Because running water is always on the go, it tends to have fewer funky microorganisms that can make you sick (microorganisms prefer to hang out in standing water, where they can live, eat, and breed undisturbed). If you can find a spring, where the water flows naturally from the ground, that's also a cleaner choice. Avoid drawing water from places that have lots of human or animal traffic, which can also mean lots of poop and other dirty stuff. But remember, no matter where you gather your drinking water, always be sure to purify it before using it—why skip a few simple steps in the beginning and risk getting the runs later on?

Filters and Other Fabulous Water Cleaners

Most water filters have a hand pump that pulls the water from the source (river, stream, babbling brook), through a filter that cleans out the impurities, and into your bottle or pot. What filters don't tackle too well is viruses (they're very tiny, so they're hard to strain out). To knock out those bad boys, you'll need water purification tablets. Always follow the directions on the bottle when using tablets, but generally speaking, you want to make sure (a) your water's not too cold (if pulling it from a frosty stream, let it warm up in the sun for a while); (b) you shake the treated water and give the tablets about 30 minutes to do their thing; and (c) you splash some of the treated water on the lip and lid of the bottle so those areas are purified, too.

Truth be told, for the greatest peace

GOOD PLACES TO FIND VERY BAD WATER

- Downstream of a beaver dam
- Water with algae on top
- Standing water like a pond or puddle
- A watering hole popular with animals
- Shallow water
- Water with anything dead floating in it
- The toilet (your cat might not mind it, but you sure will)

YOU MIGHT HEAR THE word "giardia" thrown around camp. Giardia is the name of a tiny parasite that is often found in unfiltered water. It causes what's sometimes known as "beaver fever" or—and this'll give you a better picture—"backpacker's diarrhea." It's one of the most common sources of waterborne illness, so to protect your tummy, be sure to purify your water!

of mind—and of belly—double up: Use both water purification tablets *and* a water filter. Filter the water according to the package directions and then add the purification tablets.

Boiling Water

Boiling water also gets rid of parasites and bacteria, but it's practical only at certain times—you won't want to wait around for water to boil and cool when you could be having fun. Dinner is the ideal time to get your boiling done. Put on a pot of water before you start eating, and it should be ready by the time you're done. Let the water boil energetically for three to five minutes, then let it cool. When cool, you can use it for drinking, mixing into powdered milk, or whatever else floats your boat.

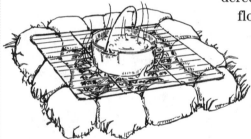

1. *Boil water for 3 to 5 minutes.*

2. *Let the water cool.*

3. *Once cool, pour the water into your bottle.*

CAMPING SKILLS

Tying Knots, Getting Around, and Staying Found

"Keep your head and your heart in the right direction and you'll never have to worry about your feet."

—UNKNOWN

When you camp out, you'll want to bring along all your gear and food and fun stuff, but even more important is what you bring along in your brain—knowledge! In this chapter, you'll learn some basic skills that'll prepare you for roughing it safely in the great outdoors.

Knots at a Glance

There are lots of different types of knots, each of which serves its own purpose. Knots are grouped into categories according to how they're used.

Binders are knots used to tie ropes together.

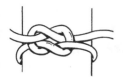

**Granny Knot
(page 101)**

**Square Knot
(page 102)**

**Surgeon's Knot
(page 103)**

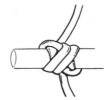

**Boa Constrictor
Knot (page 102)**

Bends
secure two ropes together.

**Overhand Bend
(page 106)**

Stoppers are knots tied at the ends of ropes to keep them from slipping through holes.

**Figure 8 Knot
(page 104)**

**Overhand Knot
(page 105)**

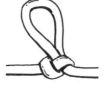

**Slipped Overhand
Knot (page 105)**

**Monkey's Fist
(page 104)**

**Fisherman's Knot
(page 106)**

Loops are for hanging or carrying equipment. Loops are very versatile and can be combined with any other kind of knot.

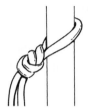

Overhand Loop
(page 107)

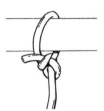

Bowline
(page 107)

Figure 8 Loop
(page 108)

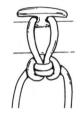

Butterfly Loop
(page 108)

Lariat
(page 109)

Hitches are used for tying a rope to an object like a pole, hook, tree limb, post, metal ring, or even another rope.

Half Hitch
(page 110)

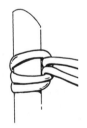

Slipped Half Hitch
(page 110)

Pile Hitch
(page 110)

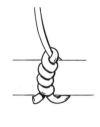

Timber Hitch
(page 111)

Rolling Hitch
(page 111)

Clove Hitch
(page 112)

IT'S A GOOD IDEA TO keep your rope coiled in even, ordered loops and tied up so you can get to it and use it easily. Also, try to keep it clean and avoid stepping on it—dirt that gets ground into a rope can wear away at the fibers and make it weak. And what's the use of a broken rope?

KNOW YOUR KNOTS

A little knot know-how can be really helpful when you're camping out. With a length of sturdy rope and a few knots expertly tied, you can tie things up, tie things down, and tie things together.

The knots on the following pages—binders, stoppers, bends, loops, and hitches—are the basics. Master these, and you'll be able to do almost anything, from tying two ropes together (handy when a game of tug-of-war calls), to securing a tent flap in the wind, to anchoring a wayward boat, to hanging your food in trees so the bears can't get to it.

Knot tying takes practice, but it's a lot of fun and can be done almost anywhere. When you're starting out, use a medium-width rope that's flexible and easy to tie and untie; with a little patience, you'll know your hitches from your bowlines in no time.

LOOPY LINGO

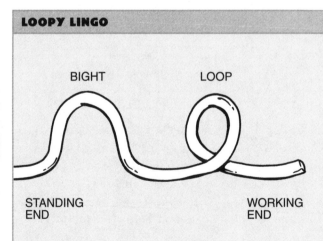

BIGHT   LOOP

STANDING END   WORKING END

I f you're going to start knot tying, it's helpful to know the lingo. The end of the rope used to make a knot is called the "working end." The "standing end" is the part that doesn't move. The "bight" is the bent part of the rope that gets all the action—it is bent, twisted, or turned to become part of the knot. Take your average bight, give it a single twist, and voilà! You have a "loop."

Binder Knots

Binders are not always the strongest knots, but they're quick and easy, and when you need to tie a few things together in a flash, these knots are really useful.

GRANNY KNOT

This binder knot is probably the first knot you ever learned to tie—minus the bow, it's the very same one you use to tie your shoes. The granny is a cinch to tie, but it's not the most practical knot for campers because it doesn't have enough gripping power to withstand a heavy strain. In fact, it's called the granny knot because it's generally considered a "granny" attempt at a square knot (page 102).

But don't knock grandma just yet! Although you won't be tying up a boat with a granny knot, you might use one to close up some of your gear or tie your rolled-up sleeping mat.

Sailors sometimes refer to the granny knot as a cow's knot, because it serves no more purpose aboard a boat than a cow would.

1. Start by twisting one end of rope around another, left side over right.

2. Cross the left strand over the right, tucking it under the left strand and through the loop (see Loopy Lingo, opposite). (A good way to remember the granny knot is "same side twice," since you're tying left over right both times.)

3. When pulled tight, the working ends (see Loopy Lingo, opposite) of the rope will exit the knot on opposite sides.

SQUARE KNOT

The square knot is similar to the granny knot (page 101) but it's a lot stronger and it's also easier to untie. Instead of crossing the right strand over left, then right over left again, as in the granny, the square knot is made by crossing left over right and then right over left (which is a smart way to remember it: repeat "left over right, right over left" as you're practicing).

The square knot is a useful basic binder to know: It's quick to tie, easy to untie, and gets stronger when you pull on the opposite ends. The square knot is great for tying up bundles, mending broken string or rope, and for tying two ropes together.

Impress the sailors and pirates in your life: The square knot is also called the reef knot.

1. Cross the left strand over the right.

2. Cross the right strand over the left.

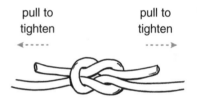

pull to tighten   pull to tighten

3. Pull on the working ends to tighten the knot. To loosen it, push the ends toward the knot.

BOA CONSTRICTOR KNOT

The boa constrictor is a sturdy knot that's fun to make. It borrows its name from the squeeze-happy snake, which hunts by wrapping its slithery body around its prey and tightening its grip. The boa constrictor knot is also a squeezer, tightly gripping whatever's in its grasp when its ends are pulled in different directions. Like the hitch knots (page 110), it is used to tie a rope around a post or a pole.

1. Start by making 2 loops like the coils of a snake.

SURGEON'S KNOT

Practice for a medical career while camping! The surgeon's knot is a square knot with an extra twist. This strong knot is ideal for securing thin, slippery plastic line, like fishing line.

1. Hold the right strand in place and wrap the left strand around it twice.

2. Now make the top half of the knot by wrapping the right strand over the left, as with the square knot.

3. Pull on the working and standing ends of the knot (see Loopy Lingo, page 100) to tighten it.

If you've ever had stitches, the doctor probably used a surgeon's knot to tie them.

TO MAKE A FIREWOOD Carrier: Wrap a rope twice around your pile of firewood and then tightly tie the ends around the bundle into a square knot (opposite), leaving the ends long. Take these ends and tie them into an overhand loop (page 107). Now you can carry your wood with elegance and ease.

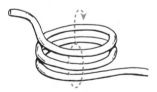

2. Stack the loops and hold them sideways. Twist the stack in the center one time to make a figure-8 shape.

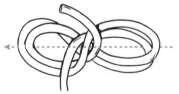

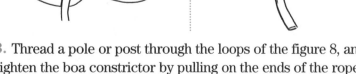

3. Thread a pole or post through the loops of the figure 8, and tighten the boa constrictor by pulling on the ends of the rope. The harder you pull, the stronger the knot will be.

FIGURE 8 KNOT

This stopper knot is shaped like an ice-skater's figure 8. It is a favorite with rock climbers, mountaineers, and wilderness rescuers because it's very sturdy and tightens on itself. It's also easy to tell when it's tied correctly (you don't want an incorrectly tied knot when it's the only thing attaching you to your lifeline).

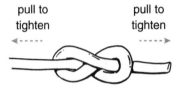

pull to tighten ⟵----- -----⟶ pull to tighten

1. Make a loop and wrap the working end under the standing end and back through the loop.

2. Tighten by pulling from both ends.

Stoppers

A stopper is a knot tied at the end of a rope. It is used to make a grip on a rope for climbing or to stop the rope from sliding through a hole.

When an overhand knot is tied in thin string, like sewing thread, it's called a thumb knot.

MONKEY'S FIST

This stopper knot adds weight to the end of a line so that it's easier to throw (as if you'd tied a ball to the end). It is tricky to tie (you may want an adult's help) and requires a bit of practice, but it's very rewarding to do. Just remember "three, three, three," and that'll help you figure it out.

Monkey's fists make great cat toys, or they can be used for a fun fetch-and-tug game with Fido (throw the knot like a ball and when your pooch catches it, tug gently on the rope).

1. Wrap the rope around your hand 3½ times.

OVERHAND KNOT

Here's a simple stopper that is really easy to tie and, once tightened, very rough to untie.

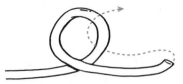

1. Make a loop. Pass the working end of the rope through the hole in the loop.

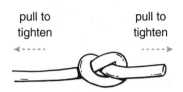

pull to tighten   pull to tighten

2. Tighten the knot by pulling on both ends at once.

SLIPPED OVERHAND KNOT

This is an overhand knot that's as easy to untie as your shoelaces. In fact, you make it the same way you make those cute little bows on your sneaks.

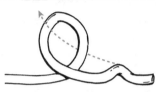

1. Make a loop and a bight (see Loopy Lingo, page 100).

2. Pass the bight through the loop.

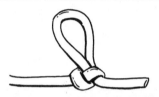

3. Pull on the bight and the standing end to tighten. Make the bight larger by pulling on it, and smaller by pulling gently on the working end.

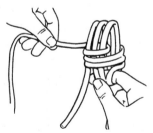

2. Holding the coils in place, wrap the working end around them 3 times. Now thread the working end through the coils.

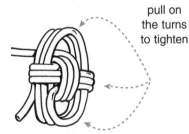

pull on the turns to tighten

3. Wrap the working end 3 times around the middle of the knot (the section of wraps you made in step 2).

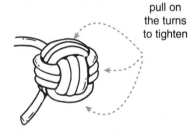

pull on the turns to tighten

4. Tighten by pulling carefully on the turns, working from turn to turn. Keep the shape of the knot stable by holding it in your hand as you work out the slack.

OVERHAND BEND

Here's a quick-tie bend that you can use to connect two light cords or strings.

Bends

Need a longer rope? Use a bend to secure two ropes together. When practicing, use two different colors of rope so you can identify what each rope is doing inside the knot.

1. Hold 2 strings side by side. Tie an overhand knot (page 105) with the double string.

pull to tighten   pull to tighten

2. Pull the standing ends in opposite directions to finish the knot.

FISHERMAN'S KNOT

This the most common knot for making one rope out of two. It's also known as the Englishman's knot and the angler's knot ("angler" is another word for "fisherman").

1. Place 2 ropes in opposite directions so that their ends overlap.

2. Make an overhand knot at the end of each rope. Pull on the working end of each knot so it's good and tight.

pull to tighten   pull to tighten

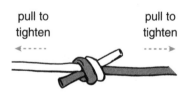

3. Pull the standing ends of the ropes away from each other to draw the 2 knots toward each other. They will slide together and form 1 large knot.

OVERHAND LOOP

The overhand loop is the simplest loop knot to tie, but very difficult to untie once it's been pulled hard.

1. Fold the rope over at the end to make a bight.

2. Tie the bight in an overhand knot (page 105), leaving the loop as large as you need it.

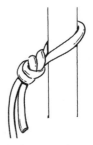

3. Thread the loop onto a pole.

BOWLINE

The bowline is a common knot among frequent knot users, from sailors to wilderness rescuers. You can tie it around an object, or thread it onto an open-ended branch or pole once it's tied.

1. Make a loop near the end of a rope (leave 5 or so inches for the working end).

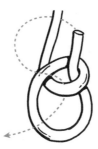

2. Pass the working end through the loop twice: up through the bottom, around the standing end, and back down again. Pull on the turns and working end of the knot to tighten it.

Loops

Loops aren't just for pretty bows and cowboy lassos—they're very versatile knots. You can use a loop to hang things like lanterns or to carry firewood, tent poles, and other cumbersome stuff.

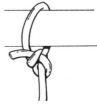

FIGURE 8 LOOP

Like the figure 8 knot, this loop is a favorite among climbers because it's easy to tell when it's tied correctly—very important when you're dangling off a cliff, held up only by a rope and a well-tied knot!

Though easy and secure, the figure 8 loop can be difficult to untie after heavy strain.

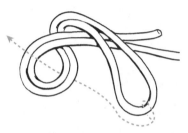

1. Double up the rope and make a bight. Tie the bight into a figure-8 shape (see page 104).

2. Tighten the knot by pulling on the bight to form a loop at the end.

3. Thread the loop onto a pole or attach a clip to it.

BUTTERFLY LOOP

The butterfly loop is strong but can be easily untied even after it's been pulled hard. It is tied in the middle of a rope instead of at the end. You can tie a number of loops on one rope, which is what some hikers do when they want to share a single safety rope among them (they use the loops as handles). In camp, you can string a rope with butterfly loops between two trees and hang pots, pans, utensils, and other odds and ends.

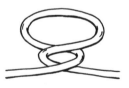

1. Make a loop and twist its top so you have a smaller circle on the bottom and a larger one on top.

LARIAT

Make a lariat, also known as a lasso, and see what you can rope in!

1. Start by tying an overhand knot (page 105) as a stopper at the end of the rope.

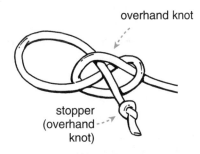

overhand knot

stopper
(overhand
knot)

2. Next, tie another overhand knot a few inches up, and thread the end with the stopper knot through the top left opening of the new overhand knot.

3. Carefully tighten the new overhand knot so the end with the stopper knot is drawn up to it. You have made a fixed loop that won't slip.

4. To complete your lasso, thread the rest of the rope through the fixed loop. Now you can toss the lasso and cinch it down on whatever you catch just by pulling on the standing end of the rope.

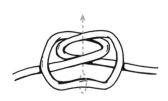

2. Pull the top circle toward you over the bottom circle and . . .

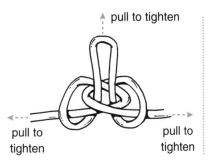

pull to tighten

pull to
tighten

pull to
tighten

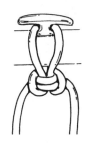

3. Tuck a bight of the top circle under and through the bottom circle. Pull it up through the circle to make a loop, and tighten the whole knot by pulling on the loop and both ends of the rope. Now you can hang the loop from an object.

HALF HITCH

Quick and easy to tie, the half hitch is the basis of a bunch of more complex hitches. It's usually tied to give another knot extra security or is used temporarily when the rope won't be under much strain.

Hitches

A hitch is a knot used to tie a rope to an object— a pole, hook, tree limb, post, metal ring, or even another rope.

1. Thread the rope through a ring or around another object. Bring it behind the standing end and then horizontally through the loop. Pull on the ends to tighten.

2. If you want to be able to open the half hitch with just one pull, run a bight through the loop (instead of running the straight end through it). This is called a slipped half hitch.

PILE HITCH

Because this simple hitch is tied from a bight, it can be tied when both ends of a rope are being used. You just need the end of a post.

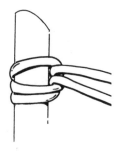

1. Fold the rope to make a bight. Wrap the bight around the end of the post.

2. Slip the bight below the standing end of the rope and over the top of the post.

3. Tighten the hitch by pulling on the free ends of the rope.

TIMBER HITCH

This hitch can turn a rope into a powerful tool for dragging poles or logs to the campsite.

The timber hitch is often used with the half hitch.

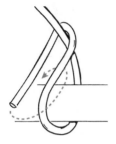

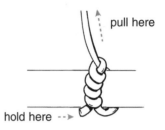

1. Pass a long working end around a pole, crossing the end over and under itself.

2. Continue to wrap the working end around itself a few times until you run out of rope.

3. Pull on the standing end, holding the tip of the working end, to tighten the knot around the pole. Use the standing end to pull the log.

ROLLING HITCH

The rolling hitch is very strong—a good choice if you're tying a rope to a pole and don't want the rope to slip down (like when you tie a tarp to a tree and don't want it to sag).

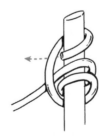

1. Wrap the rope around a post twice from the top to bottom. After the second wrap, cross the working end over the standing end, and wrap it around the post again to make a half hitch.

2. Tighten the hitch so that the working end and standing end poke out of the knot on the same side.

CLOVE HITCH

The clove hitch is versatile—like the pile hitch, it can be tied at the end of a post and/or made from a bight, making it a good choice when you don't have the ends of the rope free. It's been used since ancient times to carry loads, but if you're going to use it for this purpose, make sure to balance the weight of whatever you grasp in the knot (if one end of the load is heavier than the other, the knot will fail).

You can use the clove hitch when making the One-Tree Tent on page 34.

 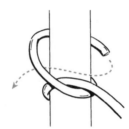

1. To make a clove hitch with one end of the rope free: Thread the rope around a post (or another standing object), keeping the standing end on top. After bringing the working end around to the front of the post, wind it around the post again. Now tuck the working end down through the loop you just made.

2. Pull on the working and standing ends of the rope to tighten the hitch.

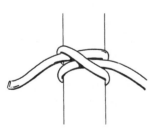

CLOVE HITCH ON A BIGHT

1. To make a clove hitch with a bight, make 2 loops of equal size.

2. Place the right loop on top of the left loop.

3. Place the stacked double loop around the top of the post.

This Is War!

T ug-of-War, that is. Impress your camping buddies with your knot know-how when you tie together two shorter strands of rope for this fun camp out classic.

2 medium length ropes

A bandanna

2 sturdy sticks or poles

What You Do

1 Fashion a long and handy tug-of-war rope from 2 shorter pieces tied together with a skillfully executed fisherman's knot (see page 106).

2 Tie a bandanna in the middle of this extra-long rope, and poke 2 sticks into the ground about 10 feet apart.

3 Divide your gang into 2 groups. Each group should grab an end of the rope and stand holding the rope so that the bandanna is exactly in the middle of the 2 sticks.

4 Now pull! Whichever team pulls the bandanna past the stick on their side wins.

KNOTTY FASHION

Use your knot-tying skills to make a couple of cool bandanna caps.

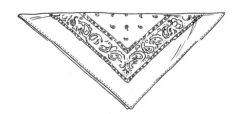

Captain's Hat

1. Fold the bandanna into a triangle and place the long side of the triangle along your forehead.

2. Hold the two points by your ears and tie them together behind your head with a square knot.

3. Tuck the third point under the knot.

Skipper's Cap

1. Take the bandanna and spread it out flat. Tie an overhand knot in each corner.

2. Try on the cap and adjust the knots so that it fits your head.

3. This jaunty cap is great for keeping your noggin shielded from the sun, bugs, or the cold night air.

GETTING AROUND AND STAYING FOUND

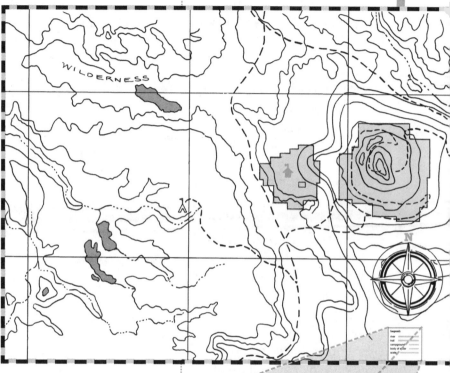

When you're out camping, nature truly calls—there's so much to see and do that you'll be popping out of your sleeping bag every morning ready to explore. But before you hit the trail, it's a good idea to figure out where you are and where you're headed. That's no problem if you've got some basic navigation skills, like reading a map, deciphering trail signs, and using a compass. And in the unlikely event you *do* get lost, you'll learn what you can do to stay safe and get found quickly.

Some of the topics in this section—especially the compass stuff—is complicated at first, so you may want to ask an adult to help you figure it out by reading along with you.

How to Read a Map

Maps are full of symbols. Decoding a map is easy once you know what you're looking at. Every map has a legend or a key, a little box that shows what the symbols on the map mean. It tells you what types of lines represent what kinds of roads or paths and what shapes stand for different types of buildings. It also gives you a compass rose, a symbol that shows the north, south, east,

Legend:

river --- ———— --- ———

trail -----------------

campground ▨▨▨ ▲

body of water ▬▬▬▬

scale: ⌊_____⌋
1 inch = 1 mile

Learn the Lingo

Bearing

The direction you're heading in based on where you start from. When you know your bearings, you know where you are and where you're going.

Magnetic North and True North

Magnetic north is the spot on the planet where a compass needle points. It moves slightly all the time—up to 26 miles a year! But true north always stays the same. It never wavers. Also called geographic north, it's the north on all the maps and the north we picture when we think of the frosty north pole.

Declination

The difference in degrees between magnetic north and true north, it changes depending on where in the world you're standing.

and west directions as they relate to the map. Every map is different. Take a look at the legend of your map to learn what the symbols mean and get the lay of the land.

All maps are drawn to scale, which means they show things exactly as they are in the real world, only smaller (which makes sense—imagine a map of your town that was the actual size of your town—not very practical!). When you look at a map's legend, you'll see a little bar that shows the scale of the map; that is, it shows you a distance on the map and its equivalent in the real world (so, for example, one inch on the map might equal 20 miles). You can figure out actual distances on a map by measuring the distance between two points and comparing that against the scale, which translates the map distance to actual distance.

Topographical Maps

These kinds of maps are really helpful for hikers and bikers. Called "topo maps" for short, they depict the ups and downs of the landscape: curvy lines represent hills, valleys, mountains, and flatlands, and numbers next to each line show how many feet above or below sea level each area is. These lines, called contour lines, are usually brown on a map; man-made trails and roads are usually black.

If the contour lines are close together, it means the area is steep, either uphill or downhill (uphill if the elevation numbers increase, downhill if they decrease). If the contours are more spread out with little elevation change, then that area is fairly flat.

You can get topographical maps from the United States Geological Service at outdoor stores like REI and L.L. Bean, and you can also download them from websites like Topozone (www.topozone.com). Your campground's website might also have simplified maps for the area where you'll be staying.

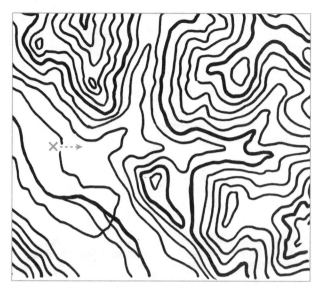

Figure 1.

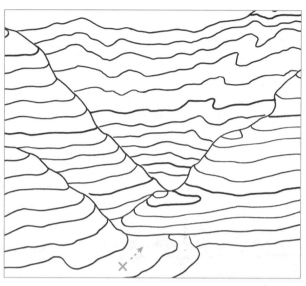

Figure 2.

How to Use a Compass

Folks have been wandering the world for a very long time, and have used compasses to find their way for thousands of years. A compass is a little gadget with an ultralight magnetic needle that rotates on a movable disk. The disk shows the cardinal points—north, south, east, and west—and all sorts of directions in between, with hashmarks that represent the degree of direction in relation to north. An orienting arrow, painted on the face of the disc, helps you "orient" the compass to find the direction you need to follow. The magnetic needle always lines up in a north–south line, and the red end of the needle always points north—it is attracted to the magnetic pull of the earth's north pole.

Before you set off on a compass-guided expedition, first you need to know how a compass works. Here are a few basic steps to follow while using this helpful device.

The squiggly contour lines on a "topo" map (Figure 1) show rises and dips in elevation. If the map were three-dimensional, you would actually see these contour lines as hills and valleys, as in Figure 2.

Look at the X in Figure 1 and imagine that it's your location. The X in Figure 2 shows you what the landscape would really look like from the same position.

Parts of a Compass

compass housing
(rotates). Turn the compass housing until the orienting arrow lines up with the red end of the compass needle.

base plate

direction-of-travel arrow

magnetic compass needle

orienting arrow (north)

These numbers provide your bearing.

1. Choose where you want to go. For starters, pick something simple and nearby, like a big tree, boulder, or tent.
2. Hold the flat base plate of the compass in your palm. The magnetic compass needle should float around and point to north.
3. Turn the round disc—also known as the compass housing—until the north arrow (the "orienting arrow") painted on the disc lines up with the magnetic compass needle. Now both the needle and the orienting arrow point toward actual north.
4. Turn the base plate of the compass until the direction-of-travel arrow points toward the object you chose. Note the number on the compass housing where the direction-of-travel arrow intersects the compass needle—it gives you your bearing and tells you how many degrees from north your object is located.
5. Walk in the direction of your bearing until you reach your object.

Make Your Own Compass!

This makeshift compass is fun to put together and will help you get a better sense of how the contraption really works. This compass isn't really practical for a hike, but if you're staying in one spot and want to get your bearings, it does the trick.

What You Need

A plastic soda bottle cap

A cup or small bowl of water

A bar magnet

A sewing needle

What You Do

1. Float the cap on the water like a small boat, with the inside of the cap facing up.

2. Magnetize the needle: Rub the needle with the magnet, running it from the eye of the needle to the tip. It's important to rub only in one direction, eye to point. Repeat about 40 times.

3. Carefully lay the needle across the cap. Watch the needle and cap spin and settle into a north–south alignment. Because you magnetized the needle in step 2, it now lines itself up with the Earth's north–south magnetic poles.

How to Use a Compass and a Map

Now that you know how to use a compass, you can pair it up with a map to navigate your way. Here are some guidelines to get you from Point A to Point B.

1. Begin with a simple map. Establish where you are and then choose a nearby landmark that marks your spot. Find this location on the map and call it Point A. Where do you want to go? Find a landmark, such as a bridge, building, or body of water, that you can see from where you are now. Find it on the map—call that Point B.

2. Draw a straight line on the map from Point A to Point B, extending the line through one of the map's north–south gridlines.

3. Put the center of the circular compass housing on the point where the drawn line crosses the north–south gridline. Rotate the base plate until the direction-of-travel arrow lines up with the drawn line. Now hold the base plate in place and turn the compass housing to line up the painted-on orienting arrow with

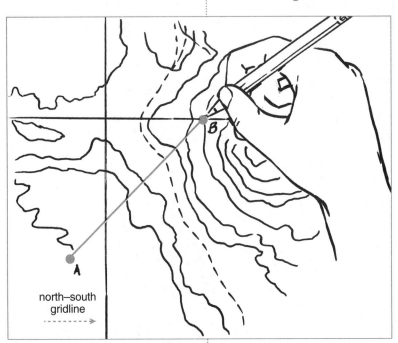

Draw a line from Point A to Point B, crossing over one of the map's north–south gridlines.

the north–south gridline. (Don't worry about what the compass needle is doing at this point.) Your bearing is the number on the compass housing that the direction-of-travel arrow lines up with.

4. Before you head off and follow this bearing to Point B, things might get a bit tricky—you may have to add or subtract degrees from your bearing to adjust for magnetic declination. (For more on this, see Dealing with Declination, page 123.) Check the declination information on the map to see how many degrees you have to add to or subtract from your compass bearing.

5. Once you've made the necessary adjustments, hold up your compass flat in your hand, with the direction-of-travel arrow pointing in front of you. Rotate your body until the red end of the compass's needle sits inside the north-pointing orienting arrow. (When the compass needle meets up with the orienting arrow, your direction-of-travel arrow will point toward your destination—Point B.) Now pick out an object straight ahead in the not-so-far distance (about 100 feet). Walk toward the object, making sure that the compass needle stays inside the north-pointing orienting arrow—this way you'll know that you're not straying off your path. When you reach the object, pick another one in the distance and walk toward that in the same way. Do this until you reach Point B. By tackling the total distance in smaller chunks, you'll have an easier time making sure you've stayed on course.

Place the center of the compass housing on the point where the drawn line intersects the north–south gridline.

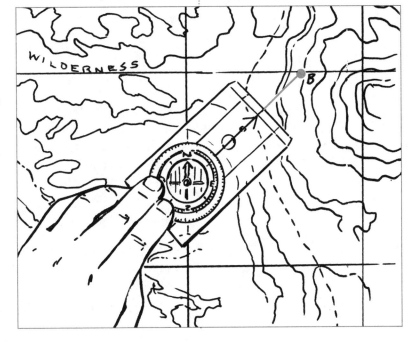

Compass Companion

There are a couple of different kinds of compasses:

An **azimuth compass** shows direction in degrees from 0 to 360, where 0 is north and all the other degrees are in relation to north. On an azimuth compass, north is 0°, east is 90°, south is 180°, and west is 270°. So a bearing of 60° is northeast, a bearing of 220° is southwest, and so on. The compass shown on page 118 is an azimuth compass.

A **quadrant compass** (right) is divided into four sections, each of which has 90 degrees. Both north and south are considered to be at 0°, and both east and west are at 90°. The numbers count up from 0 to 90 when measuring directions between north and east and north and west; the numbers count down from 90 to 0 when measuring from east or west to the south.

Your compass is built to take hard knocks, but there are a few things you can do to keep it in good shape so it can keep you found:

- **Protect your compass** while you use it. It has a cord so you can wear it around your neck. While you're hiking, you can place it in your shirt pocket or tuck it under your T-shirt so it won't bounce around so much.

- **Sometimes the needle is lazy** and can seem sticky. This happens because of static electricity buildup inside the compass. You can get rid of the extra electricity by rubbing a little water over your compass. This should disperse the extra static and the needle will move more quickly.

- **Don't leave your compass in a hot or very sunny spot** for a long time. There is liquid inside the compass housing that can rupture the plastic and leak out if it gets too toasty.

- **Don't get any insect repellent on the face**—it can cloud the glass or plastic. If you do get some on it, wash it off quickly.

- **Keep the compass away from strong magnets**, which can mess with its accuracy.

Dealing with Declination

The Earth's magnetic poles don't always run exactly in line with its geographic poles—the north and south poles. Instead, the magnetic poles are tilted slightly off-center, and this slight off-centeredness can make using a compass with a map a little tricky. To make sure your compass is in sync with your map, you need to figure in declination.

Declination is the difference in degrees between magnetic north (what the compass needle points to) and true north (what the map points to). In North America, the line of 0° declination (or zero difference) runs from Hudson Bay across Lake Michigan and down to Georgia. Along this line, true north and magnetic north

About every 250,000 years, the Earth's magnetic field does a big switcheroo—the magnetic north and south poles actually swap places.

This map shows the declinations in the U.S. in 2004. Since declinations can shift, it's important to get an up-to-date map of your location.

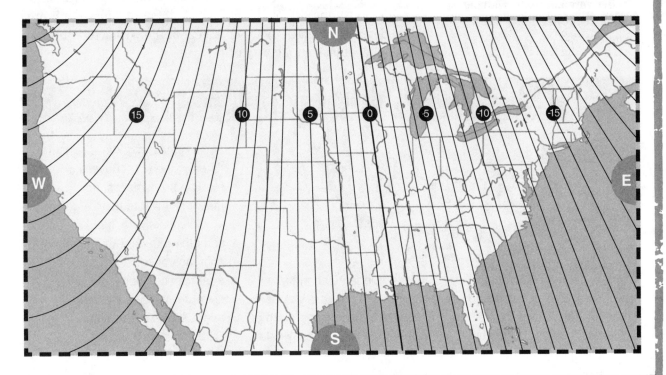

tell your folks!

Whenever you go exploring on your own—with or without a compass—your grown-ups should set boundaries so you know how far you can go. Always carry a whistle with you, too. If you get lost, blow it three times every few minutes, waiting for a response between each set.

are the same. From any point west of this zero line, the compass needle points east of true north (since the needle is attracted to Earth's magnetic poles); you have to *subtract* degrees from your heading to make sure you're going in the right direction. From any point east of this line, the compass needle points west of true north and you have to *add* degrees.

For example, if you're camping in Maine, the declination on the map will say "20°W" or "-20°." Since Maine is in the east, you'll have to add 20 degrees to magnetic north to get true north.

Since declination can change with shifts in the Earth's magnetic poles, always make sure your map is current (it will tell you how many degrees to add or subtract). You can also calculate declination online at www.ngdc.noaa.gov/seg/geomag/jsp/Declination .jsp. It's pretty important to get your declination since each mistaken degree translates to about 92 feet in the wrong direction for every mile—that's a long way off!

It's in There!

People aren't the only creatures on Earth who use magnetism to navigate. In the fall or spring, take a look up in the sky. Depending on the season, chances are you'll see flocks of birds heading north or south. Even butterflies, whales, and bacteria migrate at certain times of the year. But without a map and a compass, how do they know where they're going?

Scientists think it has something to do with an internal compass of sorts: tiny grains of a magnetic mineral inside the creatures' bodies that help them orient themselves with the Earth's magnetic poles.

NAVIGATING WITHOUT A COMPASS

Early explorers and American Indians didn't always use or have a compass or map to help them navigate through the wilderness. Instead they used natural clues—in the sun, plants, and even melting snow—to find their way. You can use these natural clues, too—you just need to know what to look for.

Follow the Sun

The sun provides crucial heat and energy, but it can also help by giving us a better sense of direction.

1. On a sunny morning, draw a circle in the dirt and poke a stick in the center of the circle. Make sure the stick is in there tight and doesn't move around.

2. Watch the shadow that the stick casts on the circle, and trace it onto the ground at 9:00 A.M., 10:00 A.M., noon, 2:00 P.M., and 3:00 P.M. Mark the time next to each shadow.

3. At sunset, draw a straight horizontal line connecting the end of the 10:00 A.M. shadow to the end of the 2:00 P.M. shadow. This line shows the location of east and west, with the end that touches 10:00 A.M. pointing west, and the end at 2:00 P.M. indicating east. The shadows made in the morning fall to the west since the sun rises in the east; the shadows made in the afternoon are in the east, since the sun sets in the west.

4. Now draw a line straight down through the center of your east–west line. With east on your right and west on your left, place an N for north at the top and an S for south on the bottom.

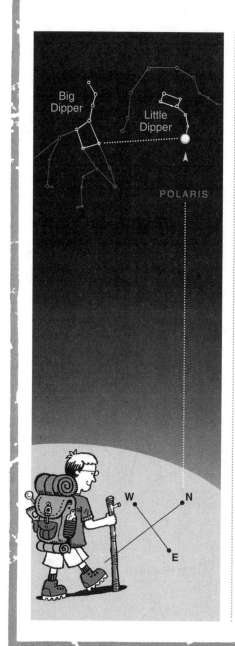

Seek Guidance from the Stars

When the sun sets, you can still find your way. Look up. Long ago, people all over the world used the stars to navigate over long distances on land and sea. If you're star savvy, you can use these tricks, too.

In the Northern Hemisphere, Polaris, or the North Star, shines in the north at all times. All you need to do is find it and you're almost there.

1. To find the North Star, first locate the Big Dipper (see page 178).

2. Find the two stars that form the outer lip of the Big Dipper's cup (see page 178). Draw an imaginary line that connects these two stars and extends beyond the cup in the same direction. The North Star is located in that direction, about five times the distance of the space between these two stars (you can measure the space by holding up your thumb against the sky). It's very bright. And it's also the top star in the handle of the Little Dipper (see page 179).

3. There you have it. North. Facing this direction, draw a line on the ground pointing directly from you to the north. Label N for north at the top of the line. Label S for south at the bottom.

4. Draw a line straight through the middle of this north–south line, as if you were making a plus sign.

5. Label the left of the new line W for west. Label the right with an E for east.

Natural Direction Decoders

What besides nature do trees, fruit, moss, ants, and snow have in common? They can all indicate direction. But just like Mother Nature herself, natural things can be unpredictable. Always back up your nature-based direction decoding with another method like a compass reading or a sun-shadow stick (page 125).

Fruit:
Because the most sunlight and warmth reach the southern face, trees that bear fruit will produce more on their southern side.

Tree branches:
A tree's north side doesn't get as much sun exposure as its south side, so it will be cooler, darker, and have fewer branches. The tree's sunnier southern side will have more growth.

Moss and lichen:
The north side of trees tends to get the least light and the most moisture. Moss and lichen love damp, dark conditions, so you'll tend to see more of both on trees' northern sides.

Snowmelt:
In the spring, snow melts faster on the southern side of a tree. Again, it's because the warm sunshine spends more time on the tree's southern side than on its northern. As a result, there will be more snow left over on the tree's north side.

Ants:
These crawlies prefer to make their homes on the drier, warmer southern sides of trees.

Backyard Bearings

When you're pitching camp in your backyard, chances are you won't get lost unless your yard is pretty darn huge. But that doesn't mean you shouldn't hone your powers of observation.

Sit down in a comfy spot for 15 minutes and look at, listen to, and smell what's around you. What kinds of things do you notice? Have a pencil and paper handy and jot down whatever you see, especially the things that surprise you. (You can also draw a picture, labeling the sights, sounds, and smells.) When you're done, you'll have a keen sense of your surroundings and will have mastered a skill that's really handy when you're camping in the wild. Here's an example . . .

Saturday, 6:00 P.M. July 21
The Davis's cat is meowing, Jean and Bobby's dog is barking, there's a woodpecker knocking on the oak tree in our backyard, there's a basketball game in Larry's driveway (Larry's dad is losing). I can smell hamburgers cooking, a freshly mowed lawn, a pine tree. I see dad's flashlight near the tent, some ants near the tree, two butterflies floating near the fence, . . .

MARKING TRAILS AND LEAVING SIGNS

Hansel and Gretel were onto something when they left their trail of crumbs. Marking a trail helps other people figure out where you've gone and helps you get back to where you came from. Preexisting trail signs also show you whether you're on the correct path or need to make a turn, or if there's danger ahead. Here are some of the universally understood symbols that you can make as you go or that you might come across during your travels. Avoid making the grass symbols unless there are no rocks or sticks available (since grasses are delicate and you don't want to hurt 'em!).

After you make each symbol, look at it from both a coming and going vantage point. Be aware of how these symbols will look to someone following your trail and how it will look to you on the way home.

This Is the Trail

This Way

Long Distance This Way

Short Distance This Way

Turn Right

Turn Left

Don't Go This Way! Stop!

Danger! Help!

IF YOU MARK A TRAIL
behind you, be sure to use
something that hungry
critters won't mistake
for lunch.

STAYING FOUND

It's a ton of fun to go exploring in the wilderness, but the outdoors can turn into the land of the lost if you're not prepared. When you start itching to check out what's behind that boulder or over that hill, be sure to both tell a grown-up before you go, and to take someone with you. Always stick to well-marked paths (shortcuts can often become paths to Lostville), and if you're taking anything more than a quick stroll, always bring a day pack with a map, compass, rain layer, extra food, water, and a whistle. (You may not need any of these things, but it sure will give you peace of mind and it is good to be prepared.)

Get your bearings in camp before you go anywhere. Take a good hard look at the landscape around you. Notice the big trees and where they are in relation to your tents. Take mental snapshots of things like rocks, water, bushes, cliffs, clumps of ferns, flowers, or open fields. Even noting things like colors, leaf shapes, and man-made objects will help you get a sense of your site.

Make a mental note about where the sun is in relation to your camp at certain times of day. In the morning, which way does the sun shine into your camp? Where does it set in the evening? This can help you get oriented if you lose your way.

Use your ears to listen for clues as well. Is there a stream bubbling nearby? Are ocean waves crashing around the bend? Are there pine trees that whistle in the wind? Where are the sounds coming from? You can use your nose, too. Breathe deeply. What do you smell when you're in camp? Camp cooking? Pine trees? Damp earth? Your little brother's dirty socks? Notice these scents and odors and file them away in your brain.

In short, you want to be plugged in to your surroundings. Be alert. Notice things. Put *yourself* in the picture. If you're going on a hike away from your base camp, a compass can tell you the direction you're heading—this can help you keep your bearings and stay on track both there and back.

As you walk around, check the direction of your camp in relation to the key landmarks you scoped out earlier. Think about your hike as a puzzle and put the pieces together as you go. If you cross a stream or a bridge, or walk through a wooded area, notice which way you are going and think about what direction you'll be heading in when you return.

WHAT IF I DO GET LOST?

You probably won't get lost if you stick with the group and pay attention to where you are and where you've been. And if you do get lost, you're most likely closer to the path or to camp than you think. The first thing to do when you feel disoriented is stop and have a seat. Pulling yourself together and avoiding panic is key. Have a sip of water, and when you are calm and have had a chance to think, you'll probably remember certain signs and landmarks that you passed on the way (write them down if you have a pencil and paper handy). This will help you find your way back.

But if you're frightened or can't get a sense of where you are, follow the guidelines of the Hug-a-Tree program, which teaches lost kids how to get found again:

- **Hug a tree once you know you are lost.** Kids and grown-ups both get scared when they're alone—it's perfectly normal and nothing to be embarrassed about. If you're lost, hug a tree or another stationary object to help you keep calm and prevent you from panicking. Hugging a

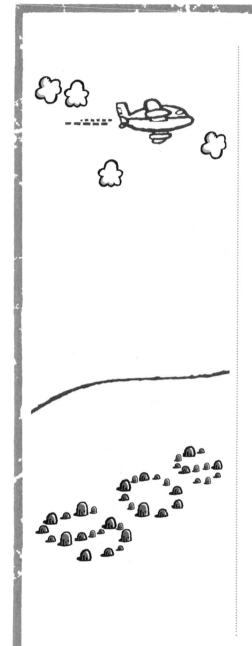

tree also keeps you in one place, which means you'll be found far more quickly and you won't risk getting injured in a fall.

● **Always carry a trash bag and whistle on an outing.** Have an adult cut a face hole in the garbage bag before you set out. In case you do get lost, you can wear the bag like a poncho (poking your face out of the hole), and it will help keep you dry and warm. At night you can sit or lie down with the poncho on and tuck your knees into it for extra warmth. The whistle is much louder than your voice and takes less energy to use. When you blow on it, give it three sharp blasts, then wait for an answer (which might also be a whistle). If you hear a response, blow the whistle three times again. A small mirror will come in handy if it's sunny out— you can move it around to reflect the sun, which will make you easier to spot (especially if people are looking for you from a helicopter or plane).

● **Remember—your grown-ups want to find you, not punish you for getting lost.** Lots of lost kids avoid res- cuers because they feel ashamed about getting lost, or are worried that they'll get in trouble for wandering off. Remember that anyone can get lost—adult or child—and your family and friends want to find you more than any- thing. Work hard to be found, and respond to any rescuers you hear or see.

● **Make yourself big.** From planes and helicopters, people are hard to see when they are standing up or hidden in a group of trees. Hug a tree near a clearing if possible. If you hear a helicopter or airplane overhead, lie down spread- eagled out in the open. If it is cool and you are rested,

FINDING SHELTER

! Rocks
Look for boulders or large rocks to protect you from wind.

If possible, find branches and lay them against the rock at an angle to create a roof and walls. Dig into the ground to make a shallow hole to sit or lie down in. Line the hole with dry leaves, grasses, and twigs. Sit or lie on top of the leaves and cover yourself with another thick layer of leaves. These will insulate you against the cold.

! Bushes
Look for a dense bush. Dig a hole in the dirt underneath if possible and line it with leaves, grasses, and twigs for warmth. Burrow in and try to get warm.

If you are really lost

and night is falling,

you will need to find shelter and drink lots of water to keep you warm and comfy while you wait to be found. When looking for shelter, just be sure to stay close to the tree you were hugging—it's easier for people to find you if you stay in the same spot.

! Logs
Downed trees provide excellent shelter.

Create a roof by laying branches, grasses, and twigs at an angle against the fallen log.

Line the area with leaves, grasses, and twigs for warmth.

! Soft dirt
If you're out in the open and there is nowhere to seek shelter, dig a long, shallow hole in the ground, line it with branches, cover the branches with leaves and grasses, and climb on top. Cover yourself with more leaves and grasses as a blanket.

FINDING WATER

! When you're lost, it's very important to stay well watered, which will help you stay warmer through the night. If you're near a stream or pond, finish off the water in your water bottle and then refill it—even if you don't have a filter or purification tablets with you. Although normally you should drink only purified water, it's more important to drink what you need now than to worry about the belly-ache you might get later. By the time you get sick from any nasty stuff in the water, someone will have found you and a doctor will take care of you.

If there's no water in sight, do your best to stay rested and cool to prevent your body from losing more fluids.

make crosses or write SOS (which means "help!") in *very* large letters using broken branches, or rocks, or by dragging your foot in the dirt.

- **Wear bright-colored clothes when you go out in the woods or desert.** People are tougher to spot when they wear dark or dull colors, or clothing that blends in with the landscape.

- **The animals out there don't want to hurt you.** If you hear a noise at night, yell at it or blow your whistle. If it is an animal, it will run away to protect itself. If it is a searcher, you will be found.

- **You have lots and lots of friends looking for you.** Rescue searchers are mainly volunteers who do what they do for free, just because they care. Sit down and stay put and searchers *will* find you. Respond to people calling you; blow your whistle, look for rangers and groups of adults.

CHAPTER 5

SOMETHING'S IN THE AIR

Watching the Weather

Mother Nature can be sweet and sunny or moody and gray. Since camping means living close to Mama Nature, it helps to understand what she's up to. How can you tell if there will be rain and storms or bright, clear days ahead? What does it mean when the clouds hang low or puff up high in the sky? You can bring a radio on your camping trip and tune in to weather forecasts. But you can also learn to read the signs in the sky for yourself. By learning about the ways weather behaves, your forecasts may be more accurate than a weatherman's predictions.

COLD FRONTS

When a cold air mass bumps up against a warm mass, the colder air—because it is denser—cuts through the warm air mass, shoving it up and out of the way. The air behind a cold front is much cooler than the air ahead of it, so as the front passes overhead, you will feel the temperature dropping. Cold fronts move fast and push hard, sometimes setting off strong weather reactions like thunderstorms and tornadoes.

EARTH, WIND, AND INQUIRE

When it comes to weather, the sun is king. During the day it heats up the atmosphere, the "blanket" of air around the Earth. At night, when it is dark, the land and water and air cool down. Just like the steam over a mug of cocoa, warm air likes to rise. When it does, it leaves behind a pocket, and cooler air charges in to take its place. All this warming and cooling of the Earth is a big balancing act: Warm air moves up, cold air settles down; heat causes water to evaporate and eventually form clouds, which release rain and cool down the ground. It is how the air moves around—and how different blobs of air, called masses, interact with one another—which causes weather.

Some air masses are cold and others are warm. Throughout the Earth's atmosphere, warm masses interact with cool ones. Sometimes the looser warm mass overtakes the cool mass, and sometimes the more tightly packed cool mass bullies its way through the warm mass. The boundary between air masses is called a front. When a front passes over your campsite, you'll notice a change in the temperature, the wind (its speed and direction), and the moisture in the air (the air may become humid or dry). Fronts generally move from west to east.

Mountain and Valley Wind

Want to know how and why the wind blows? Air masses are responsible once again. In mountainous areas there are two types of wind systems: valley breezes, which blow during the day, and mountain breezes, which blow at night. These breezes affect clouds and rainfall. How do they work exactly?

In the morning, the sun rises, and as the day goes on, it heats up the land. The land in turn heats up the air, and this warm air

rises out of the valley. If the rising air cools enough that it can no longer hold its water vapor—evaporated water—the water droplets will cling to one another and create clouds. If there is enough moisture in the clouds, the water will fall as rain or, if it is cold enough, snow. This often occurs over mountainous terrain in summer, particularly late in the day.

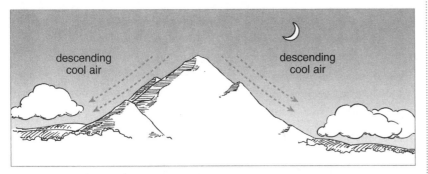

At night, the air cools down and sinks into the valley. If the air is moist enough, it will create low-lying clouds overnight—also known as fog (see page 147). Next time you're camping out in the mountains, wake up early one day and watch the sun rise over the valley below—if there's fog in the valley, it will look like a sea of clouds beneath you. It's a pretty magical sight.

WARM FRONTS

When a warm air mass approaches a cold air mass, the movement is much gentler, and therefore causes gentler weather. Because the air behind the front is warmer, you will feel the temperature heat up as this air passes overhead. The air may feel more moist, too. Though a warm front can bring rain or snow, it's usually calm and not of the hold-onto-your-hat variety.

Land and Sea Breezes

You'll appreciate these breezes if you camp by a large body of water such as the Finger Lakes, Lake Michigan, Puget Sound, or the Pacific or Atlantic Oceans.

Water heats up and cools down more slowly than land does. This means there's always a temperature difference between large bodies of water and the land nearby. This difference in temperature creates variations in air pressure, which cause local winds called shore breezes. There are two types of shore breezes: sea breezes and land breezes. Sea breezes occur when wind blows in from the direction of water. When the breeze comes from the land and blows out to the water, it's called a land breeze. Here's how these winds work: During the day, the heated-up land warms the air and the air rises. The cool air over the water sinks down and whooshes into the pocket left over the land by the rising warm air. This rising and sweeping of the air creates a sea breeze.

The Ocean Above

Believe it or not, we live underneath a huge "ocean" of air. The weight of the air pushes down on us every single day. It's called atmospheric pressure. The airy "ocean" above us sloshes around and sometimes creates areas that have more or less air at different times. When there's more air in a section, it's heavier and there's more pressure pushing (high pressure); and when there's less air, there's less pressure overhead (low pressure). Different pressures bring different weather patterns. High pressure is usually associated with clear, nice weather. Low pressure may bring clouds, wind, rain, snow, and storms.

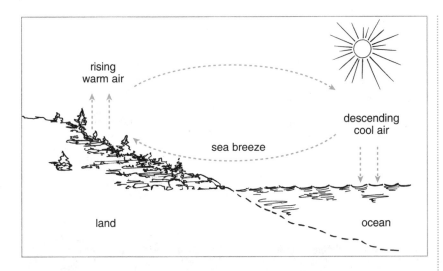

rising
warm air

descending
cool air

sea breeze

land

ocean

At night, the water holds onto more heat than the land, so the air on the surface of the water is warmer and starts to rise. Cool air is drawn from the land to fill the space over the water, creating a land breeze.

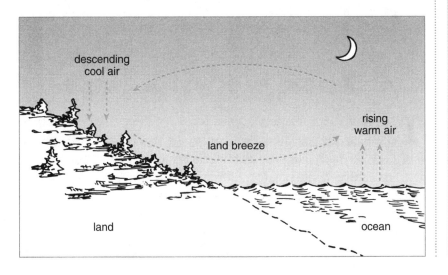

descending
cool air

rising
warm air

land breeze

land

ocean

EASY BREEZY

Which way does the wind blow? If you're camping by a mountain or by a large body of water, you can catch land and sea breezes in the act. Find a clear spot in your campsite that's exposed to the air coming from all directions and plant a 4- to 5-foot stick firmly in the ground so it stands up. Or find a tree branch hanging in a place where it is exposed to the wind on all sides. Tie a strip of plastic—about 2 feet by 2 inches—on the stick or branch and watch how it behaves throughout the day.

Does the strip show that the breezes are moving mostly in one direction? Does it switch directions at any time during the day or at night? Why do you think this happens? Reread the Land and Sea Breezes section, opposite, to explain what you observe.

IT MAY SOUND FUNNY, but the shape of the land in a given place actually shapes the climate around it. The technical term for the shape of the land is topography. A place's topography creates something called a microclimate, a mini pocket of weather that is dictated by all the lumps, bumps, and other textures of the landscape. Microclimates are all around you, whether you're in the backyard at home, on the sidewalks in the city, or camped out on the side of a mountain.

For an example of a microclimate, think of a house with a backyard. During the day the house absorbs heat, and at night radiates it back. This makes the microclimate right around the house warmer while the surrounding yard is cooler. And a tree in the yard can have its own microclimate, too. During the summer months, the shady ground underneath the tree will probably be 5 to 10°F cooler than the exposed ground around it.

Microclimates can be more dramatic in wilderness areas. Valleys, mountains, lakeshores, and beaches can all have numerous microclimates. You might have great weather on one side of a mountain and lousier weather on the other. If you travel between campsites and notice shifts in the weather, think about how the landscape changes. The shifts may just be different landscape features creating microclimates.

UNCLOUDING CLOUDS! A GUIDE

The same factors that create local weather create weather patterns across the globe. Warm air rises from the equator and cool air falls from the north and south poles. Warm air carries moisture that creates clouds—collections of tiny water droplets or ice crystals that hover in the sky.

It takes three things to make a cloud—evaporation, cooling air, and condensation. When the sun heats up any wet place on the planet—like an ocean or even a rain-soaked field (anyplace with

lots of water molecules)—it excites those water molecules and makes them leap into the air. That's called evaporation. Because these water molecules are excited, they bounce around and into one another, forming a loose group; this group is less dense than the air around it, so it rises. (To picture this it helps to think of a pot of boiling water—the heated water molecules get very excited and start to evaporate and float into the air as steam.)

As the water molecules rise, they are chilled by the cold air in the upper atmosphere. They get cooler and move more slowly, and eventually start to cling to each other. That's called condensation. When enough water molecules cling together, poof! You've got a cloud.

Clouds appear in all parts of the atmosphere and they can look and act wildly different. Ever spend an afternoon debating the appearance of a cloud with a friend? You say it looks like a kitten, but he insists that it is a racecar. You might be surprised to know that clouds' appearances and how they move can be very helpful during your camping trip. If you can tell them apart and know what each type tends to do, you might be able to tell what the weather has in store.

Learn the Lingo

Cumulus: *heap;* used for lumpy, heaped together clouds like cumulonimbus

Cirrus: *curl of hair;* used to describe wispy clouds such as cirrocumulus

Stratus: *layer;* used for clouds that blanket the sky, such as cirrostratus

Nimbo- or **-nimbus:** *rain cloud;* used to name low, dark rain clouds like nimbostratus

Clouds at a Glance

The standard system for classifying clouds is based on one devised by English scientist Luke Howard, who came up with it more than two hundred years ago.

Low Clouds form near the Earth's surface and can rise to 6,500 feet.

Cumulus

Nimbostratus

Stratocumulus

Low clouds help cool the Earth by reflecting much of the sun's heat back into space.

Towering Cumulus

Cumulonimbus

Fog

Middle Clouds form at heights of between 6,500 and 23,000 feet above the Earth.
They contain billions of water droplets as well as ice.

Altocumulus

Lenticular

Altostratus

High Clouds start at 16,400 feet above the Earth.
These thin, wispy clouds can climb as high as 42,500 feet.

Cirrus

At sunrise and sunset, high clouds produce beautiful patterns of red, orange, and yellow in the sky.

Cirrostratus

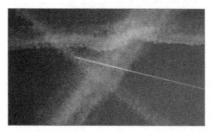
Contrails

Cirrocumulus

Low Clouds

Low clouds form near the Earth's surface and rise to heights of 6,500 feet. These low sun-blocker clouds are uniformly gray-blue and are heavy with water droplets. If low clouds form early in the morning, there's a chance the sun will evaporate the water droplets in the clouds and the sky will be clear later in the day. But these clouds can also gang up and turn into dark and wet nimbostratus; when this happens, rain will fall.

NIMBOSTRATUS CLOUDS

What you see: A dark sheet of low, wet clouds.

Forecast: Expect continuous rain or, if it's cold enough, snow.

CUMULUS CLOUDS

What you see: Cottony white clouds with plenty of blue sky and sun peeking around them. They're flat on the bottom and rounded on the top.

Forecast: A beautiful day if the clouds are small and scattered in the sky. If the clouds are large and close together, keep an eye on them! Clumped up, these clouds can bring stormy weather.

STRATOCUMULUS CLOUDS

What you see: Sheets of lumpy clouds (often with the sun shining through the lumps).

Forecast: These clouds are not as bad as they look. Unless the clouds are very thick, usually they only create a light drizzle. But sometimes stratocumulus clouds gather force and become a sign that worse weather is on the way.

TOWERING CUMULUS CLOUDS

What you see: A tall pile of cumulus clouds—like a head of cauliflower—flattish on the bottom and rounded and mounded on the top.

Forecast: Lots of moisture causes cumulus clouds to grow into these huge, upward-growing cloud towers—a sign that a thunderstorm is on its way.

CUMULONIMBUS CLOUDS

What you see: A large, white pile. The winds often blow the top part of these clouds flat—making them look like huge anvils. The anvil points in the direction the weather is moving.

Forecast: These clouds carry stormy weather with them. When they appear, you may be in for thunder, lightning, a heavy downpour, a blizzard, or even hail or tornadoes.

FOG

What you see: A thick, wet cloud that moves along the ground. Fog forms when warm, moist air moves over colder ground. The air is chilled from below and the water molecules closest to the ground start to condense.

Forecast: If the winds are light, these soupy clouds can settle into the landscape and hang around until the sun warms and evaporates the water, "burning off" the fog. Fog can roll in quickly along the shore where warm, moist air is blown in from larger bodies of water, but it can also dissipate quickly.

Middle Clouds

These clouds form at heights of 6,500 to 23,000 feet above the Earth. They are made up of a combination of ice crystals and water droplets and appear bluish-gray. Because they are so moisture-rich, they more than likely will bring rain or snow. If you see them in the sky when you wake up, pack your rain gear before you head out for the day.

Sometimes resembling a stack of pancakes, lenticular clouds are a good indicator that a snowstorm might be approaching.

ALTOCUMULUS CLOUDS

What you see: Bluish-gray, fuzzy puffs in rows and patterns. These clouds are similar to cirrocumulus clouds (page 150) and also make a "mackerel sky," but they have a sharper outline and are usually darker, larger, and denser.

Forecast: Maybe a rainstorm is coming. If it's summer and the weather is warm and humid, altocumulus clouds might become thunderclouds.

ALTOSTRATUS CLOUDS

What you see: A dreary, gray, shapeless sheet that covers the sky. Sometimes the sun shines through these clouds as a glowy disc.

Forecast: Because these clouds are heavy with moisture, once they appear overhead, it means rain or snow will probably come soon.

LENTICULAR CLOUDS

What you see: Lenticular clouds are huge U.F.O.-shape clouds that form over mountain peaks when winds travel up a mountain slope and the moisture in the air condenses. The winds are constantly blowing up the slope, so the cloud is continually renewed and appears to hang in the air.

Forecast: Strong winds, if you're very high up (and a bumpy ride, if you're passing over in a plane).

High Clouds

High clouds form at three miles or more above the Earth. Because they are so high in the atmosphere, they are in cooler air and are made up mostly of ice crystals. Watch these clouds— the direction that they move in will give you a clue about the direction of any weather coming your way.

CIRRUS CLOUDS

What you see: White, wispy clouds blown into thin streamer shapes by the frigid winds in the upper atmosphere.

Forecast: If cirrus clouds remain sparse, good weather will continue. If they begin to change to cirrostratus clouds (page 150), wind and rain may soon follow.

Long, feathery cirrus clouds are also called "mares' tails" because they look like the billowy tail of a horse.

CIRROCUMULUS CLOUDS

What you see: Small puffy ripples, often in rows. These clouds create a "mackerel sky" (as do altocumulus, see page 148), so nicknamed because it looks like the scales of a fish.

Forecast: Nothing major will happen anytime soon, so enjoy the sight of these beautiful clouds. They are created by turbulence—irregular up-and-down air currents—high in the sky. (Ever been on a bumpy airplane flight? You can thank turbulence for that.)

CIRROSTRATUS CLOUDS

What you see: A shapeless, hazy film that covers large areas of the sky.

Forecast: Rain may be on the way. Cirrostratus clouds indicate a large area of moist air in the sky. Thick cirrostratus clouds sometimes spread from the tops of advancing storm systems.

CONTRAILS

What you see: If you hear a jet plane flying overhead, look for two long clouds left in the plane's wake. These are contrails, big puffs of condensation formed when the hot, humid air from the jet exhaust mixes with air of much cooler temperatures.

Forecast: If a jet passes and there is no contrail or the contrail disappears quickly, the atmosphere is dry. That's a good sign that clear skies will stick around. If the contrail hangs out and spreads, the atmosphere is wet. Expect a change in the weather.

RAIN AHEAD

Grow Your Own Cloud

D id you know you can make a cloud from scratch? It's not the kind Uncle Harry makes after eating campfire chili, either. It's a real cloud that makes real rain, and you can make it right in camp.

What you need

Scissors

A 2-liter clear plastic soda bottle with the cap on

1 cup ice

1 cup very hot (not boiling) water

What you do

1 Get a grown-up to help you cut off the top third of the plastic soda bottle (Figure 1).

2 Scoop 1 cup of ice into the top portion of the bottle and set it aside, cap-side down (Figure 2).

3 Pour the hot water into the bottom of the bottle (Figure 3). Quickly place the top part of the bottle, cap-side down, into the bottom part of the bottle.

4 The cloud will appear as the water vapor fills the bottom part of the bottle, rises, and cools when it hits the ice. Eventually you'll see the water condense and fall just like raindrops from a real cloud (Figure 4).

Figure 1.

Figure 2.

Figure 3.

Figure 4.

CHEW ON THIS

A SINGLE BOLT OF lightning is more than four times hotter than the surface of the sun and has enough electricity to power all the buildings in a single state (for a split second, at least). Depending on what it hits, lightning can spread almost 60 feet from where it strikes.

EXTREME WEATHER

Chances are that when you're camping, you will run into some bad weather. It might rain or be foggy or cold. In rare cases you might encounter extreme weather like thunderstorms, lightning, or in some areas, tornadoes. Extreme weather is really fascinating, but if you are unprepared, it can be dangerous. Read on to find out what causes this craziness, and how you can stay safe if it makes an unexpected visit during your campout.

Thunderstorms

The clouds are hanging low in a thick, sludgy blanket, and the sky is grumbling angrily—a thunderstorm is on its way. A thunderstorm occurs when lots and lots of condensation (see page 147) comes together in an unstable atmosphere. This spells lightning, thunder, and usually lots of wind and rain (or hail or snow, depending on the temperature). These active storms are cool to listen to and watch, but it's best to do so from somewhere sheltered (see page 154), since they involve lightning, and lightning can be dangerous.

Lightning is a very large, very hot electrical current that begins inside a cloud. Water molecules and bits of ice inside the cloud bump and bash against each other and build up electric charges. As the charges multiply, the whole cloud starts to change—positive charges move to the top of the cloud and negative charges pile up on the bottom. Since opposite charges attract, positive charges start to build up on the ground beneath the cloud—piling up on higher points like buildings, trees, and even people. When the attraction between the negatively charged cloud bottom and positively charged ground becomes strong enough—BAM! A jagged bolt of lightning stretches down from the cloud.

This cloud-to-ground lightning is called forked lightning (because of its zigzaggy appearance), but lightning can strike in other ways, too. Most often it strikes within a single cloud: The positively charged section of the cloud and the negative section connect, and zap!—it's like someone flicked the lights on and off inside the cloud. Less often, lightning can strike from one cloud to another. When lightning remains in the sky, we see sheet lightning: a flash overhead accompanied by a rumble of thunder. (Heat lightning is a flash in the sky without thunder—it usually means that the storm is more than ten miles away.) And on very, very rare occasions, ball lightning can occur: It is a buzzing, hissing sphere of light the size of a cantaloupe or even a beach ball. Ball lightning is so uncommon, however, and we know so little about it, that some scientists doubt it even exists!

With the exception of heat lightning, you'll almost always hear thunder when lightning is around. In fact, thunder is the sound that lightning makes. When lightning zips through the air, it opens a small tunnel. After the electricity has passed through the air, the tunnel collapses back on itself and creates a huge sound wave that we hear as thunder. Since light travels so much faster than sound, we see the lightning before we hear it.

TO FIGURE OUT HOW far away a thunderstorm is and if and when it will arrive, count the seconds between when you see a flash of lightning and hear the next clap of thunder. For every five seconds you count, the storm is one mile away:
one-Mississippi,
two-Mississippi,
three-Mississippi,
four-Mississippi,
five-Mississippi.

IN THE UNITED STATES, tornadoes usually occur in the spring, in a region of the Great Plains known as "tornado alley," which encompasses parts of Texas, Oklahoma, Kansas, South Dakota, Wyoming, Colorado, and New Mexico. In this relatively flat area of land, huge cold fronts from Canada come crashing against warmer fronts from Mexico. The collisions cause enormous storms and high winds, which provide the perfect conditions for these unpredictable twisters.

STAYING SAFE IN A THUNDERSTORM

It can be fascinating to experience a thunderstorm when you're outdoors, but you need to take some simple steps to stay safe.

Keep away from water. If you're swimming, get out immediately, and stay out of ditches or caves, where moisture can accumulate. Water is an all-too-reliable electricity conductor, so if you're in or near water when lightning strikes, you're more likely to get caught in its path. Same goes for metal objects—metal is an excellent conductor, so you'll want to avoid metal tools and fences (though a car is okay, because it's enclosed).

A sturdy building or car with the doors and windows closed is probably the safest place to wait out the storm. If you're on the trail when a stormy light show strikes, calmly remove your pack (it has metal in it) and cover it with a garbage bag, head for low ground, and hunker down in a cluster of trees—you don't want to be out in the open. Avoid standing near the tallest tree in a group or under a tree that's all on its lonesome—tall trees can act like lightning rods (since lightning tends to hit the highest objects around). Electricity wants to make a beeline to the ground along the shortest path possible, so make yourself a small and uninviting target by crouching on the ground with both feet together. Keep a safe distance of about 15 feet from other folks—electricity likes to jump around from one object (or person) to the next—and wait calmly until the storm passes.

Tornadoes

A tornado is a wildly churning column of air that spins down out of a cumulonimbus cloud and causes winds of up to 300 miles per hour. That's wind powerful enough to toss your tent and everything inside it! How do these terrible twisters start?

When thunderstorm clouds form in the sky, sometimes the

wind can speed up and change direction, turning the air inside a cloud. The twisting air starts off moving horizontally—like tires on the road (see Figure 1)—and shifts vertically, spinning like a hula hoop, as warm air rises within the cloud (see Figures 2 and 3). When more warm air rises quickly from the ground, it causes the cloud to spin even more wildly, creating a funnel cloud. A funnel cloud that makes contact with the ground (and not all of them do) becomes a tornado.

Figure 2.

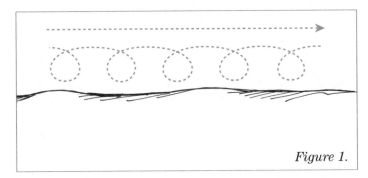

Figure 1.

STAYING SAFE DURING A TORNADO

Tornadoes are supercool to see but they're extremely dangerous and unpredictable (remember the big tornado in *The Wizard of Oz*?). If you spot one, seek shelter immediately.

If you're outdoors and there are no buildings nearby, find a depression, ditch, or hole in the ground and protect yourself by curling up in a ball. Wait out the storm like this while the winds blow over you. A tent or small shelter isn't strong enough to withstand a tornado's powerful winds, so if you're inside one, get out—a tornado can whisk these things away very quickly with you inside. If you're in a cabin, curl in a ball in the lowest part of the structure to protect yourself from flying debris. If there's a cellar or basement, go down into it and wait until the wind stops blowing.

Figure 3.

Blizzards

A blizzard is a severe winter snowstorm that has extra-chilly temperatures, high winds, and lots and lots of snow. Blizzards happen when a high-pressure area (see page 140) meets a low-pressure area (see page 140) in cold weather.

Camping in a winter wonderland can be incredibly beautiful and lots of fun, but make sure you're prepared for bad weather and pack a collapsible shovel as well as extra food, water, and layers of warm clothes (see Cool Weather Add-Ons, page 18).

If you're out and about when it starts to snow, head back to your camp with your crew. You may want to climb into the car and head home if the forecast looks bleak, but if that's not an option, get into your tent, put on lots of extra layers (don't forget a hat!), and climb into your sleeping bag for extra warmth. It's even better if you pack in like sardines—the more people in the tent, the more body heat there will be. If you have a camp stove with you, put it in the space between the tent door and the fly so that it won't get buried in the snow and a grown-up can use it to make hot drinks (keep a pot, water, mugs and cocoa handy, too!). When the harsh weather passes, unfold the collapsible shovel and use it to clear a pathway out of your tent.

WEIRD WEATHER

Warm air, cold air, wind, spinning air masses—Mother Nature has a whole bunch of weather tricks up her sleeve, including some less common weather shows like dust devils, waterspouts, red rain, and softball-size hail. These weird weather phenomena are very rare. If one strikes when you're out camping, make sure you are safe but still be sure to take a good look!

Weird Stuff Falling from the Sky

RED RAIN

In 2001, in Kerala, India, reports came of bloodred rain falling from the sky and turning everything in its path crimson. Scientists collected and analyzed samples of the rain and determined that it contained tiny red cells. One theorist proposed that the tiny red cells were aliens, though most scientists believed that they were actually spores from a rust fungus growing nearby. According to the rust fungus theory, the spores were whipped up into the atmosphere by warm winds, where they clung to water droplets and fell as rain when the water became too heavy for the cloud to hold.

HUGE HAIL

Because hail is cold, you might think it would most likely form during cold winter months. But believe it or not, hail is actually more common during the summer.

Hailstones are ice pellets formed inside storm clouds where warm, moist air cools as it rises. Ice crystals form as water molecules freeze together. When these ice crystals get heavy, they begin to fall within the cloud. Then they are lifted up by more warm air rising into the cloud; as the crystals rise, another layer of water vapor freezes onto them. These ice balls rise and fall

---

CLOUD SPOTTING

Every day of your trip, periodically write down the date and time in your journal, and describe the clouds, temperature, and weather. Using the cloud guide on pages 144–150, determine which kinds of clouds you see. Draw a picture of each one.

At the end of your trip, see what connections you've noticed between the clouds, temperature, and precipitation. Go over your data and answer the following questions:

- Which clouds belonged to each cloud group? How many kinds of clouds did you spot?

- Did the clouds predict the weather that followed?

- What kinds of clouds are associated with good weather? Rain? Snow?

- Do you think the seasons play a large role in cloud cover? Why?

many times within the same cloud, growing bigger and bigger until the cloud can no longer hold them. They fall as hailstones—sometimes the size of aspirin, sometimes the size of golf balls, or, in very rare cases, the size of baseballs. In 2003, during a hailstorm in Nebraska, one hailstone was measured and found to be about the size of a soccer ball—not something you'd want conking you on the head! If you're camping and hail begins to fall, find shelter quickly. Wait out the storm inside your tent, in a lodge, in the car, or, if there's no shelter available, hold your pack over your head. Hailstones, especially big ones, can hurt!

ACID RAIN

Rain may seem completely clean and pure, but all rainwater has some level of acidity. Acidity, which is measured on a pH scale, ranges from 0 to 14, with 7 being neutral. The lower the pH number, the more acidic a substance it is. Any rainwater measuring 5.6 or below is considered acid rain. Acid rain forms when polluting gases such as sulfur dioxide and nitrogen oxides combine with water vapor in the air. Some of the gases that cause acid rain come from the Earth (they are released by volcanoes and wetlands), but others come from us—as a result of burning fossil fuels such as coal and oil, and from our cars, electricity, and factories. Acid rain can kill plants and animals, and can even eat away at rocks and buildings over time.

IT'S RAINING FROGS!

England tends to get a lot of rain, so its residents are used to pulling on boots and carrying an umbrella. But imagine their surprise when, in 1939, it rained frogs instead of water! By the end of this historic storm in the town of Trowbridge, hundreds of frogs had fallen from the sky. People didn't dare walk outside because they were afraid to step on frogs. What happened? Probably something called a waterspout. Common in tropical areas like the Florida Keys, these spinning columns of water are formed when a funnel cloud reaches down from a cumulonimbus cloud (see page 147) and touches down on the surface of a large body of water. The spouts suck up water and debris and whip around until they exhaust themselves—sometimes spewing out fish, frogs, and other wet stuff in their wake.

Weird Wind

DUST DEVILS

A dust devil is a small, spinning column of dirt and dust that forms most frequently in hot, sandy desert places. They occur regularly in the southwestern United States, in places like Arizona, Nevada, and Death Valley, California. Hot air whips up into the atmosphere and cooler air rushes down to form a swirling vortex, kind of like a miniature tornado. These rotating tubes of wind scoop up dirt and dust as they travel. Most last only a few minutes and are not dangerous. These "devils" are also known as sand augers, dust whirls, and willy-willies. And guess what—they even occur on Mars!

Weird Light

SUN DOGS

No, these aren't just pooches that love to tan. A sun dog is a bright spot of yellow- or rainbow-colored light in the sky that is created when sunlight passes through the ice crystals in high-flying cirrostratus clouds (see page 150). The same phenomenon creates the appearance of halos around the sun and the moon.

DURING A thunderstorm you might spot a blue or green glow above a pointed object like a tall tree, a sailboat's mast, or a power pole. Aliens aren't about to land, but lightning is! Since this electric blaze often appears near the masts of ships at sea, it is named after the patron saint of sailors and is called St. Elmo's Fire.

RAINBOWS

These beautiful spectacles of nature have inspired fairy tales, songs, poems, and legends. The science is simple—combine a raindrop with sunlight and the water acts as a prism, breaking the sun's light (which looks white but is actually made up of lots of colors) into its different parts. Put a *bunch* of raindrops together with sunlight, and voilà! You now have a rainbow.

All rainbows are circular. If you could stand above the rain, you'd see the colorful circle entirely. Here on Earth, we see only a semicircle, which is the arc of the circle that's visible above the horizon.

Have you ever seen two rainbows at once? This happens when the light captured in a raindrop reflects twice instead of once, so we see a "primary" rainbow with the colors in the usual order, and a "secondary" rainbow with the colors running in reverse.

GREEN GLOW BEFORE A STORM

Sometimes the sky turns a mysterious green before a big storm or tornado hits. This effect is caused by the scattering of light, the same reason that the sky appears blue. Like all light, the light from the sun is made up of many different colors. Light travels in waves, and each of the colors has a different wavelength, some long and some short. As the sun's light travels through the sky from overhead, the colors with the longer wavelengths—like reds and oranges—tend to pass right through molecules in the air, while colors with shorter wavelengths, like blue and violet, get absorbed by the molecules and reflected back to us. Light that travels the least is always the brightest, so we usually see blue skies when the sun is overhead. But when a giant cloud blanket—like the one that appears right before a storm—covers most of the sky, we often see green: The clouds block out the scattered light nearby so we can't see blue, and green is the only color that gets through.

Weather Warners

"RED SKY AT NIGHT, hiker's delight. Red sky in the morning, hikers take warning." The presence of high clouds and dust particles at night makes the sky look red as the sun sets. This indicates high pressure and calm air, both of which mean good weather will follow. A red sunrise means there are clouds, dust particles, and moisture in the air—could be rain on the way.

WHERE THERE'S SMOKE, there's a weather forecast. Try to make a forecast by looking at the way the smoke from your campfire moves. If the smoke hangs low, chances are it could rain. But if the smoke rises up in a nice column, good weather is ahead. Atmospheric pressure dictates the smoke's movement. High pressure, a sign of good weather, forces the smoke down. Low pressure, a sign of rain, lets the smoke rise up.

"RING AROUND THE moon, rain is coming soon." Ice crystals around the moon can give it a glowing ring, indicating that a change in weather is ahead—most likely rain. The crystals come from high clouds, a sign of damp weather on the way.

SINGING FROGS
A few hours before a storm hits, frogs start singing their little hearts out. Because their skin needs to stay moist, frogs usually spend most of their time in or near the water. When a storm approaches, the air's moisture increases, making the frogs feel comfortable *outside* the pond—they climb out of the water and sing merrily.

CHIRPING CRICKETS
You can actually tell the temperature by listening to crickets. Count the number of chirps one cricket makes in 14 seconds. Add 40 to the number and you'll have a decent estimate of the temperature. For example, if you count 35 chirps in 14 seconds, it means the temperature is around 75°F (35 + 40 = 75).

SNOOZY SEAGULLS
Have you ever noticed that seagulls often gather on the ground before a storm? Scientists think the birds sense the dropping pressure in the atmosphere that occurs before a storm and choose to lay low.

SLEEPY SAMMY *and the* FORECASTERS

WHAT'S UP?

The Night Sky

"I often think that the night is more alive and more richly colored than the day."

—VINCENT VAN GOGH

When night falls and darkness settles over your campsite, you don't have to stop exploring. Spread out your sleeping bag, lie on the ground, and look up. The sky is full of twinkling light. This beautiful sight is jam-packed with history, science, drama, and other incredibly cool stuff. From planets and galaxies, to star clusters and constellations, the night offers many discoveries right over your head.

In this chapter, you'll learn about the universe and encounter the moon's phases. You'll see planets you always thought were stars. You'll explore constellations *and* hear the ancient stories behind them. So let's get going: There's lots to learn right here about all the amazing stuff up there, in our infinitely awesome, incredibly fascinating night sky.

THE UNIVERSE

Nobody knows for sure, but scientists believe that way, way, way long ago (like between 10 and 20 billion years) there was nothing but deep, dark, empty space and one tiny speck of matter. The speck was probably about the size of a grain of sand and weighed about ten pounds. It was so compact and full of energy that kept building and building with nowhere to go that one day . . . it exploded.

Scientists call this explosion the Big Bang (for obvious reasons), and they believe that after this minuscule energy-packed particle burst, everything inside it was flung far and wide into space (where it continues to expand to this day). During this eventful time other explosions occurred, stuff was pulled in on itself and attracted other stuff, and eventually all the stars, planets, moons, and everything in space formed. This Big Bang is considered the birth of our universe.

BLAM

"Universe" is the word we use to describe space and everything in it: All the stars and planets and moons and asteroids and meteors and comets and any other thing that may be out there. Our universe (there may be more universes out there, who knows?) is made up of smaller groups of stars (at least a billion or so) called galaxies. At the edge of one of those galaxies, the Milky Way, is a bright star: our sun. A handful of objects made out of rocks, gas, and chemicals orbit around the sun—those are the planets in our solar system. The third rocky, gassy planet in the solar system is Earth.

- Binoculars or small telescope

- Compass

- Star chart or wheel

- Flashlight covered with a square of red cellophane (to help you read the star chart)

- Sleeping bag to lie on or in

- Sweatshirt, fleece jacket, or coat, and fuzzy socks and hat to keep you warm

THE MOON

On a clear night, you just can't miss this bright object in the sky, and on a cloudy night it enhances the eerie mood for any scary story. From full-moon brightness to new-moon shadow, this glowing ball in the sky has been enthralling poets, astronomers, and regular folks for thousands of years.

What Exactly Is the Moon?

The moon is a big hunk of rock (about 2,000 miles in diameter) that orbits the Earth. Things that orbit around a planet are called satellites. There is a whole handful of man-made satellites out there whipping around the Earth, but the moon is the only natural satellite we have. It's about 250,000 miles away and it's trapped in a kind of tug-of-war pull with the Earth's gravity (see Learn the

Gravity

Gravity is a natural force that attracts objects to each other. Bigger, heavier objects have more gravity than smaller objects (so the Earth has a stronger gravitational pull than, say, a baseball). Gravity is the force that makes your cookie crumbs fall onto the ground instead floating off into the air.

Lingo, right). The moon's gravity pulls on us while the Earth's gravity pulls on the moon. Scientists think the moon formed around the same time the Earth did—about 4.5 billion years ago— when a chunk of space rock belted our forming planet and broke off a piece of it, and that piece got lobbed into space. Ever since then, the chunk (aka the moon) and our planet (aka Earth) have been pulling on each other.

Since the moon doesn't rotate on its axis (like Earth does), we always see the same side of it. Its other side is called the "dark side"—astronauts are the only ones who have seen it.

Don't Worry, It's Just a Phase

The moon seems to glow, but it doesn't make its own light. What's the deal? It actually reflects light from the sun. During any given

Learn the Lingo

The terminator

The boundary between dark and light or day and night on the moon (or on any planet).

MAKE YOUR OWN MOON

At night, try this little experiment. Hold a ball in your hand at arm's length at the height of your head. Get a friend to stand a few feet away from the ball and point a flashlight at it. (The ball is the moon, you are the Earth, and the flashlight is the sun.) In this position, the moon will appear dark to you (the Earth), just like a new moon. Now make a quarter-turn to the left. The sun will light up half of the moon, as it does in the first quarter (see opposite page). Make two more quarter-turns—can you see the changing phases?

month, we see the moon from different angles in the night sky. This creates the illusion of the disappearing and reappearing moon, which we call the moon's "phases." The moon's phases change over a 29-day cycle, which begins with the new moon. There are four major phases—new moon, quarter moon, full moon, and three-quarter moon—with the almost-dark crescent moon and almost-full gibbous moon both appearing between the phases (see right).

New Moon
The moon and the sun are on the same side of Earth, so we don't see any sunlight reflected—the moon looks completely dark.

➤➤➤➤ **Crescent** ➤➤➤➤

Quarter Moon
The moon has traveled one-quarter of the way around Earth and appears to be lit up halfway.

➤➤➤➤ **Gibbous** ➤➤➤➤

Full Moon
The moon has now traveled halfway around Earth. It is opposite the sun, so we get a full frontal reflection of the sun's light.

➤➤➤➤ **Gibbous** ➤➤➤➤

Three-Quarter Moon Now the moon has traveled three-quarters of the way around Earth and we see the reflection of the sun on its other side. The moon will continue to appear smaller as we head back toward a new moon.

➤➤➤➤ **Crescent** ➤➤➤➤

How can you tell if we're heading for a full moon or no moon at all? Think of this rhyme: "Bright right, growing light." When the moon is mostly lit on its right side (when it's shaped like a *D*), it is waxing, or on its way to becoming full. When the moon is mostly lit on its left side (shaped like a *C*), it is waning (getting

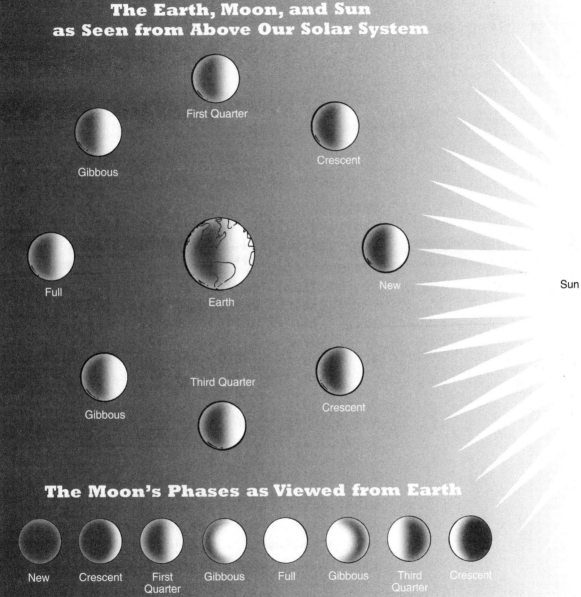

The Earth, Moon, and Sun as Seen from Above Our Solar System

First Quarter

Gibbous

Crescent

Full

Earth

New

Sun

Gibbous

Third Quarter

Crescent

The Moon's Phases as Viewed from Earth

New

Crescent

First Quarter

Gibbous

Full

Gibbous

Third Quarter

Crescent

Have you ever heard the saying "Once in a blue moon"? It originates from the moon's phases. In a normal month we get one full moon. On rare occasions, there will be two nights of a full moon in one month. The second full moon is called a blue moon. No one knows why, since it's not blue at all, but folks have been referring to this phenomenon as a blue moon since the 1500s. So when someone uses the phrase "Once in a blue moon," they're talking about something that doesn't occur very often.

narrower) and about to disappear from view. You can also remember the phases by using the word "DOC." The moon comes in like the belly of the D, fills out to an O, and leaves like a C.

More Than Just a Pretty Face

The moon is close enough to Earth that you can explore its surface with a pair of high-powered binoculars. There are three basic features on the moon's surface: seas, mountains, and craters. Grab a pair of binocs and take a better look.

MOON SEAS On maps of the moon you'll see seas all over the place. But they're not watery seas—these dark spots are actually ancient lunar lava beds. It is believed that they were created when comets and asteroids hit the moon so hard that lava leaked out from beneath the moon's surface. The spots were mistaken for seas by astronomers in ancient times, and the name stuck. (You may also see the labels "mare" or "maria" used on a moon's map; these words mean "sea" and "seas" in Latin, which is the language ancient astronomers used to name objects in space.)

When the moon is full, try to spot the Sea of Rains and the Ocean of Storms in the northwest quarter (see map, opposite).

MOON MOUNTAINS You can identify mountains by finding the lighter areas on the moon's surface. The Apennine Mountain Range is just northwest of the center of the moon, between the Sea of Rains in the northwest and the Sea of Vapors in the center.

MOON CRATERS Ever think the moon looks like Swiss cheese? That's because it's covered with craters—indentations in its surface created when comets and meteors collided with the moon long, long ago. Through binoculars, craters look like circles, sometimes with lines radiating from their edges. Two of the most prominent craters on the moon are Plato, near its top, and Tycho, near the bottom.

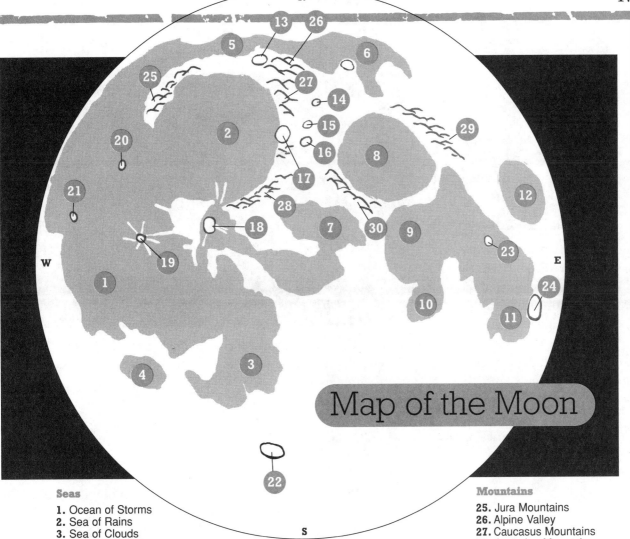

N

W

E

S

Map of the Moon

Seas

1. Ocean of Storms
2. Sea of Rains
3. Sea of Clouds
4. Sea of Moisture
5. Bay of Dew
6. Sea of Cold
7. Sea of Vapors
8. Sea of Serenity
9. Sea of Tranquility
10. Sea of Nectar
11. Sea of Fertility
12. Sea of Crises

Craters

13. Plato
14. Eudoxus
15. Aristillus
16. Autolycus
17. Archimedes
18. Copernicus
19. Kepler
20. Aristarchus
21. Marius Hills
22. Tycho
23. Taruntis
24. Langrenus

Mountains

25. Jura Mountains
26. Alpine Valley
27. Caucasus Mountains
28. Apennine Mountains
29. Taurus Mountains
30. Haemus Mountains

CHEW ON THIS

IN EXTREME NORTHERN and southern parts of the world, you can see a shimmering light show called the Northern Lights (aurora borealis) in the north or the Southern Lights (aurora australis) in the south. The lights are caused by a stream of high-energy particles, called solar wind, emitted by the sun. When solar wind approaches Earth, it interacts with the magnetic field near the north and south poles and begins to get pulled in. The excited molecules in the "wind" collide with gas molecules in the atmosphere and start to glow. The resulting auroras look like swirling multicolored clouds of light—pretty cool.

MOON ROCKS Humans first set foot on the moon in 1969, when the astronauts on America's *Apollo 11* lunar module landed. The *Apollo* astronauts took a short walk, and gathered a few rocks to study. The oldest of these rocks are about the same age as the Earth itself—a mere 4.5 billion years old. Scientists believe this similarity in age is due to how the moon was formed—by a huge meteor that slammed into the Earth and broke off chunks of the Earth's crust. The globs of crust formed a ring around our planet and eventually came together as the moon.

THE PLANETS

Our solar system is made up of a group of celestial bodies called planets, which orbit around the sun. There are eight planets in this group: Mercury, Venus, Earth, Mars, Jupiter, Saturn, Uranus, and Neptune. (Wondering what happened to Pluto? See Not Round Enough, right.)

You may not realize it, but you can actually spot some of these planets with your bare eyes. Of course, it's always easier to make them out with binoculars, and you can see them even better with a telescope, but it's fun knowing that there are a few you can pick out on your own.

Planet-spotting is tricky. The size and brightness of the planets differ wildly. And their positions in the sky vary as well. (To determine the planets' locations in the night sky before you go camping, consult an astronomy website such as www.stardate .org/nightsky/weekly.php.) Here's a short guide to what you might see. (Remember that planets don't twinkle like stars.)

MERCURY Mercury is the smallest planet in our solar system and the planet closest to the sun. Even though you can sometimes spot it with binoculars or the unaided eye, it is usually too near the sun to pick out.

VENUS Venus is the second planet from the sun and it's the sixth largest. It has been spotted in the skies since ancient times.

Because Venus is always by the sun, we can't see it during the day or late at night. The best time to find it is just after sunset or just before sunrise. In the early morning, before dawn, look east. If you see a point of light that doesn't twinkle and doesn't move, it's probably Venus. After sunset, look west. From your perspective, as the sky darkens, Venus will set as it follows the sun to the

NOT ROUND ENOUGH

It's not so easy to be a planet. In fact, according to the "official" definition, an object must not only orbit the sun, but also have a strong enough gravitational pull to make itself round. In 2006, the big cheese of space-object naming, the International Astronomical Union (or IAU), decided that Pluto no longer fit the "planet" bill—it's a little too lumpy and shaped more like a bumpy potato than a round, ball-like sphere. So the IAU pushed Pluto off the planet list—poor guy—and demoted it to a dwarf planet.

Dwarf planets orbit the sun and have enough gravity to be almost round. According to the IAU definition, our solar system has three dwarf planets—Ceres, Eris, and now, Pluto.

AUGUST IS THE BEST
month to find shooting
stars. See below.

southern hemisphere. Because of location and visibility, it is sometimes called the "morning and evening star." Like the moon and the other planets, Venus reflects light from the sun and it is easy to mistake for a star. You can tell it's Venus because other than the moon, it's the brightest object in the night sky.

MARS This planet is the easiest to recognize because it is red, but it takes a keen eye to find it. At first Mars may look like a star, but when you peer closer, you'll notice that it doesn't twinkle and it glows orangish-red. Its ruby color comes from the rusted iron on the planet's surface. Take a look for Mars right after the sun goes down or just before dawn—like Venus and Mercury, that's when it's simplest to spot.

Shooting Stars

Stare at the sky long enough, and you may see a shooting star streak across the heavens. But did you know shooting stars aren't stars at all? They're bits of space junk—like dust, rocks, and ice—that enter our atmosphere and whiz through, burning up as they go. They appear as a bright white light streaking across the sky. When they're in the sky, these burning bits of debris are called meteors; if they land on the ground,

they're called meteorites. They travel thousands of miles an hour and usually burn up about 30 to 80 miles above Earth.

During the middle of August, look up in the sky around midnight and chances are you'll see a bunch of shooting stars. Every year the Earth travels through the tail of the Swift-Tuttle comet. Some of these icy-rocky bits enter the atmosphere and we see a "meteor shower" as they burn up.

For the best viewing, find a comfy place to lie on your back and allow your eyes to get used to the dark. Ideally this place should be far away from the city and streetlights. The nights with a new moon are best because they are darkest—the bright light of a full moon can make viewing meteors more difficult. Be patient and keep looking. You may see as few as three to four per hour or as many as hundreds per hour.

JUPITER Jupiter is considered the fourth brightest object in the night sky. It is the largest planet in our solar system. Observed since ancient times, it has long been called a "wandering star," because its position changes in the sky as it orbits the sun. With a telescope you can see the Great Red Spot on the surface of Jupiter. This is a huge storm that never stops raging.

SATURN Best known for its rings, Saturn is the second largest planet in our solar system. You can't see the rings with your naked eye, but you can with a telescope. Saturn is not as bright or as big as Jupiter, but both are called "gas giants" because of their size and their makeup.

URANUS AND NEPTUNE These guys are really far away, so they can't be spotted with the naked eye. If you have a pair of binoculars, you can try to find Uranus in the Aquarius constellation (page 190); it's easiest to see in late August and early September. Neptune is also visible in the late summer, near the constellation Capricornus (page 193), but you'll need a telescope to see it.

Learn the
Lingo

Light-year

Light is fast. In fact, it's the fastest thing we know of in the universe—it can zip around the Earth about seven times in one second. Talk about speedy! It travels at about 186,000 miles per second (300,000 km/sec) in empty space, where it doesn't bounce into anything.

Things in space are *hugely* far apart, so scientists use the speed of light to help measure the enormous distances. They rely on a unit called a light-year—which is how far light can travel in one year. Think about it. If light can travel 186,000 miles a second, in one year it travels about 5,899,000,000,000 miles or 9,460,000,000,000 kilometers. The nearest star to us, Centauri, is about 4.3 light-years away.

THE STARS

L ooking up at a starry sky can be amazing, awesome, and also a bit confusing. But it doesn't have to be. Learning the patterns of stars up there will open up a whole new world for you.

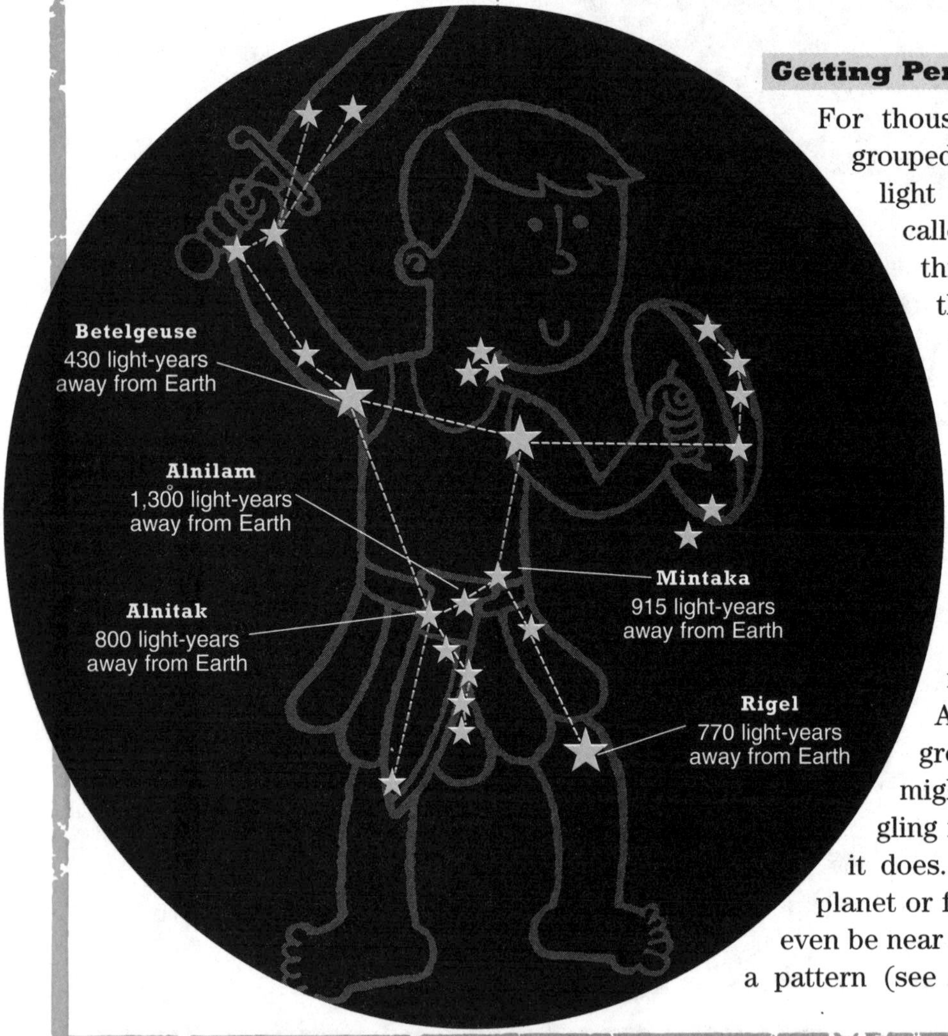

Betelgeuse
430 light-years
away from Earth

Alnilam
1,300 light-years
away from Earth

Alnitak
800 light-years
away from Earth

Mintaka
915 light-years
away from Earth

Rigel
770 light-years
away from Earth

Getting Perspective

For thousands of years people have grouped the stars, making the points of light into connect-the-dot-pictures called constellations. The funny thing about constellations, though, is that although the stars look like they're next to each other, they're often very far apart. In fact, the stars are related to each other only from *our* perspective here on Earth.

Take the famous Orion constellation, which is visible high in the sky during the fall and winter months. The Ancient Greeks thought this grouping of stars looked like a mighty hunter with a sword dangling from his belt. And from Earth it does. But if viewed from another planet or from space, the stars wouldn't even be near enough to each other to make a pattern (see the illustration on the left).

Alnitak, the star on the left side of Orion's belt, is 800 light-years away (see Learn the Lingo, page 175). (That means it takes the light from this star 800 years to travel to Earth, which is nearly six trillion miles!) Alnilam, the next star to the right in Orion's belt, is a whopping 1,300 light-years away. And Mintaka, at the right side of the belt, is 915 light-years away. Because they all appear to shine with the same degree of brightness and look similar to us, we group them together.

So Fa-a-a-r Away

Not only are stars far away from each other, they're very far away from us—trillions of miles away, in fact. So far it's hard for human beings to even imagine the distance. Light travels at 5,899,000,000,000 miles per year (that's almost six trillion miles!) and yet the stars are so far away that it takes their light many, many years to reach Earth—which means that when we look up into the night sky, we're not seeing the stars as they are now, but as they were hundreds of thousands of years ago, when that light first left the stars. In a way, you are actually looking back in time. When the light that you're looking at right now started its journey, it's possible that the earliest humans were walking around—maybe even where you're camping right now.

POINTING THE WAY

Learning about the constellations and finding their dot-to-dot shapes on a map is pretty easy. Finding them in the night sky? Not so much. But there are some stars and groups of stars that are easy to spot no matter the time of year or your location. Using these "pointer stars" you can begin to piece together and discover the many constellations up there.

THE NORTH STAR

Polaris, also known as the North Star, is located above the North Pole. As the Earth spins on its axis, the stars in the sky seem to move—all of them except Polaris. Because of its seemingly stationary appearance, many people use Polaris to find different constellations. The most reliable way to find it is by using the Big Dipper pointer stars (see page 178). Some think Polaris is the brightest star in the sky, but it is, in fact, only the 49th brightest. The brightest star in our sky is the sun. The next brightest is called Sirius and can be spotted in the Canis Major (or Great Dog) constellation (page 187).

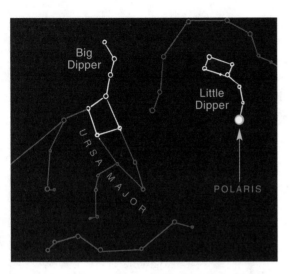

The Big Dipper

Pointer stars can be found in a constellation you might already know—the Big Dipper. (The Big Dipper isn't actually a true constellation, it's part of a bigger constellation called Ursa Major, or the Great Bear—see below).

Once you find the Big Dipper, find its pointer stars. These are the last two stars on the cup (on the far side from the handle). Follow the line out of the top of the cup, about three hand-lengths from the pointer stars, and you will see Polaris, the North Star.

Now that you've found the Dipper's pointer stars and Polaris, you can use these to find other constellations.

STAR ★ STORY   Ursa Major and Ursa Minor

These two constellations were seen as bears by ancient civilizations across the globe. According to ancient Greek myth, the ursa story (ursa means "bear" in Greek) began with Zeus, king of the gods, and his wife, Hera. Zeus was a real ladies' man and his wife, Hera, was very angry about it. So when Zeus tricked an innocent woman named Callisto (who later bore him a son named Arcas), Hera was furious. And she did what any god's jealous wife would do— she turned poor Callisto into a bear.

Years later, Zeus and Callisto's son, Arcas, went out hunting. Callisto spotted him in the woods and was so overjoyed to see him, she forgot she was a bear and barreled toward him to hug him. Surprised, Arcas drew his bow to kill the crazed bear he believed was about to attack him. Zeus, having kept tabs on Callisto, saw the tragedy that was about to happen and immediately turned Arcas into a bear, too, so he would recognize his mom. Zeus then flung them both up into the heavens, where they remain to this day—Callisto as Ursa Major (Big Bear), and Arcas as Ursa Minor (Little Bear).

The Little Dipper

Polaris is the last star on the handle of the Little Dipper, which is the nickname of the constellation Ursa Minor, or Little Bear.

Cepheus, the King

From the Little Dipper, continue the line from the Big Dipper's pointer stars through Polaris, until you spot Cepheus. It kind of looks like the outline of a house. If you have binoculars, look below the constellation for the bright red Garnet Star, the largest star discovered so far.

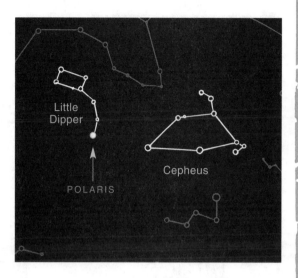

Little Dipper

Cepheus

POLARIS

STAR ★ STORY Cassiopeia and Cepheus

According to Greek myth, Cassiopeia and Cepheus were queen and king of the ancient kingdom of Ethiopia. Cassiopeia was very beautiful but a little on the vain side. (In ancient mythology, this is never a good thing.) Cassiopeia bragged out loud that she was prettier than the daughters of Poseidon, the god of the sea. Even a queen shouldn't go around comparing herself to the daughters of a god. When Poseidon caught wind of the vain queen's comments, he sent the sea monster Cetus to wreak havoc on Ethiopia's coast.

Cepheus and Cassiopeia worried about the fate of their nation, and sought the advice of a fortune-teller. The fortune-teller told Cepheus and Cassiopeia that they must sacrifice their own daughter, Princess Andromeda, to save the country. They agreed to toss Andromeda into the mouth of Cetus to stop him from destroying their land. But just as Andromeda was about to be swallowed, she was rescued out of the blue by the hero Perseus, who couldn't bear to see the princess become a sea monster's lunch. Cassiopeia, Cepheus, Cetus, Andromeda, and Perseus are all together now as part of the night sky.

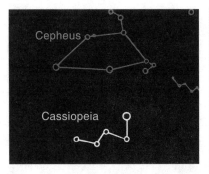

STAR ★ STORY

Draco

Draco, the Dragon, made the mistake of attacking Athena, the Greek goddess of wisdom, war, justice, and skill, among other things. Athena wasn't very happy with Draco's decision, so she grabbed him by the scruff of the neck and flung him through the air. He flew up so high that he wrapped around the North Pole, which is where you can still see him today—stuck around the northern center of the night sky.

Cassiopeia, the Queen

Other stars in the Big Dipper are useful as pointers, too. Find the third star in the Big Dipper's handle, and imagine a line that runs from that star through Polaris, up, and out. You'll arrive at Cassiopeia. In the summer, this constellation looks like the letter W (or a crown).

Draco, the Dragon

To find the constellation Draco, which resembles a dragon, start from the fourth star in the handle of the Big Dipper (where the handle meets the cup). Make an imaginary line to a boxy set of stars—Draco's head. His long body snakes toward Cepheus then winds westward and ends between the Big and Little Dipper.

Draco is nearly impossible to see at nighttime in a city. A combination of smog and artificial light will blot out the constellation because the stars themselves are faint. Out in the wild, however, without streetlights and smog, you can see Draco clearly.

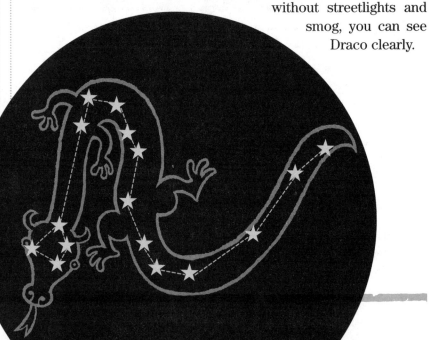

STAR ✦ STORY The Pleiades

Cultures from all over the world have their own stories associated with this bright and clear grouping of stars. In Japan, the group is known as Subaru, the Tortoise. Ever heard of a Subaru car? Take a look at the car's logo, and you will see the Pleiades!

To the Vikings, the stars represented Freya, goddess of love, taking a stroll with her hens.

To the Celts, the Pleiades were associated with mourning because they appear in the heavens around All Souls' Day (in early November), when the dead were remembered.

In Greek mythology, they represent the Seven Sisters—the daughters of Atlas. Atlas was the leader of a group of giants called Titans, and he waged war on the gods of Mount Olympus. Zeus, king of the gods, was pretty ticked off about this, and when the gods won the war, Zeus punished Atlas by making him carry the heavens on his shoulders. When this happened, Atlas was too busy to keep an eye on his daughters.

The burly hunter Orion had always been interested in the Seven Sisters, and while Atlas was busy bearing the heavens, Orion saw his chance. He began to chase after the girls. Zeus saw what was going on and—because he had a soft spot for the ladies—decided to protect them by turning them into doves and then finally into stars, which he placed in the heavens so they would be safe and could comfort their father. You can still see Orion pursuing the sisters in the sky—follow the line of the three stars in Orion's belt up and out to the right.

Learn the Lingo

Zenith

The **zenith** is the point straight above your head when you look up into the sky.

"There wouldn't be a sky full of stars if we were all meant to wish on the same one."

—Frances Clark

Learn the Lingo

Asterism

Asterism is the astronomical term for a distinct group of stars that are not constellations, such as the Summer Triangle. The most famous asterism of all is the Big Dipper—part of the constellation Ursa Major (the Great Bear). Other asterisms are the Teapot of Sagittarius, the Pleiades (the Seven Sisters) in Taurus, the Belt of Orion, and the twin stars, Castor and Pollux, in the constellation Gemini.

Summer Triangle

In addition to Polaris and the pointer stars of the Big Dipper, there is another group of easy-to-spot stars that can help you find constellations. In the summer, once it gets dark, three bright stars high in the night sky will catch your eye right away. They are the brightest stars in three neighboring constellations, and form what's known as the Summer Triangle. The stars in the triangle connect three constellations: Lyra, the Harp; Cygnus, the Swan; and Aquila, the Eagle. You can also use the stars to find your way around other constellations in the summer sky, such as Draco, the Dragon; Pegasus, the Flying Horse; and Cepheus, the King.

The first star in the triangle is Vega. In the month of August, Vega is almost directly overhead. It is the brightest star in the constellation Lyra, the Harp.

Deneb is the second star in the triangle, and is what's known as a supergiant star (an enormous star that is a thousand times larger than our sun). Deneb is the tail feather of the constellation Cygnus, the Swan. Cygnus is easy to find because it contains some of the brightest stars in the summer sky.

The last star in the Summer Triangle is Altair. It is the brightest of three stars in a row. This row forms the wing of the constellation Aquila, the Eagle.

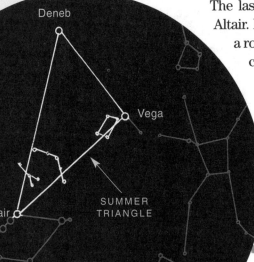

CONSTELLATION ROUNDUP

Many constellations twinkle in the night sky. Depending on where you're standing, you'll see different constellations at different times of the year.

A Moving Scene

The Earth is always in motion—it makes its way around the sun once a year and takes one day to spin all the way around on its axis. Our view of the stars also changes throughout the night as well as throughout the year.

As the Earth rotates on its axis each day, the sun appears to rise in the east and set in the west. Just like the sun, which is a star, the constellations also rise in the east and set in the west, appearing to glide across the heavens all night.

If you had a speed-'em-up camera, you would also see that through the year, as the Earth twirls on its tilty axis, the sun moves along a higher and then lower arc depending on the season. And so do the constellations. The sky is full of constellations, and some rise higher into view and some disappear below the horizon. The result is that each season presents a new window into the sky.

When you're stargazing on your campout, take a look at the seasonal sky maps on the following pages and find the map for the correct season. It will give you an idea of which constellations appear at this time of year, and where they are in relation to each other. Then take a look at A Month-by-Month Walk Through the Stars (page 184). It describes some key constellations to look for in each month. This way, if you're camping in July, you'll be able to get a good snapshot sense of the summer sky and will know what special stuff to look out for.

STAR ☆ STORY

The Little Fox

Named in the seventeenth century by the Polish astronomer Hevelius, the Little Fox constellation originally depicted a fox with a goose in its mouth. Nowadays, because of the dimness of the stars, the goose seems to have flown the coop, and people mostly refer to this as just the Little Fox.

Walk Through the Stars

Here's a seasonal guide to what you might see in the skies of the Northern Hemisphere, with highlights for each month. (The Northern Hemisphere is the part of the world that's north of the equator, including the United States and Canada.) The star maps will show you some of the constellations that appear in the sky during a particular season, but keep in mind that the stars shift, so you may only see a portion at any given time.

winter

December

Facing northeast, you'll find two bright stars near each other: Castor and Pollux in the constellation Gemini, the Twins. Around December 13, the constellation is host to a meteor shower known as the Geminid (check at your local library or on the Internet for the shower's exact timing).

Low in the northeast, the Big Dipper stands on end, with the stars of its handle below the horizon.

In the southeast, Lepus is just below Orion. Among the stars of Lepus is the coppery red Crimson Star. Observe it with binoculars or a telescope.

January

The star Capella (of the Charioteer constellation) is easy to spot and is almost directly overhead.

Also near the zenith (overhead) are the Pleiades, a star cluster in the constellation of Taurus, the Bull. To the naked eye, the Pleiades looks like a group of six faint stars. With binoculars, you can see many more stars in the cluster, and with a telescope, you can see hundreds.

The Pleiades' neighboring star cluster, a V-shaped grouping called the Hyades, outlines the face of Taurus, the Bull. Outside the Hyades, a bright orange star, Aldebaran, can be seen in the bull's eye.

February

Look for Orion, the Hunter. Find the three stars that make his belt, then the two stars that make his shoulders. Can you spot Betelgeuse, the red star that is Orion's left shoulder?

Look down and find Rigel—at the lower right corner of Orion's toga.

Draw an imaginary line moving to the left of Orion's belt to find Sirius, the brightest star in the night sky. Sirius is part of the constellation Canis Major, the Great Dog. Follow a line eastward from Betelgeuse to the nearest bright star. It's Procyon, of the constellation Canis Minor, the Little Dog.

The Winter Sky

To use this map, hold it in front of you vertically, and turn it so the direction you're facing is at the bottom. The outer circle of the map represents the horizon, and the center of the map represents your zenith, the spot directly overhead in the sky.

STAR ★ STORY Boötes

Who was Boötes? In one ancient Roman myth, he was a farmer who invented the plough. Pleased by the invention, the gods placed Boötes in the heavens as a constellation after he died.

Another Roman story portrayed Boötes as a grape grower who showed his fruit to Bacchus, the god of wine. Bacchus shared the secrets of winemaking with Boötes, and the farmer and his friends drank too much and got sick. Boötes's friends mistakenly thought he had poisoned them, and they killed him. Feeling sorry for Boötes, Bacchus placed the grape farmer in the heavens to honor him.

Although the constellation is meant to depict a person, at first glance, Boötes resembles a kite with a tail.

STAR ✦ STORY Orion

According to Greek mythology, Orion was a mighty hunter who had two faithful dogs—Canis Major and Canis Minor—who traveled with him wherever he went. When pursuing all of the Seven Sisters (you can see them in the Pleiades constellation, page 181), Orion fell madly in love with one of them, a maiden named Merope. Merope wanted nothing to do with Orion. According to legend, Orion was so cuckoo about Merope that he stepped on a scorpion by accident and was stung. Though he destroyed the scorpion with his club, its venom ultimately killed the hunter. Feeling sorry for him, the gods placed Orion in the sky with his two dogs at his heels and the animals he liked to hunt nearby. Lepus, the Rabbit, is at his feet. In his left hand, Orion holds a shield (the line of stars below Aldebaran).

He appears to battle Taurus, the Bull, in order to protect and impress the Seven Sisters of the Pleiades. The scorpion is also up there, though he and Orion never appear in the sky together (Orion shines in the winter and Scorpius in the summer). It is said that Orion avoids Scorpius by staying on the opposite side of the sky.

The Spring Sky

To use this map, hold it in front of you vertically, and turn it so the direction you're facing is at the bottom. The outer circle of the map represents the horizon, and the center of the map represents your zenith, the spot directly overhead in the sky.

spring

March

The star Regulus (located in Leo, the Lion constellation) reaches its zenith in March. It begins its rise in December, reaches its zenith, and then starts to set. By July, the constellation will be gone from the sky, but it will rise again in December. Regulus (which means "little king") has also been known as Cor Leonis ("lion's heart") because of its position in the Leo constellation.

Boötes, the Farmer, rises in March. Its bright star, Arcturus, can be found by following the arc of the Big Dipper's handle.

April

Wave good-bye to Orion. This month, you'll see the winter constellations sink in the sky while summer constellations rise. Low in the northeast, the group of stars forming the boxlike body of Hercules begins to appear. By July, this constellation will appear fully overhead.

Also arriving this month is the dazzling white summer star Vega, in the constellation Lyra, the Harp. It will rise in the northeast, near Hercules.

Between Hercules and Boötes, you can see the semicircular constellation called Corona Borealis, or the Northern Crown. Its brightest star, Gemma (also called Alphecca), stands in the center like a glittering jewel in a tiara.

May

A small constellation appears near the zenith this month: Canes Venatici, the Hunting Dogs. They are near Boötes, who is chasing the bears (Ursa Major and Minor) around the sky.

On the southeastern horizon, you might see a rising red star, Antares, which is the brightest star in Scorpius, the Scorpion. According to legend, this is the scorpion that killed Orion. Scorpius rises as Orion sets (see page 191).

Scorpius's neighbor is the constellation Centaurus. It resembles the centaur, a creature who has the head and chest of a man and the body of a horse. We only see a part of Centaurus in the northern hemisphere (and unfortunately, it's the least exciting part—pretty much just the torso). Look for him in the middle of May. Try to find the star Spica in the southeastern sky (it's the only bright star in the constellation Virgo) and look due south.

summer

June

Directly overhead, Boötes and the Summer Triangle (Vega, Deneb, and Altair) shine brightly in the north eastern sky. (Look for the semicircular Corona Borealis nearby.)

Low in the northeast is Lacerta, the Lizard. Lacerta stretches across a very dense area of the Milky Way, so it is a neat constellation to explore with a telescope.

July

Low on the eastern horizon, Aquarius is rising (see page 192). Aquarius is the Water Bearer. As a boy he was tending his sheep—giving them water—when Zeus spotted him and decided to put him in the sky. Zeus took the form of a bird and swept down to the field, picked the boy up, and carried him off to the skies where he was made into this constellation. Around July 28, you can see a meteor shower radiate from the constellation. The shower is called Delta Aquarids (check online or at your local library for more information about the exact date, time of night, and duration).

Near Aquarius, you'll find Sagittarius—half man, half horse. Can't find a half-man, half-horse shape in the stars? Look for a teapot shape instead. Inside the constellation is a smaller group of stars called the Teapot of Sagittarius. Beneath the Teapot is a faint semicircle of stars known as the constellation Corona Australis, or the Southern Crown.

High in the sky, look for Draco, the Dragon. You'll find him stretching from the northwest above Polaris to the northeast.

August

You'll see the only constellation that is broken into two separate parts: Serpens Caput (the Head of the Snake) and Serpens Cauda (the Tail of the Snake). The two ends of the snake are separated by Ophiuchus, the Serpent Bearer or Snake Charmer. During August, both constellations are prominent in the southwest sky. Above the southern horizon is Sagittarius, the Archer, rising to the highest point in the night sky.

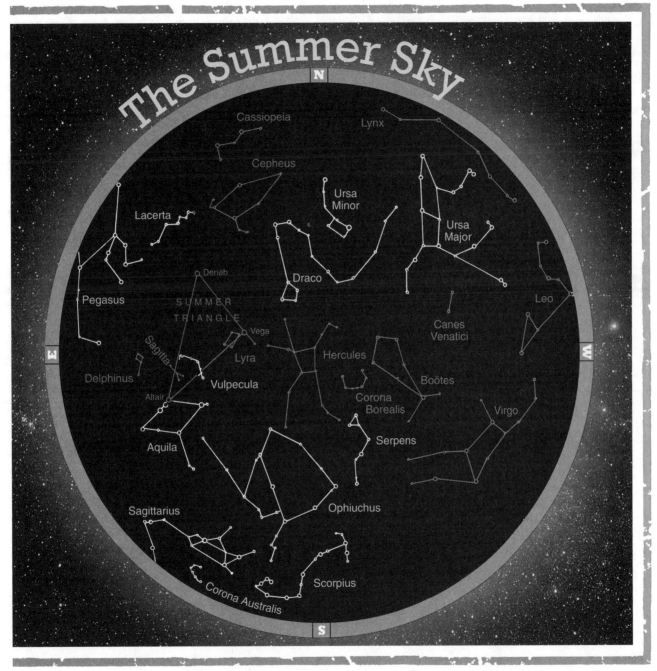

To use this map, hold it in front of you vertically, and turn it so the direction you're facing is at the bottom. The outer circle of the map represents the horizon, and the center of the map represents your zenith, the spot directly overhead in the sky.

To use this map, hold it in front of you vertically, and turn it so the direction you're facing is at the bottom. The outer circle of the map represents the horizon, and the center of the map represents your zenith, the spot directly overhead in the sky.

fall

September

Many of September's constellations have only one or two bright stars; others, while still visible, have no bright stars at all. This month, two dim constellations shine at their brightest. Near the star Altair is a triangular constellation, Capricornus, the Sea Goat. The other constellation with peak visibility is tiny Delphinus, the Dolphin.

Between Altair and Cygnus (at their zenith in September) is a small, straight line of stars. It is Sagitta, the Arrow, the third-smallest constellation.

South of Cygnus is a group of three stars that looks a little like a boomerang. This grouping comprises the tail of Vulpecula, the Fox. It is made of dark stars, so it's hard to recognize. Once you find it, and if you have a telescope, look for the Dumbbell Nebula, a grouping of stars shaped like—what else?—a dumbbell.

October

Pegasus, the Winged Horse, reaches high in the sky. Directly south is Pisces, the Fish. It has a faint pentagonal shape of stars in the west (pointing toward Aquarius, the Water Bearer) and a long, faint V-shaped line of stars to the east (pointing toward Cetus, the Sea Monster). On the horizon in the southern sky are the dim stars of Eridanus, the River.

The only bright star in the lower southern sky is also one of the least known: Fomalhaut, a star in Piscis Austrinus (the Southern Fish). Fomalhaut's name comes from an Arabic word that means "mouth of the fish."

November

Orion is back! He's on the rise in the east as the Summer Triangle sinks low in the northwestern sky. Deneb, Vega, and Altair, the Summer Triangle, are the most noticeable stars in their part of the sky.

In November, more of the constellation Eridanus is visible. It is always faint, and it tends to blend in with Orion at the star Rigel, so look really hard. Also blending in with Orion and peeking up above the eastern horizon is Lepus, the Rabbit (see page 185).

STAR STORY

Lepus and Aquila

According to an ancient legend, Lepus, the cautious Rabbit, rises only when, on the opposite side of the sky, Aquila, the Eagle, is setting. Makes sense for a rabbit to be wary of his natural predator!

Lepus appears in fall, but the constellations put on their best show in winter. See page 184.

STAR ✦ STORY Pegasus

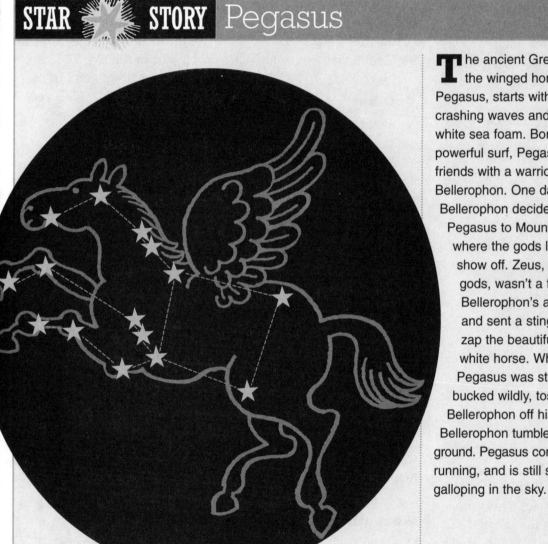

The ancient Greek story of the winged horse, Pegasus, starts with wildly crashing waves and brilliant white sea foam. Born in the powerful surf, Pegasus became friends with a warrior named Bellerophon. One day Bellerophon decided to ride Pegasus to Mount Olympus, where the gods lived, to show off. Zeus, king of the gods, wasn't a fan of Bellerophon's arrogance and sent a stinging fly to zap the beautiful flying white horse. When Pegasus was stung, he bucked wildly, tossing Bellerophon off his back. Bellerophon tumbled to the ground. Pegasus continued running, and is still seen galloping in the sky.

FAR OUT! GALAXIES

O nce you've spotted the constellations, it can be really cool to explore some galaxies (especially with a pair of binoculars or, even better, a telescope). A galaxy is a huge group of stars, gas, and dust held together by gravity in a shape that can be recognized as a unit. Our sun and most of the stars you can see without a telescope belong to a family of millions of stars that we call our galaxy, the Milky Way. On clear, moonless nights you can see a misty haze in the sky toward the constellation of Sagittarius (page 190). This misty band is made up of the light from the countless stars in our galaxy. But ours isn't the only one—millions of other galaxies exist out there. Since we don't have millions of pages in this book, here are some of the easier-to-find galaxies to look for.

M81 and M82

Back in the 1700s, French astronomer Charles Messier began to catalog all the objects people were finding in the sky. M81 and M82 (M stands for Messier) are two galaxies that were spotted and cataloged. Use your binoculars to see these two galaxies near the head of Ursa Major (where the Big Dipper is found, see page 178). They'll look like small, milky, cloudy disks. The brighter of the two is M81.

Andromeda

On a very clear dark night, scan the sky between Pegasus and Cassiopeia (page 179), and you will see a fuzzy oval of light: It is the Andromeda galaxy (also known to astronomers as M31). At a distance of two million light-years away, it is the most distant object that can be seen from Earth without a telescope.

CREATE YOUR OWN CONSTELLATION

T ake a look at the stars and find the Big Dipper. Choose a few random stars nearby and draw an imaginary line between them—can you create a picture from what you see? What have you drawn in the sky? Is it an animal, a person, a heroic character, an object? Use some of the pointer stars in the Big Dipper as part of your constellation or to point toward it, so you can find it again. Then come up with a myth—what's the story behind your stars? Challenge your fellow campers with the same task, and then share your constellations and star tales.

HEY BABY!

What's Your Sign?

Ever heard that question? When people ask about your sign, they're referring to your zodiac symbol. The word "zodiac" comes from a Greek word meaning "circle of little animals." The zodiac consists of the 12 astrological signs that correspond to a circle of 12 constellations. The constellations lie along the path of the sun throughout the year, and your zodiac sign is determined by where the sun passed the constellations on the day you were born.

People called astrologers believe a person's birth sign can say a lot about him. They chart the positions of the planets and the sun against a person's zodiac sign in order to gain information about his or her personality and destiny. Want to know what your sign is? Look for your birthday in the list below.

January 21–February 19
AQUARIUS,
the Water Bearer
Traits: friendly, helpful, loyal, unpredictable

February 20–March 20
PISCES, the Fish
Traits: imaginative, caring, secretive, eager to escape

March 21–April 20
ARIES, the Ram
Traits: adventurous, confident, impatient

April 21–May 21
TAURUS, the Bull
Traits: patient, loving, peaceful, jealous

May 22–June 21
GEMINI, the Twins
Traits: witty, adaptable, energetic, nervous

June 22–July 23
CANCER, the Crab
Traits: loving, imaginative, street-smart, moody

July 24–August 23
LEO, the Lion
Traits: warm, faithful, creative, bossy

August 24–September 23
VIRGO, the Virgin
Traits: practical, reliable, hardworking, fussy

September 24–October 22
LIBRA, the Scales
Traits: easygoing, idealistic, charming, indecisive

October 23–November 22
SCORPIO,
the Scorpion
Traits: passionate, lively, intuitive, stubborn

November 23–December 21
SAGITTARIUS,
the Archer
Traits: good-humored, honest, philosophical, unrealistic

December 22–January 20
CAPRICORNUS,
the Sea Goat
Traits: patient, practical, humorous, pessimistic

THE LIST OF CONSTELLATIONS

For thousands of years many cultures have grouped stars into constellations. So to make it more official, an organization of astronomers and scientists from around the world—called the International Astronomical Union—met and agreed upon 88 official constellations. Some of the constellations are strictly in the Southern Hemisphere and others are strictly in the Northern. Some can be seen in both, depending on the time of year. Take a look at a star chart or the seasonal star maps on pages 185–192. How many of these official constellations can you see?

1. Andromeda
2. Antlia
3. Apus
4. Aquarius
5. Aquila
6. Ara
7. Aries
8. Auriga
9. Boötes
10. Caelum
11. Camelopardalis
12. Cancer
13. Canes Venatici
14. Canis Major
15. Canis Minor
16. Capricornus
17. Carina
18. Cassiopeia
19. Centaurus
20. Cepheus
21. Cetus
22. Chamaeleon
23. Circinus
24. Columba
25. Coma Berenices
26. Corona Australis
27. Corona Borealis
28. Corvus
29. Crater
30. Crux
31. Cygnus
32. Delphinus
33. Dorado
34. Draco
35. Equuleus
36. Eridanus
37. Fornax
38. Gemini
39. Grus
40. Hercules
41. Horologium
42. Hydra
43. Hydrus
44. Indus
45. Lacerta
46. Leo
47. Leo Minor
48. Lepus
49. Libra
50. Lupus
51. Lynx
52. Lyra
53. Mensa
54. Microscopium
55. Monoceros
56. Musca
57. Norma
58. Octans
59. Ophiuchus
60. Orion
61. Pavo
62. Pegasus
63. Perseus
64. Phoenix
65. Pictor
66. Pisces
67. Piscis Austrinus
68. Puppis
69. Pyxis
70. Reticulum
71. Sagitta
72. Sagittarius
73. Scorpius
74. Sculptor
75. Scutum
76. Serpens
77. Sextans
78. Taurus
79. Telescopium
80. Triangulum
81. Triangulum Australe
82. Tucana
83. Ursa Major
84. Ursa Minor
85. Vela
86. Virgo
87. Volans
88. Vulpecula

Taurus

BACKPACK NATURALIST

Experiments and Projects

You've got your tent pitched and your fire pit set up—
you're finally at home in the wilderness. But one of the
best parts of being in nature is exploring it, discovering
the plants and animals that call your campsite home,
sweet home.

In this chapter you'll find lots of fun projects and interesting
experiments to help you get in touch with the Earth's wild side.
You'll see how seeds spread, how some creatures recycle organic
material, and how water moves through plants. You'll acquire a few
recording and observation skills for becoming a crackerjack
backpack naturalist. And you'll craft a pond peeper for water
viewing and use the tilt and turn of the planet to tell time.

Keeping a Field Journal

What You Need

Sketchbook

Pencil

Colored pencils or markers

Watercolor set with brushes (optional)

Camera (optional)

Envelopes for holding any leaf, flower, feather, or other natural treasures that you may find along the trail

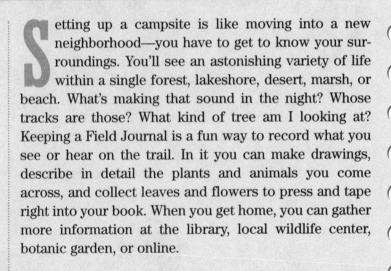

Bring along a pair of binoculars if you can. They will help you scope out wildlife from a safe distance.

Setting up a campsite is like moving into a new neighborhood—you have to get to know your surroundings. You'll see an astonishing variety of life within a single forest, lakeshore, desert, marsh, or beach. What's making that sound in the night? Whose tracks are those? What kind of tree am I looking at? Keeping a Field Journal is a fun way to record what you see or hear on the trail. In it you can make drawings, describe in detail the plants and animals you come across, and collect leaves and flowers to press and tape right into your book. When you get home, you can gather more information at the library, local wildlife center, botanic garden, or online.

What You Do

1 Get Organized
Before you begin, think about how you want to organize your journal. Here are some ideas to get you started.

● **Organize by environment.** If you camp in areas that have different climates and types of plant and animal life—say, the woods one weekend, the desert another—you might want to make sections in your journal for every kind of place you go.

● **Organize by topic.** Have an animal section, plant section, bug section, and rock section. Add new entries to each part according to what you see.

● **Organize by camping trip.** Keep a running journal of your trips. Gather your information, make sketches, and record your thoughts by journey.

● **Keep two journals.** Make one a free-form forum for notes, sketches, and collages of leaves, bark, and feathers. Then keep a second, more polished book where you can categorize the random info from the other book.

2 Gather the Essentials
Before each entry, write down the date, time, name of your location, and other information that will provide the what, where, and when.

● **Date.** Time of year can play a big part in what you see in the wild. In the autumn, many animals migrate and others are busy gathering food for the winter. Leaves begin to turn colors and fall. This season is great for watching foragers—animals that gather their food and hide it for safe-keeping—such as squirrels and chipmunks. In the spring, many animals search for mates, graze for food, and have babies. Trees begin to bud and flowers bloom. Spring is a great time to look and listen for songbirds. Winter is sort of quiet for some animals, but you'll see lots of activity in the summertime.

● **Time of day.** Most critters are more active at dawn and dusk (though some, like owls and snakes, are more lively at night). So if you want to spot these animals or insects, plan to get up early or stay up late. Some plants are more active at different times of day as well, like the morning glory, a flowering vine that usually blooms in the morning and closes during the day.

Keeping a Field Journal, contd.

● **Notes on the environment.** Are you exploring a pine forest? Wading in a brook? Sitting on a rock at the ocean's edge? Describe where you are and what it looks, sounds, and smells like.

● **What's the weather?** Is it sunny, snowy, or somewhere in between?

3 Gather Information
A Field Journal can document more than just animals—it can include bugs and plant life, too. Here's a general list of questions to ask yourself:

ANIMALS

● **Describe the animal.** What did it look like? What was its behavior? Did it make a sound? Where did you see it? Was it alone?

● **Did it leave behind any tracks?** How many toes were on each foot? Are there claws? What is the shape and size of the toe pads and the heel? What kind of pattern do the tracks make as a group? Sketch the track(s) in your journal, then look at Who Goes There? (page 332) and try to identify them. (It takes time to learn to read tracks, but you'll get the hang of it eventually. And after a while, you'll learn to read other things as well, like chewed bark, uneaten food, bent grass, or broken twigs.)

● **Don't forget the poop.** Recognizing the different types will help you learn what animal it came from (again, see Who Goes There?, page 332). Remember: Look, but don't touch. It is poop after all!

● **Identify the animal.** Is it a mammal, bird, reptile, or amphibian (see A Class Refresher, page 206)? When you get home, you may want to research the animal further. Leave space to write your findings. Some questions to consider: Does the male look any different from the female? What kind of home does it live in? What are its feeding habits? How does its body develop or change over its lifetime?

Keeping a Field Journal, contd.

INSECTS

- **Carefully collect an insect** (for observation only—see page 246 to make your Bug Lab) and describe it. What color is it? Does it have wings? How many legs does it have? How many antennae? Any weird behavior?

- **Identify the insect.** Leave room in your journal for answers to these questions (you may need to do some research: —see Truth or Flies, page 207, for help with this). Where does the bug live? Does the male look different from the female? Is the insect part of a colony? What is its life cycle?

PLANTS

- **Choose a plant.** Draw it, and if there are any leaves, flowers, branches, or bark on the ground nearby, paste them in. (Be careful of certain plants, though—see Leaves to Look Out For, page 237.) You can press the leaves and flowers to make them last longer (see page 240).

- **Describe the plant.** What kind of leaves does it have? How tall is the plant or tree (to estimate, see page 231). What is its overall shape? Are there any flowers? If so, what do they look and feel like? What color and texture are the bark or stems? Where does the plant live? Is the soil wet or dry, dirt or sand? What do the seeds look like? Can you tell how the seeds move around (see page 234)?

- **Identify the plant.** Using information you gathered, do some research at home to figure out what kind of plant it is. If you like, leave room in your journal to answer the following questions: What is the life cycle? Does the plant serve as food or shelter for any animal? Does the plant lose its leaves in the fall?

4 Write Your Field Journal Entry In case you need a little help getting started, use the description of a beaver on the following pages as a model.

Date: 7/6/2006

Time: 8:30 P.M.

Location: Appalachian Trail, New York

Environment/Weather: I'm sitting at the edge of the pond. It's the end of a warm, sunny day. Stars are just starting to pop up.

Animal/plant/insect spotted: Beaver

WHAT IT LOOKED LIKE: The beaver has webbed feet and a broad flat tail that it uses for swimming. It looks a little like a medium-size dog, but with a round head, flat tail, and buck teeth. It uses its big teeth to gnaw through wood.

WHAT IT WAS DOING: I saw the beaver when I was walking

along the edge of the pond. I tried to stand still, but I accidentally stepped on a twig. The beaver looked up when it heard the twig break, and jumped into the pond. It started slapping the water with its tail, which made a loud sound. Maybe it was trying to warn other beavers?

ADDITIONAL INFO: Beavers can be found almost anywhere in the United States in places where woods surround a lake, pond, or stream. The most noticeable signs that a beaver colony is nearby are fallen trees and a beaver lodge—made of mud and sticks—in the water. They are mostly active at night, when they use their sharp teeth to feed on tree bark.

Keeping a Field Journal is a little like writing in a diary, except instead of writing about yourself, you write about what you observe all around you. After your camping trip, you can look up extra info online or at the library to explain or flesh out what you saw in the wild.

A Class Refresher

Scientists group all living beings into different categories according to what they have in common. This is called classification, and the groups (from larger to smaller) are: domain, kingdom, phylum, class, order, family, genus, and species. Animals with backbones, called vertebrates, are grouped into five classes based on skin covering, how they maintain body temperature, how they make babies, and what their limbs are like.

Mammals

This class of animals is warm-blooded and has hair covering their skin. Female mammals produce milk from their mammary glands to nourish their young. They give birth to their young live (though there are a few, like the platypus, that actually lay eggs).

Guess what? You're a mammal. So are your parents. Other mammals include cows, monkeys, elephants, dogs, cats, horses, dolphins, pigs, mice, and giraffes.

Birds

Instead of hair, birds are covered with feathers. They have beaks instead of teeth. Instead of arms or forelimbs they have wings, giving many of them the ability to fly. They are oviparous, which means they give birth to their young in hard-shelled eggs.

Some birds are really small, like the hummingbird; others are large, like the ostrich. All are warm-blooded. Some, like the penguin, can't fly, even though they have wings.

Reptiles

Like birds, these cold-blooded creatures give birth to their young in eggs. Their bodies are covered by hard scales or horny plates.

Turtles, snakes, lizards, alligators, and crocodiles are reptiles, as were the dinosaurs. Some people think reptiles are mean or scary, but they're just misunderstood.

Fish

These scaly-skinned animals live underwater. They are cold-blooded and reproduce by laying eggs, although unlike birds and reptiles, they lay their eggs in water. Instead of arms, fish have fins, which help them swim.

Amphibians

These cold-blooded animals live both in water and on land. Their young stay underwater and breathe through gills (just like fish do). As they mature, they breathe through lungs and glands in their skin.

Frogs, toads, and salamanders are all amphibians.

Truth or Flies

True insects have three body segments, three pairs of legs, two antennae, and sometimes wings. Some of the most common groups:

Beetles have hard, shiny wings that fold over their backs, giving them a rounded appearance.

Bees, wasps, and ants are social insects that live in hives or nests and work together as a community.

Flies have wings and complex eyes (made up of many-faceted smaller eyes called omatidia). They sometimes bite or sting.

Butterflies and moths often have beautifully colored, scaled wings. The wings can even be iridescent (meaning they appear to change color in different light or from different angles).

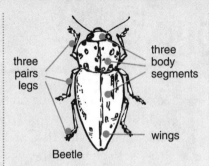

three pairs legs

three body segments

wings

Beetle

Cicadas, crickets, and grasshoppers rub together their wings or legs to create a "cheee-cheeee" chirping sound to attract mates or establish territories.

Dragonflies have long bodies and two pairs of wings. They can be a rainbow of colors, with iridescent blues, greens, and reds.

Damselflies are easily mistaken for dragonflies, but they're actually pretty different. Damselflies are weaker fliers than dragonflies, so they tend to flutter about.

Dragonfly

Their eyes are also farther apart, and unlike dragonflies, their wings come together against their long body when they're at rest.

Not Really Insects

Spiders have two body segments and four pairs of legs. They belong to a class known as arachnids.

Ticks and mites are also arachnids. They have one body segment and four pairs of legs.

Millipedes have two pairs of legs per body segment, and centipedes have one pair per segment.

Little sow bugs, crabs, and lobsters are crustaceans. They have two pairs of antennae and at least five pairs of legs.

Damselfly

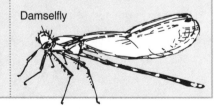

Camping Activity

Pond Peeper

What You Need

Heavy-duty clear plastic wrap

A large empty can (a coffee or tomato can is great); have an adult remove the top and bottom

3 rubber bands

Rubber boots, old sneakers, or surf shoes

A pond or lake

Your Field Journal (page 200), pen or pencil, (optional)

P onds have a lot going on beneath the surface, with an incredible array of frolicking insects, fascinating plants, flashy fish, and other living things. Want to peek beneath the water without getting your face wet? Make this easy-to-use scope, and you can take a long look at the world of wonders that awaits. Refer to the chart on pages 210–211 to get a sense of what you might see through your peeper.

What You Do

1 Take a large square of clear plastic wrap and put it down on a flat surface.

2 Place the bottom of the can in the center of the plastic wrap.

3 Bring the sides of the plastic wrap up around the outside of the can.

4 Secure the plastic wrap to the lower edge of the can with a rubber band. Move up an inch and wrap another rubber band around the plastic and can. Move up another inch and wrap the last rubber band in the same way.

5 Make sure the plastic wrap is stretched tight across the bottom of the can—you may need to pull on the plastic wrap here and there to adjust it. Your Pond Peeper is ready for use!

6 Wearing your boots, take a short step into the water, up to your ankles. Crouch down and hold the plastic-covered end of the peeper so it just touches the water. Stay very still and look through the peeper. What plants, animals, and insects do you see (check out Surface Dwellers, page 212)?

7 Push the peeper into the water until the water comes up to the second rubber band. Look at Water Dwellers, page 213, to get a sense of what you might see.

8 Now push the peeper down until it's just an inch from the muck on the bottom. (Be careful not to let the water go above the third rubber band, or it will flood the peeper.) You may need to wait a bit until the kicked-up mud settles back down. Look through the peeper again and see if you spot any of the creatures listed in Bottom Dwellers, page 215.

9 If you like, describe and draw your observations in your Field Journal.

What You Might See IN A POND...............

These are some of the freshwater plants and critters that just may be

Whirligig

Mosquito

Water Strider

Backswimmer

Tadpole

Water Boatman

Diving Beetle

Crayfish

Leech

Caddisfly Larva

Key

floating, swimming, or slithering around in the the pond under your peeper.

Duckweed

Pond Lily

Snail

Giant Water Bug

Sunfish

Stickleback

Frog

Mayfly Larva

Dragonfly Larva

Damselfly Larva

WHENEVER YOU'RE
exploring around water,
make sure a grown-up
knows where you are
and always take a buddy
with you.

LIFE IN A POND

Surface Dwellers

Pond Lilies: Pond lilies have large, leathery leaves and waxy pink, yellow, or white flowers that bloom from May to October. Spreading three to six feet over the water's surface, the plants' flowers can grow up to 23 inches tall. Pond lilies provide food and shelter for many fish and insects.

Duckweed: These clusters of small, round, budding leaves float on the surface of the water, their tiny roots dangling into the water below. Also known as "water lentils," duckweeds are the smallest known flowering plants. They grow in still or slow-moving water and multiply quickly, taking over large surface areas at a rapid rate.

Snails: There are two types of snails that you may see in or near a pond—land snails and freshwater snails. Freshwater snails breathe through gills, while land snails breathe through lungs. Protected by coiled shells, snails move by contracting and stretching their bodies at a very slow speed (one millimeter per second); they create mucus to reduce friction, which helps them go faster.

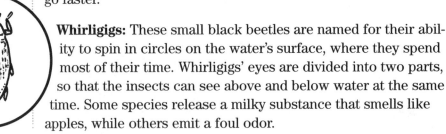

Whirligigs: These small black beetles are named for their ability to spin in circles on the water's surface, where they spend most of their time. Whirligigs' eyes are divided into two parts, so that the insects can see above and below water at the same time. Some species release a milky substance that smells like apples, while others emit a foul odor.

Water Striders: These insects have four long, oarlike middle and hind legs that help them skate across the water's surface, and two short front legs for grabbing prey. They release oil as they walk, which repels the water and keeps their feet dry. The even proportions of the insects' bodies prevent water striders from sinking, allowing them to move over the water quickly. Adult water striders also have wings, which they use to fly from one body of water to another.

Mosquitoes: Mosquitoes are commonly found on the surface film of water, while their larvae (see page 216) hang just below the surface. Female mosquitoes, known for their itchy bites, use their antennae to find a meal nearby by sensing an animal's warmth and moisture. Thin needles in their mouths pierce skin and withdraw blood, leaving behind an uncomfortable bump.

Water Dwellers

Frogs: Frogs have webbed toes, short bodies, and long hind legs; their elongated ankle bones help them jump long distances. These amphibians have the unique ability to "breathe" through their skin; oxygen passes directly through the thin skin (which must stay moist at all times) into the bloodstream. The males are known for their "ribbit" mating sounds. The females lay egg masses that contain thousands of eggs. Most of the eggs get nibbled up by predators, but once the remaining eggs hatch, tadpoles drop directly into the water. Later the tadpoles undergo metamorphosis, transforming into adult frogs.

Sunfishes: There are 27 species of sunfish, including the black bass, rock bass, bluegill, and crappies. Most range from 8 to 12 inches long, although some species can reach up to three feet in

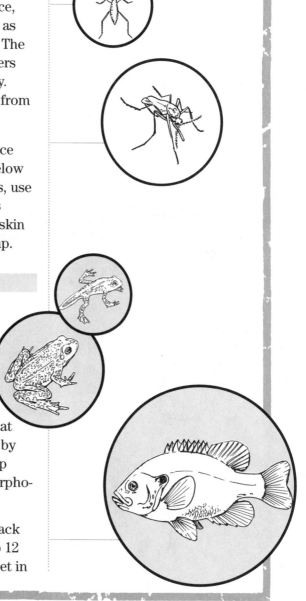

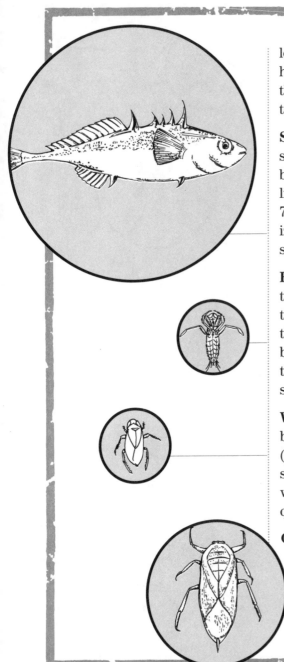

length. To make a family, first the male sunfish builds a nest with his tail. After the female lays the eggs in the nest, the male guards them until the baby sunfishes have hatched safely. Sunfishes tend to live in large, cold bodies of water, like northern lakes.

Sticklebacks: These scaleless, finger-length fish have a row of small spikes along their spines and range in color from green to black. The sticklebacks produce young from April to July; these little ones grow up to four inches in length. The female fish lay 75 to 100 eggs on nests built by the males; the males then fertilize the eggs and protect the young until they are large enough to survive on their own.

Backswimmers: These small insects swim upside down, using their long, oar-shaped back legs to propel themselves through the water. They capture oxygen in silvery air bubbles, which they hold against their bodies with tiny hairs; once they have breathed in all of the air in the bubble, the insects somersault to the water's surface and capture a new supply of air. Preying on small fish and tadpoles, backswimmers also bite humans.

Water Boatmen: These insects look similar to backswimmers, but they swim right-side-up; they have flattened, hairy arms ("oars"), which they use to row through the water. Unlike backswimmers, they feed mainly on plants and algae. In Mexico, water boatmen are considered a delicacy and are eaten in large quantities.

Giant Water Bugs: Also known as "toe-biters," these dark brown bugs can grow to be the size of your palm. They are voracious hunters, feeding on crustaceans, fish, and amphibians; these insects kill by injecting digestive saliva into their prey and then sucking out the broken-down material. Giant water bug bites can be very painful to humans.

Diving Beetles: While larvae, diving beetles are between a half an inch and two inches in size. When hunting, they cling to the pond's bottom, keeping perfectly still until they see their prey (tadpoles and other small creatures); they then lunge, capture, and bite into the prey with their pincers. When they are ready to become adults, the larvae crawl out of the water and bury themselves in the mud. They emerge a week later as fully formed adults. The adult beetle traps air under its wings, which it breathes from as it dives and looks for food.

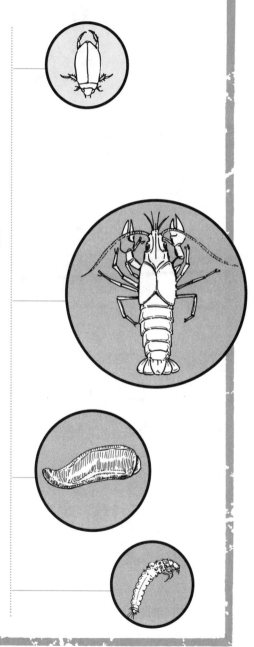

Bottom Dwellers

Crayfish: These small crustaceans look like tiny lobsters: Each has a shell, two antennae, and ten legs. They usually hide under plant debris, but, when startled, move swiftly by flapping their tails backward. Because their outer skeletons don't provide room to expand, crayfish molt—or shed their outer shell—as they grow. First they find a hiding place, then they rub their back against a hard surface until the outer shell cracks. The new, softer shell then pierces and detaches the old one. The crayfish eats the old shell, which helps strengthen and harden its new protective coat.

Leeches: Leeches look like flattened worms, ranging in color from black and brown to green and gray. They are hermaphrodites, which means that they have both male and female reproductive organs. Carnivores, leeches attach their "suckers" to their prey and drink their blood. Once full, the leeches detach from their prey and digest their meals separately.

Caddisfly Larvae: These wormlike larvae (see page 216) have three pairs of legs on the first three segments of their body, and

Learn the Lingo

Larva

A larva is an immature, not fully developed insect or animal that has recently emerged from its egg and must grow into its adult shape. Some larvae look like worms, and most look very little like the adult animals they'll eventually become. The plural of "larva" is "larvae."

hooks on the last segment. Their bodies are usually covered in a protective silky case, which the larvae hold onto with their hooks; often, they build their own cases from gravel, twigs, needles, sand, or other debris they find in their habitats.

Mayfly Larvae: These grayish-brown, six-legged larvae have two antennae sprouting from their heads as well as two or three pointy tails sticking out of their segmented bodies. Rows of flat, paddlelike gills line their lower bodies. Mayflies spend much more time as larvae (one year in the water) than they do as adults (a few hours or days on land). There are around 2,500 species of mayflies.

Dragonfly Larvae: Brown and hairy, these larvae blend in well with the muck at the bottom of a pond. They have six legs, stubby antennae, thick tails, and internal gills, which they use to breathe. Like mayflies, dragonflies live the longest in their larva stage; when disturbed, they sometimes release bursts of water from chambers in their butt (ew!), which propel them to a safer spot.

Damselfly Larvae: These larvae have thin, elongated abdomens with three long "tails" at the end. The "tails" are actually respiratory organs that the larvae use to breathe. Damselfly larvae are a half to one inch in length and are often similar in color to their habitats (a good thing when trying to hide from hungry predators). They molt several times before becoming fully formed adults.

Camping Activity

Pond Peeper at the Beach!

Ever noticed rocky, sandy pockets of water sitting on the ocean's shore? They're tide pools, and they contain fascinating underwater worlds filled with remarkable sea plants and colorful creatures. These life-filled water holes are created by the ocean's tides, regular changes in the water level caused mainly by the moon's gravitational pull. (Tides occur in bays, gulfs, and inlets, too.) Every day there are two high tides where the water level rises, and two low tides where the water recedes. Throughout the day, tide pools fill up with water when the tide rises and leak it away as the tides fall.

A tide pool is a perfect place to peek around underwater with your Pond Peeper (page 208), and you can find them up and down the coast. While there will be differences between a tide pool on the Atlantic Ocean and one on the Pacific, you may recognize many of the same residents—seaweeds, mussels, hermit crabs, and other critters. Take a look at pages 220–223, to get a sense of what you might spot.

What You Need

A tide pool

Your Pond Peeper (page 208)

Rubber boots, old sneakers, or surf shoes

Your Field Journal (page 200), pen or pencil (optional)

Pond Peeper at the Beach, contd.

What You Do

1 At low tide take a wander with a grown-up and look for a tide pool. Rocky places tend to have good ones. Once you find it, sit quietly and observe in a place where your shadow doesn't fall across the pool. (Some animals may sense your presence and hide. If you sit quietly, you will see life in the pool reemerge.)

2 Observe the area around the tide pool. What kinds of birds are there? Do you see seaweed around the rocks of the pool or inside the pool itself? What does it look like? Look at the seaweeds described on pages 220–221—do you spot any of these?

3 Now take a peek into the pool. Gently place your Pond Peeper about an inch under the water and wait while the water settles. What kind of movement do you see? What types of animals are cemented on the rock sides and bottom? Can you spot any movement from these hard-shelled creatures?

4 Take a closer look: Move the Pond Peeper deeper into the water, between the second and third rubber bands. Watch for feathery arms waving from barnacles as they comb the water for food. Gently lift up seaweed and see if there's anything beneath it. What sorts of animals and plants do you see? Are they active, and if so, what are they doing? Are they anchored or floating?

5 Try to determine what part of the tide cycle you are watching. Is the pool almost submerged (which means it's moving toward high tide) or is the water leaking away, leaving the pool drier and drier (moving toward low tide)?

6 Visit the tide pool at a different time of day. What's changed? Do creatures like mussels, clams, and barnacles look and behave the same or differently than they did at low tide? What about the seaweed? How does it look when it's dry versus when it's wet? Keep notes and pictures in your Field Journal, if you like.

What You Might See IN A TIDE POOL..........

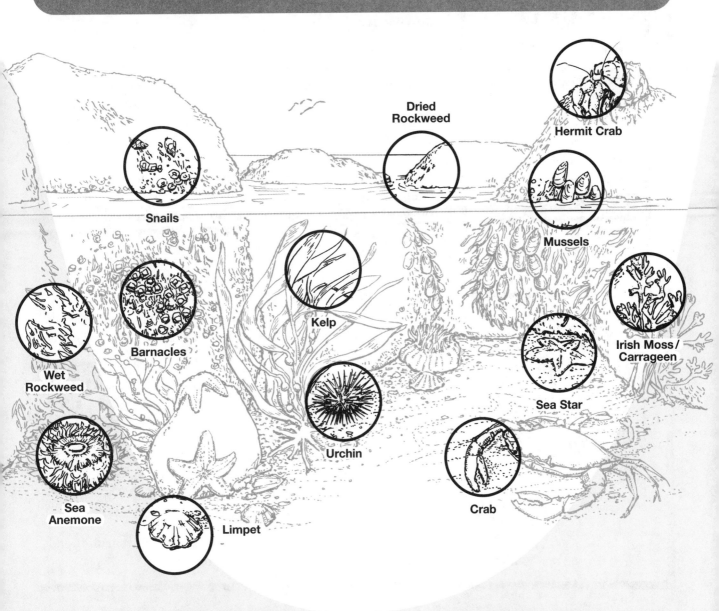

Dried Rockweed

Hermit Crab

Snails

Mussels

Kelp

Barnacles

Wet Rockweed

Irish Moss / Carrageen

Sea Star

Sea Anemone

Urchin

Crab

Limpet

TIDE POOLS ARE NOT only fascinating but also fragile and tough to navigate. The rocks around a tide pool can be very slippery and sharp, and you should take care walking around so you don't crush the animals that live there. If you pick up anything, make sure to put it back exactly where you found it.

LIFE IN A TIDE POOL

Seaweeds

Seaweeds aren't weeds at all. In fact, all of them belong to a group of living things called algae. Like land plants, they make energy from sunlight. They don't have the internal structure to stand up (like land plants), so they depend on the water for support. They cling to the ground with holdfasts, which look like roots and anchor the bottom of the seaweed. When the tide is low, most seaweeds lie flat along the rocks, drying out until they're paper-brittle. But when the water comes back to the pool, the seaweeds rehydrate and thrive. At low tide, many creatures hide under seaweeds trying to keep cool and moist; other creatures crawl around beneath the seaweed gardens as they float in the current. Some common seaweeds you might spot:

Kelp: This seaweed anchors itself to the bottom of a tide pool. When the tide is high, the kelp's large brownish-green blades reach up and sway in the water. Take a look at a kelp blade and see if you can spot a little air-filled bubble inside it. This is called a bladder and helps keep the kelp leaf afloat.

Irish Moss or Carrageen: If you peek into an Atlantic tide pool, you may see this lacy red seaweed beneath the rockweed. Carrageen is harvested for use as a thickener in toothpaste, lunchmeat, and ice cream. Check the ingredients on the back of an ice-cream container and see if you can find carrageenan, which is the thickener made from this seaweed.

Rockweed: These brownish sea plants have many small, round bladders in their leaves, which help them float.

Sea Anemones

These may look like brightly colored flowers, but they're actually animals that anchor themselves to solid objects like the bottom of a tide pool (or the shell of a hermit crab!). Many anemones are predators. They wait, waving their poisonous tentacles, until their prey (usually small fish or shrimp) swim by. When dinner swims past, the anemone stings it with its tentacles and draws the now-paralyzed animal into its mouth.

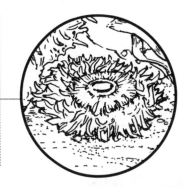

Zoning Out

A tide pool is often called an intertidal zone—a place between tides. But it has a whole lot of mini zones within it as well.

● **Splash/Spray Zone:** This is part of the tide pool that is splashed by high tide. It's not typically underwater unless there's a storm or an unusually high tide. You can find a lot of barnacles in this zone. Birds hang out here, too.

● **High-Tide Zone:** A tough spot for tide pool inhabitants, this zone alternates between long exposures to salt water from crashing waves, followed by stretches in open air and hot sun. This area is only underwater during the high part of high tide. You can find different seaweeds here, as well as more barnacles, mussels, and limpets that are stuck to the rocks. Take a look for hermit crabs, too.

● **Mid-Tide Zone:** As tides move in and out, this region is submerged underwater, then exposed to open air twice daily. This zone is home to anemones, snails, sea stars, and many other creatures. When the tide comes in, the anemones open up, the sea stars begin to move slowly, and the snails start to hunt for food. When the tide goes out, the anemones close up, the sea stars stay put, and the snails seek shade and moisture in the seaweed that limply drapes along the rocks.

● **Low-Tide Zone:** This portion of the tide pool is covered by water most of the time. The seaweeds anchor here. In the low tide-zone, crabs, urchins, and sea slugs hunt for food, and shrimp and fish dart around under the protection of the seaweed.

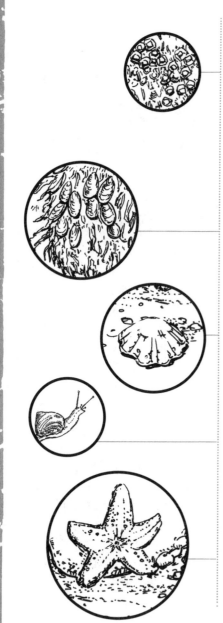

Shelled Critters

Barnacles: These little invertebrates (see Learn the Lingo, right) live in hard, white volcano-shape shells. They cement themselves to rocks and other hard things (like the shells of other animals). When the water in a tide pool is low, barnacles retreat into their shell. But when barnacles are submerged, they extend their feathery feet and comb the water for tasty treats. Baby barnacles float around without a shell until they find a suitable place to live. When they find one, they glue themselves to the spot headfirst using special cement glands in their antennae, and then grow a shell.

Mussels: These pinkish bivalves (see Learn the Lingo, right) live in blue-black teardrop-shape shells. They hang out in groups and anchor themselves to rocks with tough strings called byssus threads.

Limpets: These soft-bodied sea snails have a hard, flattish, cone-like shell that protects them from predators. They cling to rocks with their muscular feet. They move slowly along the bottom of the tide pool, licking algae from the rocks with their raspy tongues. You can see limpets in cooler waters of the Pacific and Atlantic.

Periwinkles or Snails: These soft-bodied animals have a whorled shell with a "trap door" that they can pull in tightly to protect themselves from predators and from drying out. The shells are tough and unique, with beautiful markings. Sometimes a periwinkle will open its trap door if you hold it in the shade and hum. Cousins of land snails, they can survive in salty environments.

Sea Stars: You probably know these guys as starfish, but since they're actually nothing like fish, people now call them sea stars. Most have five (or a multiple of five) arms with thousands of tiny tubelike feet underneath. The arms are pretty cool—if the sea star loses one, it will grow back—and the feet help the star move gracefully and slowly along the tide pool or ocean bottom as it hunts for food.

Sea stars eat limpets, snails, and other larger shellfish. If its prey is bigger than its mouth (which is in the center of the sea star's underbody), the star will squish its stomach through its mouth, dissolve the prey with its nasty stomach juices, and then suck the whole thing back up. Yum. There are more than 2,000 varieties of sea stars worldwide, and they come in almost every color of the rainbow.

Sea Urchins: These dome-shaped, spiky, hard-shelled creatures can be found at great ocean depths as well as at the bottom of tide pools. Ranging in color from deep purple to brown to green, they eat mostly rotting matter from kelp to fish to crabs. They have tiny tube feet that they use to move, gather food, and hold on to rocks when the currents rage. Some of the spines are poisonous, so look but don't touch!

Crabs: Crabs are hard-shelled animals with eyes on long stalks at the front of their bodies. They use a pair of large claws to gather food and defend themselves—watch out! With three pairs of walking legs, and a pair of swimming legs in the back, they are fast sideways walkers and can dig quickly and swim. There are almost 5,000 species of crabs in the world. Most crabs will pretty much eat anything from plants to animals to rotting stuff.

Hermit Crabs: These creatures lack a hard shell and use other animals' discarded shells for protection. As a hermit crab grows, it has to find newer, bigger shells to squeeze its vulnerable body into. Look for large snail shells, the favored homes of hermits (if one is inside, you'll probably see its little legs poking out).

Learn the Lingo

Invertebrates and bivalves

An invertebrate is an animal that doesn't have a backbone, such as an octopus, anemone, sea star, crab, or sea cucumber. A bivalve has a soft body and a hinged shell with two halves. Clams, scallops, and mussels are bivalves.

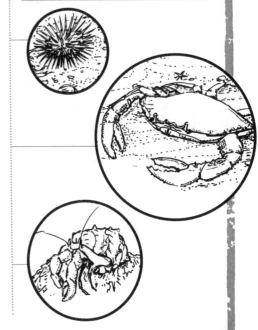

Old Trees, New Life

What You Need

A rotting log

A pair of garden gloves

A magnifying glass

Your Field Journal (page 200), pen or pencil

When a tree falls, its life is over. But the tree can still *give* life to others. The dead tree becomes its own ecosystem (see Learn the Lingo, page 230), where plants, insects, and microorganisms thrive—from the mosses, ferns, and fungi that make the rotting tree their home to a whole host of bugs and bacteria that eat the tree and break it down into soil for new plants.

Next time you see a dead log, take a close look and record your observations in your Field Journal. You just might be amazed by what you see.

What You Do

1 Find a rotting log: Look for a tree that has fallen and that has wood breaking apart in pieces. It may be slightly damp.

2 Describe what the log looks like. What is growing on it? Can you see any mushrooms, ferns, mosses, or lichens? Are there baby trees or any other plants sprouting out of the wood?

3 Do you see any insects? Where are they doing their thing? Look for tiny piles of sawdust at the base of the log. This is evidence that insects have drilled into the wood, starting the decomposition process. The holes left behind create highways for fungi and bacteria to come in and break down the wood even further.

4 Tap the log with your fingers. Is it hollow? Wet? Bone-dry? What does it smell like?

5 Put on your gloves and, with a grown-up's help, gently and carefully lift the log a few inches to see if you can take a peek underneath. (Only lift the log if it's flat on the ground; if it's perched on a rock or another log, it might roll over and land on your foot or worse—ouch). What do you see? Are there insects underneath? What are they doing? What do they look like? When you're done, put the log back.

6 Use your magnifying glass to peek at the log itself. Do you see insects breaking it down? What do they look like under the magnifying glass? What about the plants growing on the tree? What do the mushrooms look like up close?

7 Draw and describe what you've seen in your Field Journal. Try to identify plants, animals, and insects by looking at What You Might See, page 227.

CHEW ON THIS

YOU CAN LEARN A LOT about the life of a tree by looking at its stump. Take a look at the stump's rings. Are they thick or thin or do they vary? Count the rings. Each ring represents a year in the tree's life. Thick rings mean that year was a good one for the tree—a nice wet spring and summer full of solid growth. A thin ring means the tree had a tough year and may have struggled through a lack of water or even insect infestations.

LIFE ON A ROTTING LOG

The world on, in, and under a rotting log is teeming with activity. Here is a sampling of what you might see when you look up close.

Insects and Animals

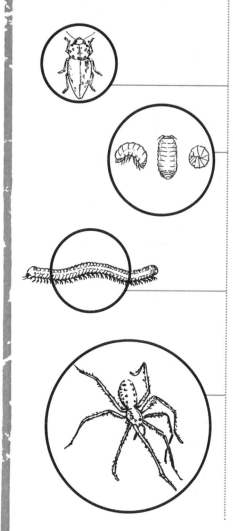

Wood-boring Beetles: Many beetles are able to eat and digest wood and turn it into nutrients in the soil that help new plants live.

Pill Bugs: Aptly named because they are oval-shaped like a pill, these guys have seven overlapping plates along their backs that allow them to curl up in a ball to protect themselves from predators. They eat decaying plants, and they like things dark, cool, and wet.

Millipedes: You can find these scavengers under leaves, rocks, or rotting logs, where they feed on decaying plant material on the forest floor. Millipedes are rounded like a worm but they have many shell-like segments with two pairs of legs sprouting from each. Millipedes are related to centipedes, which have only one pair of legs sprouting from each body segment and can sting.

Spiders: There are thousands of different kinds of spiders. They all have eight legs and usually two rows of four eyes. Spiders don't have ears but they can sense sound vibrations through the tiny hairs on their legs. They all eat insects and some eat small animals.

Daddy Longlegs: Commonly believed to be spiders, daddy longlegs belong to a group of bugs called harvestmen. They like dark, wet, quiet places. They have small round bodies with long, thin legs. These creatures won't hurt you—unless you're another daddy longlegs (these bugs eat each other!).

What You Might See ON A ROTTING LOG

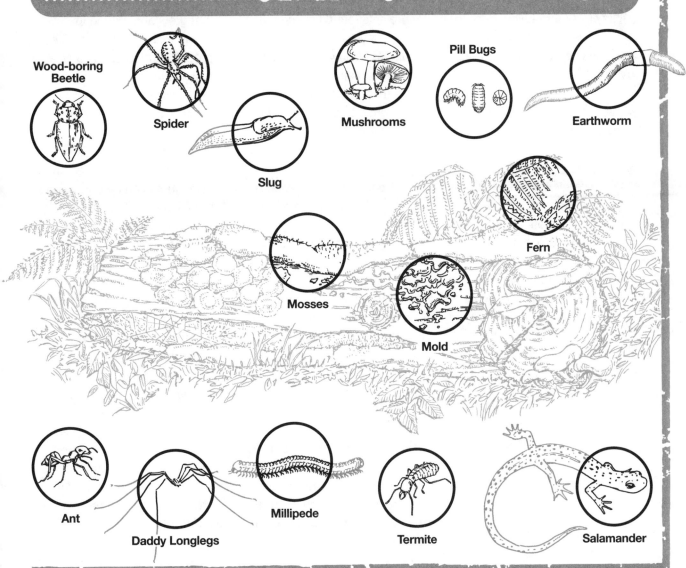

Wood-boring Beetle

Spider

Slug

Mushrooms

Pill Bugs

Earthworm

Mosses

Mold

Fern

Ant

Daddy Longlegs

Millipede

Termite

Salamander

Forest Layers

There's more to forests than meets the eye. Forests are actually made up of three basic layers:

- **Canopy or Overstory:** This is the upper level of the forest, made up of leaves and branches of the tallest trees. Because the tall trees get so much sunlight, they grow ever bigger and stronger, and shade the sunlight from the trees below. In fact, less than 50 percent of the available sunlight makes it through the canopy to the rest of the forest.

- **Understory:** This layer is made up of the young trees, shrubs, and plants found between the canopy layer and the forest floor. Just below the canopy are the saplings, younger trees that haven't yet grown tall enough to elbow their way into the canopy. The saplings struggle to grow because they don't get that much sunshine. When a mature tree dies and falls, a sapling has the opportunity to take its place. The sapling that grows the fastest at this point will fill the gap and mature.

  Animals such as squirrels and birds live in this layer, too; here they build nests and search for food.

  The shrub layer is also part of the understory. Plants that grow about three to seven feet tall live here. They provide food for many animals that live in the forest, such as deer and bears, which forage for leaves and fruits here.

- **Forest Floor:** This is the ground level, where dead leaves and fallen trees can be found. Tiny organisms feed off and break down the dead vegetation, creating nutrients that help new plants and trees flourish. Animals such as skunks, porcupines, and mice live here, too—building dens and munching on insects like grubs that live under logs and rocks and in the decaying leaves.

Ants: There are more than 12,000 species of ants in the world. They all have three body segments, six legs, and two antennae. Some even have wings. They live in ant cities, where each ant has a role. Some gather food, some care for the baby ants, and some defend the city. So chances are if you see one ant, you'll see more.

Slugs: Slugs are snails without shells. They slide along the ground on a path of their own mucus. Whee! They like dark, wet places where they don't have to worry about drying out.

Termites: These insects eat 24/7 and have huge sawtooth jaws that help them chew through wood. They live in massive underground colonies.

Salamanders: Salamanders look kind of like smooth, wet lizards, but they're amphibians, not reptiles (see A Class Refresher, page 206); that means they need to be in moist places so their skin won't dry out. They seek the dark sponginess of rotten logs.

Earthworms: These pinkish-brown recyclers break down plant matter and turn it into nutrients for rich soil.

Fungus and Plants

Mushrooms: These are fungi, not plants. Unable to make food from the sun because they have no chlorophyll, they get their food from decaying matter. The mushroom is actually the seed spreader of the fungus, which is made up of an underground network of fungus threads. When conditions are right, the mushroom pops up from the ground and dries out, releasing the fungus's seeds, or spores, from the gills in its cap.

Mosses: These small, soft plants grow together in low clumps that can be vibrantly green. They thrive in shaded, moist areas.

Ferns: They also thrive in dark, wet places. Ferns have a single stem with smaller fronds growing off in pairs. They use spores to reproduce (look for small dark spots underneath their leaves.)

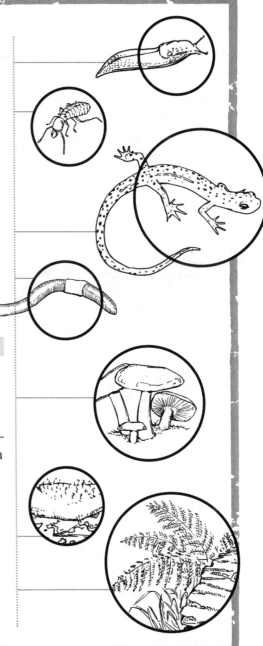

Biodiversity

Bio means life and *diversity* means variety. When you put the two together you get *biodiversity*, which is the wide variety of living beings that inhabit a single environment. That environment can be as limited as the woods behind your house or as vast as the whole wide world.

Biome

A biome is a region on Earth that has its own unique characteristics. These are large areas such as: tundra, taiga, alpine, temperate forest, tropical rain forest, desert, grassland, and ocean. Each biome has its own specific soils, plants, animals, and weather patterns. Within the biomes are more specific communities of plants and animals called ecosystems.

Biosphere

Are you familiar with the phrase, "everything under the sun?" Encompassing air, land, surface rocks, and water, the biosphere contains all the regions in which

Learn the Lingo

living organisms are found. It is the thin, outermost part of the planet's shell and the inner layers of its atmosphere. Everything—from the birds in the sky, to the worms in the dirt—lives in the biosphere.

Ecosystem

An ecosystem is a group of plants, animals, insects, and microorganisms (tiny beings like bacteria) that live in the same place and function as a unit. To get a better sense of what this means, let's imagine a forest ecosystem where a wolf eats a rabbit, which was eating some grass. Later bacteria decompose the wolf's poop and convert it into nutrients. These nutrients enrich the soil, which helps more grass grow, the grass feeds more rabbits, and the cycle repeats itself. In this way, we can see how all the different beings in an ecosystem—from very big

to very small—are connected.

An ecosystem can be large like a meadow or it can be as small as a puddle of rainwater where a whole community of microorganisms, plants, and insects lives and survives off each other.

Habitat

Habitat is Latin for "it inhabits." It is the envirnonment in which a particular species naturally lives and grows. It's made up of a variety of factors, including the type of soil, the range of temperature, the amount of light, the availability of food, and the presence of predators. Except for birds that migrate, most animals stay within their habitats. For example, an alligator's habitat is a swamp or marshland, so you wouldn't find one living in the Arctic.

Organism

Organism is another word for a living being. Plants, animals, insects, and bacteria are all examples of organisms.

Measuring a Tree Without a Giant Ruler

So you're dying to know how tall that huge tree by your campsite is but you don't have the climbing skills of Spider-Man? No problem. Here's a way to estimate the height of a tree without climbing a single branch.

What You Need

A tree

A ruler

A tape measure

A partner

What You Do

1 Stand at the base of a tree, facing its trunk. Grasp the bottom of the ruler in your right hand so it points up. Extend your arm and close your left eye—the ruler should be lined up with the tree.

2 Now carefully walk backward (look where you're going every once in a while so you don't fall in a hole or trip on a raccoon).

3 Stop walking when the ruler appears to be the same size as the tree.

4 Have your partner measure the distance between your feet and the base of the tree. That distance is about equal to the height of the tree. Neat, huh?

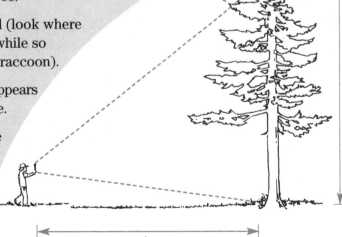

Decomposers at Work

What You Need

An apple slice

A small zip-top bag

A few days (see Note)

Your Field Journal (page 200), pen or pencil

Decomposers—bacteria, fungus, mold, and various other organisms such as worms—break down material and turn it into nutrients that can be absorbed by plants. Decomposers are the unseen heroes of rot. If not for them, we'd be up to our eyeballs in dead trees, leaves, animals, and lots and lots of garbage.

Try this experiment and see the effects of decomposers doing their thing. Start this project on the first day of your trip and see how the apple changes over your visit.

What You Do

1 Put the apple slice in the bag, squeeze out the air, and zip the bag tight so no air can get in or out.

2 Put it in a sunny spot and wait 3 or 4 days.

3 Watch how the apple changes every day. Does it change color? Does anything fuzzy or slimy grow on it? Does it change shape or texture?

4 Note your observations in your Field Journal each day.

5 After the fourth day, bury the apple in the soil so it can be reabsorbed into the environment: Dig a small hole in the dirt, open the zip-top bag, and drop the rotten apple from the bag into the hole. Cover the apple with the dirt you scooped aside, and throw away the plastic bag.

What's Going On

When you first put the apple slice into the bag, it isn't alone. There is a whole invisible party of bacteria, mold, and fungus spores hanging out on the apple and in the air. When given the right conditions—warmth and food—this gang of decomposers goes on a feeding frenzy.

For a decomposer, this means taking plant or animal matter and turning it into nutrients. It's the process of rotting something and changing it from one phase (an apple phase) to another (a fertilizer phase). When you bury the apple in the ground, it will continue to rot, breaking down further and further until it eventually becomes nutrients that will enrich the soil and the plants living in it.

Note: If you like, try extending this experiment at home. Keep the apple zipped tight in the bag and place the bag on the windowsill. How does it change after a month? Chances are you won't even recognize that it was once an apple. The decomposers will turn it into a nutrient-, mold-, fungus-, and bacteria-filled mush fit for the compost pile. When you're done, make sure to dispose of the rotten apple appropriately (see Step 5).

The Seedy Side of Things

What You Need

A place to walk

A pair of nubby wool socks

A magnifying glass (optional)

Clear tape

Paper

Your Field Journal (page 200), pen or pencil

Plants have developed a few interesting ways to spread their seeds. Some seeds are flyers that catch the wind and land in new places. Some simply drop to the ground encased in delicious fruit; animals eat the fruit (seeds and all), then poop out the seeds. Other seeds are exploders, launching into the air at the slightest touch. And there are hitchhikers, which stick to passing animals (and people) and then get dropped farther afield.

In this experiment, you will catch and look at some of those hitchhiker seeds. Take a walk through a field or forest and see what you can pick up.

What You Do

1 Find an interesting natural area to walk through, such as a field, park, backyard, or forest.

2 Put on the wool socks over your shoes.

3 Walk around for 10 to 20 minutes, making sure you wander past shrubs, flowers, and grasses.

4 Have a seat and take off the socks. Take a close look at them. Look on the bottoms, on the ankles, and on the tops. Do you see any hitchhiker seeds (see the chart at right)?

5 Pick off all the different kinds of seeds you find and organize them into groups based on their shape or size. Tape a few of each seed into your Field Journal. Look at the chart and try to identify each one.

6 Now walk back through the area and see if you can find the seeds sticking out of any of the flowers or plants nearby. (For example, you may find a dandelion that's covered with seeds, or a milkweed.)

7 When you get home, go online or check the library and look up the seeds you found. Try to identify the ones you don't know. Add any interesting facts about the seeds or the plants they come from to your Field Journal.

Beggar's lice

Burdock

Foxtail

Milkweed

Burr Clover

Dandelion

Sprout Your Socks

What You Need

A pair of nubby wool socks

A large zip-top bag

About $\frac{1}{4}$ cup water

A place that gets sun for most of the day—indoors or out

What happens after a seed hitches a ride? Seeds can stay in a state of suspended animation until they land in a place with all the right conditions. Seed a sock and see for yourself.

What You Do

1 Find an interesting natural area to walk through (a field, park, backyard, or forest).

2 Pull the wool socks over your shoes. Hike around the area, making sure your feet brush up against plants.

3 Have a seat, take off the socks, and slip them into the zip-top bag. Sprinkle the water over the socks (they should be damp but not soaked) and seal the bag.

4 Put the whole thing in the sun and wait a few days. After a while, the hitchhiking seeds will sprout.

5 See what happens if you separate the socks for a few days, keeping one in the sun and the other in a new zip-top bag in the dark. What happens?

6 Try planting your socks and see if you get a mini meadow!

STEER CLEAR OF SOME PLANTS WHEN you're collecting leaves and when you're outdoors in general. Plants like poison ivy, poison oak, and poison sumac can give you a nasty, oozy rash if you touch them.

It's a good idea to wear long pants in areas where these plants are common, and avoid them when gathering firewood (burning these poisonous leaves can give you a rash inside your lungs—ack!). If you touch one of these plants by accident, wash the area with soap and water, and tell your grown-ups. Most important, know what to look for. A good rule of thumb:

Leaves grouped in three? Let them be!

Poison Ivy: Look for leaves grouped into threes. Poison ivy varies in shape and can grow as bushes, vines, or single plants. It grows throughout the country, usually at the edges of forests, in fields, or in sunny areas. Its leaves are bright green in the spring and red in the fall.

Poison Oak: These leaves are grouped into threes as well and are scalloped at the edges. The plants can appear in different forms, just as with poison ivy. The leaves are generally bright green in the spring, dusty green to reddish in the summer, and bright red or orange in the fall. The Pacific or western poison oak

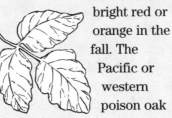

is found in shrubby areas all along the Pacific Coast; the Atlantic poison oak is found mostly in woody areas in the southeast and west.

Poison Sumac: This tall shrub or small tree has six to twelve leaflets arranged in pairs along a long stem, giving its branches a featherlike appearance. It grows mostly in swamps, bogs, and wetlands in the eastern part of the country and can be found as far west as Texas. Bright green in the spring, the leaves turn red and orange in the fall. You can tell the difference between poison and nonpoisonous sumac by looking at the seeds: Poison seed pods sit between the leaves and branches, while the nonpoisonous pods are at the ends of the branches.

Working Leaves

What You Need

An easy-to-reach tree branch with leaves (not an evergreen)

A clear plastic bag (like the kind you put veggies in at the grocery store)

A foot-long piece of string or duct tape

A sunny day

Y ou can't see it, but trees everywhere are sucking up and spitting out gallons and gallons of water. Trees pull water through their roots into their trunk and branches, and out to their leaves, where they release it into the atmosphere as water vapor. If you have a clear plastic bag, you can see the effects of this amazing process for yourself.

What You Do

1 Gently place the plastic bag over the end of the branch so that some leaves are inside the bag. Being careful not to crush any leaves, wind the string or tape around the bag about an inch from the opening, so that the bag is secured snugly to the branch. You want the string or tape tight enough that no air will enter or leave the bag.

2 Keep the bag on the branch for a few hours in full sunlight. Check on it after an hour or so. You should see condensation starting to bead up on the inside of the bag. What's happening? This condensation is water coming from the leaves. The roots of the plant suck water up and vessels inside the tree called xylem and phloem disperse it to the leaves. Tiny pores in the

leaves called stomata release water back into the air.

3 When you finish observing the leaves, gently take the bag off and reuse it or throw it away. This experiment won't hurt the tree at all if you clean up, but if you leave the bag on the leaves for more than a day you may cause some damage.

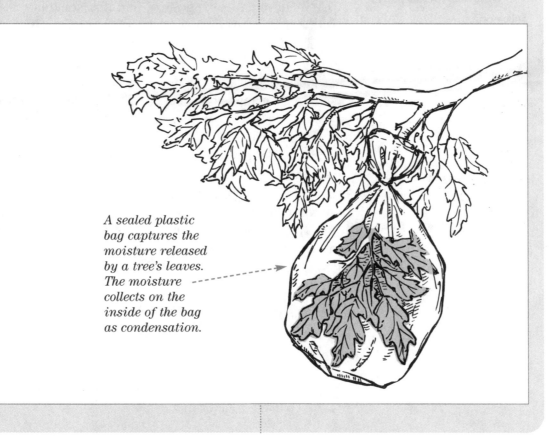

A sealed plastic bag captures the moisture released by a tree's leaves. The moisture collects on the inside of the bag as condensation.

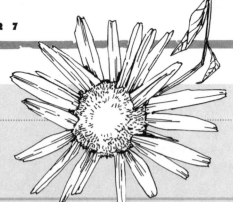

Plant Pressing

What You Need

Scissors

Paper towels (at least 2)

Notebook or any thick book that you can let sit for a week

Assorted leaves and flowers with at least 2 to 3 inches of stem (remember to use leaves and flowers that have fallen naturally; avoid poisonous plants (page 237)

A large, heavy rock

6 wide rubber bands (optional)

Envelope or folder, for storage

When you're out and about hiking and making observations, you may find that some interesting leaves or flowers have flung themselves on the ground in your path. Why not take them home? It's a great idea, but if you pack even a few straight into your journal, they may end up looking more like a pile of dust than the beautiful plants they once were. Not to fear! Plant pressing is here!

Pressed leaves and flowers can keep their shape and color for a long, long time—scientists still study specimens that were dried in the field more than a hundred years ago! These preserved plants are perfect for pasting into your Field Journal and great for other projects as well. They'll need to be squished for at least a week, so press them right in camp and keep them flat in your notebook for easy transport.

What You Do

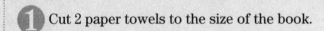

1 Cut 2 paper towels to the size of the book.

2 Place 1 trimmed paper towel on a sturdy, flat surface like a rock or picnic table.

3 Place as many leaves or flowers on the paper towel as will fit comfortably. Try to lay them as flat as possible. If you're using a flower, you can press it with all the petals together, like a bud, or with the petals opened, which will give you more detail. If you want the petals to be open, place the flower face down and gently arrange the petals as you wish.

4 Lay another paper towel on top of the leaves and flowers. Smooth it out so it lays flat.

5 Place the whole thing between the pages in the back of your book and close it firmly.

6 Put the heavy rock on top of the book and let the whole thing sit in a warm, dry place (like the car) for a week.

7 If you're on the move, wrap the rubber bands around the book tightly to keep it closed firmly and to keep the pressure on the leaves.

8 After a week or so, carefully remove the pressed leaves and flowers from the book.

9 Store them flat in an envelope or a folder until you're ready to use them. (Pressed flowers look great on posters, notecards, placemats, and more— use clear contact paper to secure them.)

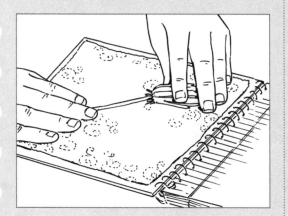

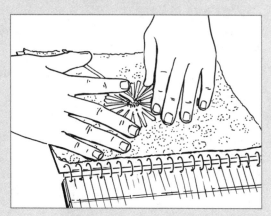

Leaf Rubbing

ake a look at a leaf. Notice its texture. Look at the veins underneath. By making a rubbing of the leaf, you can show all this detail on paper. Try this with leaves of different shapes and sizes. Experiment with rubbing the top and the bottom of each leaf—which works best? Which do you like better?

What You Need

An assortment of leaves

A few pieces of white or light-colored construction paper

Crayon(s) with the paper removed

Your Field Journal (page 200), pen or pencil (optional)

White glue

What You Do

1 Put a leaf down on a flat, sturdy surface like a picnic table or rock. (If the surface has some texture to it, put a piece of paper under the leaf.) Place a piece of paper over it.

2 Press lightly on the paper and leaf to hold both in place. Gently rub the side of a crayon over the whole leaf until all of its details appear on the paper.

3 Repeat with other leaves and crayon colors. (You can also do a bunch of rubbings on the same paper, or rub part of a leaf with one color and then the rest of it with another.)

4 When you're done, you can cut out the leaf shapes and paste them into your Field Journal.

Make and Take Tracks

A ll sorts of other animals, big and small, may walk the very trails you do. If you're lucky enough to find some tracks, you can capture a footprint and take it home.

You'll need to pick up some special supplies for this activity, but it's cool to be able to make an actual copy of a moment—a footprint to keep forever—long after the actual print and even the animal have moved on.

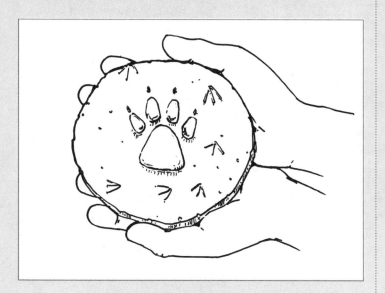

What You Need

An animal track

4 sticks, each at least 8 inches long

Scissors

An empty plastic gallon milk jug

Plaster of Paris (available at art supply or hardware stores)

Water (follow the directions on the plaster package for specific amounts)

A sturdy arm-length stick

A large paper clip, partway opened

A permanent marker

Your Field Journal (page 200), pen or pencil

continued on page 244

Make and Take Tracks, contd.

3 Put the four 8-inch-long sticks around the track like a frame. They will prevent you from stepping on the track by accident and will make it easier to find again).

4 With a grown-up's help, cut off the top of the milk jug to create an opening about 4 inches wide. Be careful not to cut too far down—you want the handle to stay on.

5 Following the directions on the plaster of Paris package, combine some plaster and water in the plastic milk jug. (You should need only a cup or so of plaster to cover and fill the track, unless it's very large.)

What You Do

1 Look for tracks in soft soil, mud, or sand in areas that animals frequent, such as the shores of a pond or lake.

2 When you come across a track that looks interesting, stop and clear the area of sticks, leaves, or any other debris.

6 Stir the mix with the sturdy stick until it becomes as thick as pancake batter.

like. (When the plaster hardens completely, overnight, thread a string through the hole to hang your track.)

9 Pick up the hardened plaster and turn it over. Brush off the dirt.

10 Describe the track in your Field Journal. How big is it? Are there claw marks? How many toes are there? What is the shape of the foot pad? Are there a lot of tracks in the same area? What does all of this tell you about your track and the animal that made it?

11 Identify your track using the clues you've gathered and Who Goes There? on page 332. Write the date, location, and name of the animal on the back of the track with the permanent marker.

7 Gently pour the plaster into the track. Stop pouring when the track is full and the plaster overflows at least an inch on every side of the track.

8 Wait for the plaster to harden. Depending on its thickness, it will take about 10 minutes. While the plaster is firming up, you can poke a hole in the top with the end of the paper clip, if you

Camping Activity

Bug Lab

What You Need

A 2-liter clear plastic soda bottle with the cap

A hammer

A nail

A big leaf, stick, or flat rock

Insect

Your Field Journal (page 200), pen or pencil (optional)

There are more than two million species of bugs out there. Insects inhabit almost every ecosystem (see page 230) on Earth, so you're bound to run into a few when you're out camping. Why not take a closer look and get to know a few of your many-legged friends a bit better?

Many bugs are pretty harmless, but some bite or sting, so you shouldn't pick one up with your hands. Instead, gently nudge a leaf or other flat object underneath it and then coax it into this cool Bug Lab. The Bug Lab is a great place to hold your insect specimen while you observe, describe, and sketch it. It lets the bug breathe and keeps both you and the bug safe.

What You Do

1 Carefully peel off and throw away the label on the soda bottle. Rinse out the bottle and put the cap on.

2 With a grown-up's help, use a hammer and nail to make 12 holes around the upper third of the bottle.

3 Use a leaf, stick, or rock to carefully pick up an insect. Coax the bug into the mouth of the bottle.

Once the bug is safely inside—no legs poking out!—put the cap on the bottle.

4 Observe your insect.

- How many body parts do you see?

- How many legs?

- Are there wings?

- Antennae?

- What color is it? Does its color help it blend into its environment or does it shout out "Back off Jack!" to any would-be predator?

- What do its mouth parts look like?

- What is it doing?

5 Record your observations in your Field Journal if you like. Include such specifics as where you found it (under a leaf, on your head) and what it was doing when you found it. Make a drawing so you can do more research when you get home.

6 Make sure to release the insect when you are finished observing it. Open the bottle cap and rest the bottle on its side. The bug will eventually leave on its own, but if it seems to be camping out, you can try tapping the bottle gently.

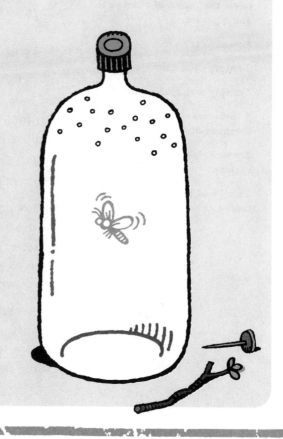

Solar Water Heater

What You Need

Black poster paint (enough to cover the inside of a soda can and a pie tin)

A paintbrush

2 empty soda cans

2 empty disposable pie tins

A thermometer (a digital oral thermometer works great)

A watch, to time your observations

Your Field Journal (page 200), pen or pencil (optional)

The sun has the power to really heat things up down here on Earth. This great experiment shows you how to take advantage of this power and really get the temperature rising.

What You Do

1 Paint the outside and top of 1 can and the inside of 1 pie tin with a coat of black paint. Let the paint dry completely (you can do this before you leave home if you like).

2 Fill both cans and pie tins with cold water and put them in a very sunny spot.

3 Record the temperatures of all 4 containers: Place the thermometer in each container and wait for a reading. (This should take only a few moments. Make sure to clear the thermometer after every reading.) Write down the temperature of each container.

4 Feel the water in the tins and cans with your hand. Do any of them feel warm? Which ones? At what point does the water start to feel warm? Write down your observations in your Field Journal.

5 Repeat Steps 4 and 5 every 15 minutes for an hour.

6 Ask yourself the following questions and note your observations in your Field Journal: Did any of the tins or cans have water that was bath-warm (above 95°F)? Did the water in any of the containers heat up faster? Which ones? How hot did each one get after a half hour? An hour? Why do you think the water in certain cans or tins heated up more or faster than the water in the others?

What's Going On

The black paint absorbs the sun's energy while the metal surface reflects it, so the water in the dark containers absorbs more heat than the water in light ones. The pie tins warm up faster than the cans because there is more surface area for the sun to heat.

Stick-in-the-Mud Sun Clock

What You Need

A sunny spot with soft dirt (so you can draw in it)

A straight, sturdy stick, about 3 feet long

A watch, to set the clock

Before there were mechanical and digital clocks, people used natural materials such as hourglasses, water clocks, and candles to tell time. But the most reliable natural time-telling tool was the sun.

People figured out how to tell time by measuring the shadows created as the sun "moved" across the sky. You can do the very same thing by building this simple clock. You'll need to check it every hour for an entire day, but once you've done that, you'll have a reliable clock as long as it's daytime and the sun is shining.

What You Do

1 Find a sunny spot with soft dirt that's out in the open (so it won't get shady during the day). Push the stick into the dirt so it points straight up.

2 If you want to make an all-day clock, get up early and start this experiment when the sun starts shining. (But be reasonable—you are on vacation after all.) A good time to start is around 7:00 in the morning. At 7:00 A.M. exactly, make a mark in the dirt where the end of the stick's shadow falls. Write "7:00 A.M." in the dirt right next to the line.

3 Repeat Step 2 every hour on the hour until 7:00 at night. (Each hour, mark where the stick's shadow falls and the time right next to it.)

4 Starting the next day you'll be able to tell time with your sun clock. When you wake up, see where the shadow falls. Read the time. For example, if it's halfway between the 7:00 A.M. and the 8:00 A.M., you'll know it's 7:30 A.M.

Note: This clock will only work accurately for a week or so. As the year passes, the days get longer or shorter. The angle of the sun and the amount of time the sun shines and casts shadows changes as well. You won't notice this shift over a few days, but it would become obvious after a month and you'd have to "reset" your clock.

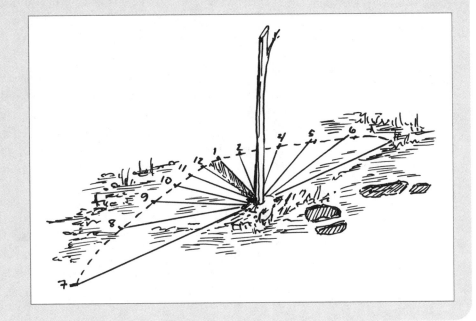

Camping Activity

Egyptian Stick Clock

What You Need

A sunny spot

2 big rocks, each about the size and shape of a brick

A straight, sturdy stick, about 1 foot long

A watch, to set the clock

A sheet of paper and a pencil

The ancient Egyptians used a device like this one to tell time with the sun. As with the clock on page 250, you'll need to check this each hour on the hour for one whole day to make the complete clock.

Get up early to start this experiment—say just before 7:00 A.M. Give yourself about fifteen minutes to set this up so it will be ready at 7:00 A.M. on the dot.

What You Do

1 Find a sunny spot out in the open (so it won't get shady over the course of the day) and place the paper down with the short sides running north to south. (Look at your shadow to figure out the directions. The morning sun rises in the east, so your shadow will point west. North will be between the two, with east on the right.)

2 Place the 2 rocks across from each other in the middle of each long side of the paper to anchor it. Lay the stick across the top of the rocks so the stick (and its shadow) is parallel to the short edges of the paper. The stick should run north to south.

3 At 7:00 A.M. on the nose, mark exactly where the shadow falls on the paper and write the time next to it.

4 Repeat Step 3 every hour on the hour until 7:00 at night. (Each hour, mark where the stick's shadow falls and the time right next to it.) Make sure you don't move the paper or the stick during the experiment or after.

5 You can tell time the next day with your sun clock. Just look at the shadow that the sun makes on the paper, and you can see what time it is. For example, if the shadow falls directly between two numbers, say 8:00 A.M. and 9:00 A.M., it's 8:30.

Note: *This clock will only work accurately for a week or so. As the year passes, the days get longer or shorter. The angle of the sun and the amount of time the sun shines and casts shadows changes as well. You won't notice this shift over a few days, but it would become obvious after a month and you'd have to "reset" your clock.*

Fast-Food Sundial

What You Need

A pencil

A large paper cup with a lid

Sand or water

A drinking straw

A sunny spot

A permanent marker

A watch, to set the time

Y ou can make this sundial out of a recycled cup and straw. And this clock is portable, so you can bring it to any sunny spot and it will still tell you what time it is.

The clock takes a little while to set up, so you may want to make it the night before you use it.

What You Do

1 Use the pencil to poke a hole in the side of the cup about 2 inches down from the top.

CHEW ON THIS

THE SUN IS 110 times larger than the Earth. If the Earth were the size of a bean, the sun, in comparison, would be the size of a beach ball. Talk about big!

2 Remove the lid of the cup and fill the cup about halfway with sand or water to weigh it down.

3 Stick the straw through the lid and down through the hole in the cup's side. The straw should stick up out of the lid about 2 to 3 inches.

4 Just before 7:00 A.M., find a sunny spot and set down the sundial so that the straw points north. (Look at your shadow to figure out the directions. The morning sun rises in the east, so your shadow will point west. North will be between the two, with east on the right.)

5 At 7:00 A.M. on the dot, carefully use the marker to trace the shadow that the straw makes on the cup's lid. Make sure you don't move the cup or the straw. Write the time next to the line.

6 Repeat Step 5 every hour for 12 hours until 7:00 at night.

7 Once you have the times written on the clock, you can move it. You can tell time the next day with your portable sun clock. Simply place it in the sun and align the straw so it points north (see Step 4). Look at where the shadow lands on the cup lid to read the time.

CRAFTY CAMPING

Outdoorsy Arts and Crafts

"Some touch of Nature's genial glow."

—Sir Walter Scott

Nature has provided inspiration and materials to lots and lots of artists. People have painted pictures of rolling hills, soaring mountains, and rollicking rivers. Sculptors have created incredibly lifelike forms out of wood, clay, and stone. Potters have made lovely and useful clay vessels, and jewelers have created ornaments from metals, shells, and grasses. And back when people still lived off the land, they used natural materials not only to make art but to make household objects, such as woven reed baskets and hollowed-gourd water jugs, that would improve their lives.

In this chapter you'll find inspiration, too, from the nature that surrounds you. You'll use your imagination to create amazing works of art and neat crafts that you can wear or use to decorate your camp. You'll make a cool sign to stake out your site, a woven grass bracelet to show off to your friends, a T-shirt stamped with green fern fronds, a wildlife menagerie out of sticks, rocks, and leaves, and lots of other amazing stuff. We'll give you the basic steps, and you'll do the rest!

Camping Activity

Smash Berry Camp Sign

What You Need

Brown Bag "Hide" (page 259)

A big handful of dark-colored berries (huckleberries, blueberries, and blackberries work well)

A straight stick, about 3–4 feet long and the width of your pinky

Twine, for hanging the sign

After you've set up camp, make this neat natural sign to mark your turf. If you're not using safe-to-eat berries, wash your hands well after you use them (some berries can make you sick).

What You Do

1 Choose a name for your camp. You could name it after your family, but you might want to get more inventive than that. How would you describe your fellow campers? Are you guys always munching on hot dogs? Maybe you should be "Camp Weenie Roast." Or do you spend so much time in the water that your fingers look like prunes? Maybe try "Camp Soggy Bottom." You could also choose words from another language. (Look at the Native Language box on page 263 for inspiration.)

2 Tear the Brown Bag "Hide" into a rectangle big enough to fit your camp name and any pictures you want to add (see page 262 for ideas). Using the stick, poke a small hole near the top right corner of the rectangle and another small hole near the top left corner. (You will thread the stick through these holes to hang the sign.)

3 To write your camp name and draw pictures on the "hide," smash a berry into the paper until its juice runs. Drag the berry across the "hide" to write and draw on it, replacing it with another berry when it runs dry.

4 Let the sign dry for about an hour in the sun.

5 Thread the stick through the hole on the top right corner of the sign, from front to back. Pass the stick behind the sign to the hole on the left, poking it through the hole from back to front. Adjust the stick so that equal lengths poke out on either side of the sign.

6 Tie the twine to both ends of the stick so that you can hang the sign. Display your sign in a prominent place—on a low tree branch or over a tent pole.

BROWN BAG "HIDE"

This paper bag "hide" almost looks and feels like the real thing.

1. Open up a large paper grocery bag. Tear it along one side until you reach the bottom. Now tear off and discard the rectangle that forms the bag's bottom. You now have a large sheet left over. (Don't worry about keeping the edge straight—it looks better if it's a little messy.)

2. Crumple the sheet into a ball. Really smush it. Beat it up. (But try not to rip it.)

3. Smooth out the sheet.

4. Repeat Steps 2 and 3 until the sheet is wrinkly all over and feels soft and flexible, about 8 times.

5. Now the sheet will be easy to tear, so you can rip it into any shape you like.

Campsite Pictographs

What You Need

Large, smooth, flat rocks or a smooth rock wall

Nontoxic chalk (white or a variety of colors)

Camera, optional

Your Field Journal (page 200) and a pencil, optional

In the American Southwest, there are hundreds of sites where the early Pueblo people carved or painted symbols into the walls of canyons, cliffs, and caves. These images—some created more than 3,000 years ago—are called petroglyphs (when carved) and pictographs (when painted). They include symbols of deer, buffalo, humans, lizards, the sun, even water, and their meaning is complex. Some images are historical, depicting specific events, others are spiritual and ceremonial.

You can make pictographs to tell your own story or to create your own sacred space around camp. Make up your own symbols, or use some from page 262.

Ancient pictographs were carved or painted, but you should use chalk when creating yours, so they will eventually wash away in the rain, leaving your campsite clean.

These ancient rock carvings were found in Petrified Forest National Park in Arizona.

What You Do

1 Design your own pictograph symbols or use the ones in Worth a Thousand Words, pages 262 to 263. To come up with your own, think about what is meaningful to you and your family or fellow campers. Have you seen memorable things on your trip? What designs might represent what you've seen? Do you have a special pet, sport, activity, or book that you cherish? If you want to convey a feeling or idea, you could use a picture of the sun to mean energy and light; a star to indicate distance, travel, and wishes; or a spiral to mean truth or the passage of time. Specific animals can also represent certain qualities (for example, a bear could be strength, a snail could be patience, a wolf could be wisdom). Use your imagination to come up with symbols that mean something to you.

2 Use the chalk to draw your images on the rocks. You can arrange the images in a line or telling a story, as a paneled cartoon. If you want to decorate the rock with symbols, choose your own design.

3 Since the chalk will eventually wash away, you may want to take pictures or copy the images into your Field Journal so you can bring home a memento of your work.

Try This! *If you want to make portable pocket pictographs, find small, smooth pebbles and draw your symbol(s) on them in permanent marker. You can keep them in your pocket as a reminder of your adventure.*

Worth a Thousand Words

It's true what they say: A picture's worth a thousand words. All images have some meaning, whether they tell a story or convey an emotion.

This design is a form of the Hopi *nakwách* symbol. The interlacing lines represent friendship.

The hunched flute player, Kokopelli, is a common symbol seen throughout the Southwest. In his flute he carries music of warmth and love. *Koko* means "wood;" *pelli* (or *pilau*) means "hump."

The handprint is believed to have several sacred meanings. Placed next to another symbol such as clouds, it was a prayer for rain. It was also used as a signature.

The tree symbolizes life.

Many rock paintings depict animals. This is a squirrel.

This is a form of the Mother Earth symbol. It can be used to represent birth and motherhood.

Wavy lines indicate water.

The turtle symbolizes courage, patience, and strength.

The thunderbird is a sacred bird that brings rain.

The spiral represents a journey.

Native Language

In America, many place names incorporate American Indian words. There are many American Indian tribes and languages—the terms below are just a small sample. Can you incorporate any of these into your Smash Berry Camp Sign?

ooljee: moon (Navajo)

mapiya: sky (Sioux)

abina: outdoor camp (Choctaw)

apelka: laughter (Creek)

oske: rain (Seminole)

wasa: far, distant (Ojibwa)

cola: friend (Lakota)

heecha: owl (Lakota)

ina: mother (Lakota)

iyotake: sitting (Lakota)

mato: bear (Lakota)

shunkaha: wolf (Lakota)

wicasa: man (Lakota)

giannahtah: always ready (Apache)

golinka: skunk (Apache)

inju: good (Apache)

Simple Rock Sculpture

What You Need

A bunch of fist-size flat rocks of different shapes and colors (the number depends on what you build with them)

Open space to make your sculpture

Beaches and riverbanks are great places to find interesting rocks. The moving water rounds off the rocks' hard edges, leaving them smooth—perfect for gathering, for gazing, and for making interesting sculptures.

This activity will give you some ideas, but feel free to play around with your own.

What You Do

1 Choose rocks of different shapes and colors. Some rocks will be a single color, others will be flecked with different colored crystals or striped with another type of rock. Pick the rocks that appeal to you (be careful not to disturb the habitats of any creatures living nearby).

2 Make a sculpture from the rocks you found. Do this in a space that doesn't get too much traffic, so you can leave your sculpture there without worrying that it will get knocked over or kicked around. Here are a few ideas:

● Try stacking rocks into short columns to mark the entrance to your campsite.

● Make a rock spiral on the beach or around your campfire. Make a really small one out of pebbles and a much larger one out of bigger rocks.

● "Draw" a meaningful symbol with rocks of the same color. (See Worth a Thousand Words, page 262, for symbol suggestions.)

● Place rocks next to one another to spell out the name of your camp or to leave messages for your friends and family.

● Build houses or structures out of long, flat rocks by pressing their sides into the dirt and balancing other rocks across the tops.

● Create your own sculpture garden. Lay down a long, winding path that runs through your campsite. Maybe it ends at the stream, or a nearby field of wildflowers. Place smaller sculptures along the way so people can follow the path and discover your creations as they go.

Berry Ink Winter Count

What You Need

2 handfuls of fresh berries (blueberries, huckleberries, and blackberries work well)

A small plastic container with a lid (see Note)

A spoon

Water

A Brown Bag "Hide" (page 259)—keep the bottom of the bag for testing the ink

A skinny stick or a feather with a pointed tip

Note: *If you have different colored berries, you may want to make different color inks in separate containers.*

For thousands of years people have drawn pictures to record history. In the past, pictures were often drawn on animal hides using inks created from natural materials like flowers, leaves, and berries.

In the American Indian tradition, these picture stories were called "winter counts," so named because they recorded the events from the first snowfall of one year to the first snowfall of the next. Winter counts often included images of momentous events such as meteor showers, feasts, and visiting tribes—they documented the community's shared experiences.

The experiences you have when you go camping are special. There may be firsts—like catching a fish, spotting an eagle, or hiking up a mountain. There also may be events you'd like to forget, like being chomped on by mosquitoes, getting a sunburn, or dropping your marshmallow into the fire. You may want to remember a beautiful sunset, shooting stars, or a swim in a crystal-clear lake.

In this activity you'll create your own version of a winter count and record the fun, funny, memorable events from your camping trip.

What You Do

1 Make the ink. Pour the berries into a container and squash them well with the spoon. Add water, a teaspoonful at a time, to thin out the berry juice ink a bit. (After adding each teaspoon of water, test the ink on the bottom of the brown bag to make sure it's not too thick; add another teaspoon of water if needed.)

2 Gather information about your camping trip. Who is with you? Where did you go on your trip? Describe your campsite. Have there been any firsts? What made you laugh? What amazed you? Talk about your trip with your friends and family, collecting their favorite stories about the experiences you have shared. Decide how you'll represent the information you gathered. Will you draw scenes of various events? Will you draw a picture of each person who is with you? Will you show the tents you slept in and the lake they're next to?

3 Make the winter count. Dip the pointed stick or feather tip into the ink and start drawing and writing on the hide.

4 Let your winter count dry completely (at least 1 hour). Share it with your group, and let other people add to it if you like. When it's totally done, let it dry again and then roll it up to take home.

Camping Activity

Tiny Eco-Houses

What You Need

A collection of natural found objects: twigs, bark, pinecones, leaves, seeds, grasses, and pebbles (see right)

A flat spot with soft ground in a quiet, tucked-away location

These teeny-tiny houses are fun to make, and when you pack up camp, you leave behind a fantastic treasure for someone else to discover. Before you get started, think about who would live in your little house. Would you live there if you got zapped by an incredible shrinking machine? Is it a home for a family of mice, or a group of wood sprites? Make your house as simple or as elaborate as you like. Collect twigs, leaves, pebbles, pinecones, and other stuff you find along the trail or forest floor. The object is to make your house look as much a part of the natural surroundings as possible.

There are no wrong answers when it comes to making tiny eco-houses, but you'll need some basics: specifically, walls and a roof. When building walls, try to use similar-sized objects (all twigs should all be about the same height and width, all stones should be roughly the same shape). There are a few different ways to build walls and roofs, but you can combine types to create a bunch of unique designs—no two tiny houses are alike! When you're done setting up the house, don't forget to decorate the outside with bushes, a path, and anything else you can think of.

What You Do

 Build the walls (choose one of the following wall types):

STOCKADE WALLS: These look kind of like a picket fence, in which the pickets are touching. Poke twigs into the ground one after the other so they touch and are pushed in to the same height (see Figure 1). This is your first wall. At a right angle to the first wall, poke an equal number of twigs into the ground, again at the same height. This is your second wall (see Figure 2). Continue poking the sticks into the ground until you've built 4 walls of equal height and width (see Figure 3 and Figure 4).

Figure 1.

Figure 2.

Figure 3.

Figure 4.

BARK WALLS: Poke 4 equal-size slabs of bark into the ground. Make sure they're the same height and width. You could also use just 2 pieces of bark, and lean them together to make an A-frame house (without a roof).

ROCK WALLS: Lay flat rocks in a small square. Layer on more flat rocks until you have walls that are as high as they are wide. Try to make the walls even in height.

continued on next page

Tiny Eco-Houses, contd.

LOG CABIN–STYLE WALLS: Lay down 2 twigs of equal length 2 to 3 inches apart (see Figure 1). Lay 2 more twigs of equal length across the bottom of the first twigs to make a square (the second set of twigs should be on top of the first, see Figure 2). Now layer 2 sticks across the bottoms of the sticks you've just put down. Continue in this way, laying 2 sticks across the sticks in the previous layer, until you have the walls of a house (see Figure 3). If you like, you can gently smear mud over the sticks as you build higher—it will help keep the walls together.

2 Put on the roof: Place a layer of twigs about the same length as the walls are wide across the top of the walls. You can decorate it with leaves, moss, or long grasses. You can also try propping pieces of bark against each other to make a pointy roof.

3 Decorate the outside: Ball up pieces of moss or clusters of grass to make bushes to place in front of the tiny house. Create a front door by propping a leaf, flat pebble, or piece of bark against one wall. Build a pathway to the door by laying down pebbles or bark pieces in a line or use coarse sand to make a "gravel" driveway. Use your imagination—the possibilities are endless!

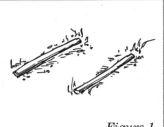

Figure 1.

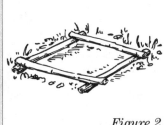

Figure 2.

Figure 3.

Fluttery Fishes

Gather a handful of interesting leaves (watch out for poisonous ones, though; see page 237) and turn them into a school of fish. All you need is some water and a flat surface.

What You Need

A collection of leaves in different shapes, sizes, and colors

A small pot of water

A flat surface, such as a car window, picnic table, or the side of your tent

White glue (optional)

Paper (optional)

What You Do

1. Look through the leaves for fishy shapes: pointy maple or aspen leaf fins, ferny fish tails, spearlike leaves for sea star arms, or wavy leaves for octopus legs.

2. Choose a fish body and fins. Lay them out flat so you can see what the fish will look like.

3. Dip the leaves in the water. This will make them sort of sticky and will keep them from blowing away when you make your picture.

4. Press the wet leaves onto a window, tent wall, or table to make your design— the leaves will stick.

5. When the leaves dry, they will no longer be sticky. If you want to make fish that are more permanent, glue your finned friends, once dry, to a piece of paper.

Rock Bugs

What You Need

A collection of smooth pebbles in different shapes, colors, and sizes (for the body)

A collection of small twigs bent in half, blades of grass, and pine needles (for the legs and antennae)

A collection of leaves in different shapes, colors, and sizes (for the wings)

White glue (see Note)

A flower with fluttery petals (optional)

You can watch bugs all day long—especially when you make them yourself. Create your own insects out of natural materials and pose them around your campsite. Perhaps you'll have guard beetles by the entrance, dragonflies by the campfire, or butterflies that sit gently outside your tent. You'll find some suggested bugs below, but use your imagination to come up with other ideas, too.

What You Do

1 Build the body:

- Dragonfly: Glue a small round rock (the head) to a long skinny rock (the body).

- Beetle: Use a simple oval-shaped rock.

- Ant: Glue together 3 small pebbles, end to end.

- Spider: Glue a small pebble on top of a larger one.

2 Add the legs (put a drop of glue on the end of each leg before tucking it under and pressing it to the rock or rocks):

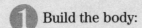

- Dragonfly: Glue 3 short, bent pieces of grass to each side of the long skinny rock (for a total of 6 legs), placing them just below the head.

- Beetle: Glue 3 short stubs of grass or pine needle to each side of the rock (for a total of 6 legs).

- Ant: Glue a short leg to both sides of each pebble (for a total of 6 legs).

- Spider: Bend 8 small twigs in half and glue them to the larger pebble, 4 on one side and 4 on the other.

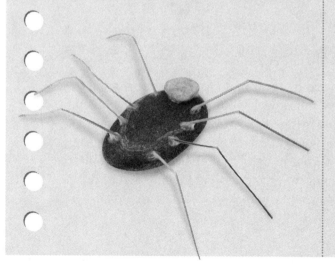

3 Add the wings and antennae:

- Dragonfly: Glue 2 long slender leaves, pointing out to the side, on top of the long skinny rock to make wings. Place them just above the legs. (To turn the dragonfly into a butterfly, substitute a flower with fluttery petals for the leaves—center the flower on the rock and glue it stem-side down)

- Beetle or Ant: Add 2 short pine needles or blades of grass (or small, twisty twigs for a zanier look) to the head to make antennae.

Note: *White glue can take more than an hour to dry, so you'll need to be patient and let your bugs sit still for awhile until the glue hardens. Ask a grown-up to help you prop up the rock pieces so that they continue to touch while the glue is drying.*

Branch Weavings

What You Need

An interesting branch with a fork at the end, about the width of your finger and the length of your forearm

Lightweight string or embroidery thread (long enough to wrap around the fork in the branch at least 5 times)

A collection of leaves, grasses, flowers, bark, shells, feathers—anything cool, pretty, or unusual you come across

White glue

Spiders are amazing weavers. Working between the twigs on a branch and using silk spun directly from their bodies, they create the most intricate and delicate webs. If you look closely at the branches in trees and shrubs, you might be lucky enough to see some spider handiwork.

What do the webs look like? What's caught in them? Some webs contain the most unexpected and beautiful things—brightly colored leaves, bits of grass, water droplets, animal fur, even feathers. You, too, can weave the objects you find around camp into your very own woven keepsake web.

What You Do

1 Sit down and place the long end of the branch between your knees so the forked end points up. Press your knees together to hold the branch steady. (If you prefer, you can poke the end of the stick in the ground or secure it under a big rock on a picnic table.) Wrap one end of the string around the left side of the branch's fork, where the fork begins, and tie it in a tight knot.

2 Stretch the string across to the right side of the fork and wrap it around once.

3 Stretch the string back to the left fork and wrap it around the branch above the first wrap you made. (As you wrap back and forth, be careful not to pull the string so tight that you accidentally snap the branch—you want the string to be taut, but not so much so that it starts to bend the branch.)

4 Continue to wrap and stretch the string, moving up toward the tips of the forked branch, until you get to 1 inch from the end of the branch. Use an overhand knot (page 105) to tie the string to the branch.

5 Weave your collected materials up and down, going over one string and under one, and so on. You can place feathers, leaves, grasses, seeds, mosses, and sticks in your web by weaving them in between the strands of your loom.

6 Use a dab of glue here and there to secure the items in your weaving so they won't fly out the window on the car ride home.

Weave interesting objects into your branch web and you'll have a fantastic memento of your trip.

Sand Paintings

What You Need

Different colors of nontoxic chalk

Sand

Sandpaper

A long, sturdy stick

Posterboard, marker, large gluestick, and a large trash bag (optional, if you want to take your artwork home)

This contemporary Navajo sand painting depicts a medicine man restoring balance to the universe.

The Navajo people of the American Southwest make two kinds of sand paintings. Some are created during sacred ceremonies and are rarely seen by non-Navajos—the completed paintings are destroyed when the ceremony is finished. The second type of sand painting borrows elements from the sacred ceremonies, but is created in a more permanent form so that it can be shared. These artists coat a board with glue and then apply sand and crushed stone to create images and symbols.

If you're camping in the desert or by the beach, you can use sand to make some interesting sand paintings around your campsite. Invent or choose symbols that mean something special to you and your family (see page 262) and surround your site with your own art-on-the-spot. Create your masterpiece out in the open where people can enjoy it before nature washes it away, or use glue and paper to make something more long-lasting that you can tote home.

What You Do

1 Decide which colors to use and set those pieces of chalk aside.

2 Create a small pile of sand for each color you want to make. For each color, rub the chalk on the sandpaper, holding the sandpaper over the pile so the colored chalk dust falls on it. Stir the dust in with the stick to make the color uniform. Repeat with the rest of the colors.

3 Choose the symbols you'll use in your sand painting. Maybe you want your painting to bring good luck. What symbols seem lucky to you?

Are there letters or numbers that mean something to you and your family? Experiment with geometric shapes: A circle could mean the sun or the moon; a square could mean home; a triangle could be your tent. Think up freeform shapes: A wavy line could be water or change; a spiral could be life; a bird could be freedom.

4 Think about how to arrange your symbols. You could tell a story with a cartoonlike panel, create a big square with small symbols inside, or "draw" individual symbols with other shapes around them. Use your imagination—it's up to you!

continued on next page

Sand Paintings, contd.

 Create your painting.

To make an in-camp-only sand painting:

- Clear a flat space for the painting (a patch of dirt works well). Choose a place away from foot traffic (and other traffic, for that matter) that doesn't get too much activity.

- Draw your design in the sand with the stick.

- Pick up a small handful of sand and slowly drizzle it over your design, filling in the spaces. Repeat with the other colors until you're happy with your artwork.

To make a take-home sand painting:

- Place the cardboard on a table or flat surface and use a marker to draw your design on the board.

- If your design covers the whole board, use the glue stick to coat the board with a layer of glue (otherwise just coat the parts of the design that you want to fill in).

- Pick up the sand in small handfuls and slowly drizzle it over the glue-coated areas to fill in the spaces. (You'll want to do this kind of quickly so the glue doesn't start to dry out.)

- Let the glue dry completely before moving the board, at least 1 hour. When it's dry, tip the board gently and blow on it to remove the excess sand. Carefully wrap the board in the trash bag and store it flat to transport it home.

Tree Bark Rubbings

Bark is a tree's protective skin. It keeps bugs out and water in. But it's more than just that: It's really cool to look at. Tree bark comes in a wild variety of colors and textures. Some barks are smooth, some rough, some flaky, and some even shaggy or scaly. Bark is so beautiful and interesting, why not start a bark collection? Well, that'd be great for you, but not so nice for the tree. Since you never want to peel bark from a living tree (it would hurt the tree), you can collect the textures by making bark rubbings.

What You Need

Trees with interesting bark

Masking tape

White or construction paper

A crayon (or an assortment of crayons) with the paper wrapping removed

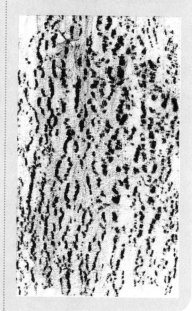

What You Do

1. Find an interesting section of bark about eye-level on a tree and tape your paper in place.

2. Using the side of your crayon, gently rub in an up-and-down motion until you see the bark's pattern emerge. The flat side of the crayon will only make marks from the highest parts of the bark, giving you a really cool image. Experiment with different textures and crayon colors.

3. You can use finished rubbings as placemats or tape them together to make awesome gift wrap.

Seed and Petal Pictures

What You Need

A variety of seeds, bark pieces, pebbles, fallen flower petals, dried leaves, sand, dirt, twigs, and other natural found objects

A flat patch of dirt

A long, sturdy stick

2 long sticks of equal length and width

2 slightly shorter sticks of equal length and width

A small bunch of tiny twigs or pebbles, for signing your picture

You can decorate your campsite with a really cool seed-and-petal picture, and then, when you break camp, you can leave it behind for someone else to discover and enjoy.

What You Do

1 Organize your objects into piles according to texture or color.

2 Decide what kind of picture you want to make. You will be using the objects to give the picture color and texture, and to separate areas from each other. For example, if you make a flower, you may choose to use pink pebbles for the petals, yellow dandelion heads for the round center, and a line of leaves for the stem. Use your imagination to come up with an image you'd like to draw—maybe it's a plant, animal, or person. Here are some ideas to get you started:

- An abstract geometric design
- An animal or plant
- A landscape or scene
- Someone's portrait

3 Create your "canvas" by drawing a rectangle in the dirt with a stick.

4 Use the stick to draw a picture on your canvas. (You may want to keep the shapes large so it's easier to fill them in with the found objects.)

5 Fill in your picture with seeds, pebbles, leaves, flower petals, shells, and other found objects. Group the objects according to color to create larger sections, or alternate colors and textures to get different effects. Play around with the stuff you found and see what works for you!

6 After you're done, frame your picture by placing the 4 long sticks around the edges.

7 Sign your artwork by writing your name with the tiny pebbles or twigs.

BY JIM

ALWAYS TELL YOUR GROWN-UPS where you're going before you head off on your own to find neat stuff for your projects. Adults tend to worry when they don't know where you are!

So Cool Seed Jewelry

What You Need

A collection of seeds, cones, pods, nuts, and dried beans and corn kernels in all different shapes, colors, and sizes

A pot of hot water

Paper towels

Embroidery thread

An embroidery needle

Scissors

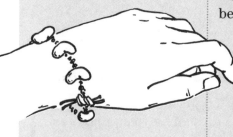

Human beings have always made beautiful jewelry out of the natural objects around them—pebbles, shells, pine needles, animal bones and teeth, seeds, even porcupine quills (not to mention metals and clay). You can make some amazing natural jewelry, too.

Plant seeds and pods can make really neat beads—from pine cones to maple tree "helicopter" seeds to corn kernels and acorns. Dried beans work very well, too. Hunt around for a few you like, string 'em up, and adorn yourself.

What You Do

1 Pods and other hollow beads should be easy to thread, but dried beans, kernels, and seeds need to be softened.

- For dried beans like black, pinto, kidney, and fava, as well as kernels of Indian corn: Soak overnight in the pot of hot water.

- For fresh seeds such as sunflower, squash, or pumpkin: Soak in hot water for about 20 minutes. Have an adult test the seeds; they are ready when you can poke a needle through the center.

2 Drain the beads on the paper towels and pat dry.

3 For a necklace, make a loose loop around your neck with the embroidery thread (it should be big enough to slip over your head). For a bracelet, make a slightly loose loop around your wrist; for an anklet, make a slightly loose loop around your ankle. Once you have your length, add 2 inches to it and double that entire length.

4 Get your grown-up to help thread the needle. Pull the thread through the hole halfway and knot the two ends together (tie the knot about 1 inch from the ends).

5 If you like, figure out a pattern for your jewelry by arranging the beads on a flat surface before you start. (But if you'd rather just figure it out as you go along, that's fine, too.)

6 Working one by one, poke the needle through the center of the beads and string them onto the thread. If you want to space the beads apart, tie a knot after each before stringing on the next, or put a small bead (or a bunch of small beads) between larger beads. Leave enough room to tie the open end of the thread to the knotted end, about 2 inches.

7 Tie a knot after the last bead and cut off the needle.

8 Let your jewelry dry in a sunny spot for a day or two. Tie the ends of the necklace together using a square knot (see page 102). For the bracelet or anklet, have a buddy wrap it around your wrist or ankle and tie the ends in a square knot.

Camping Activity

Rockin' Rock Necklace

What You Need

Scissors

Rubber, leather, or plastic cord, for stringing around your neck

Waterproof glue (such as Krazy Glue)

24 or 26 gauge wire (available at craft or hardware stores)

A small, smooth rock

Nail clippers

A pencil

Y ou can use small round stones to make one-of-a-kind necklaces for friends and family. Stones carry the power of place with them. Wearing a necklace with a stone from a memorable campout can bring you good vibes all year.

What You Do

 Cut a piece of cord as long as you want your necklace to be (it looks good worn high up on the neck, like a choker). Now add 2 inches so you'll have room to tie a knot.

2 Find the midpoint of the cord.

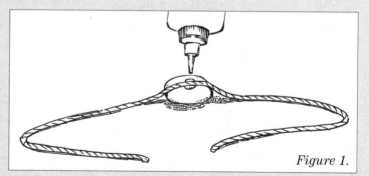

Figure 1.

3 Place a small dot of glue in the center of the rock and glue it to the midpoint of the cord (see Figure 1). Wait for the glue to dry.

4 Place one end of the wire against the cord and the back of the stone; one end of the wire should point down below the cord/rock by ½ inch and the rest of the wire should point up.

5 Holding the stone and the cord together, tightly wrap the wire around the middle of the stone in a vertical direction, until you reach the back of the stone again. Wrap the stone 4 more times (see Figure 2).

6 After the last wrap, bring the wire to the back of the stone and, leaving a ½ inch end, snip it with the nail clippers. Twist the new ½ inch end around the first ½ inch end so the wire doesn't unwrap (see Figure 3).

7 Ask an adult to place a small dot of glue on the wire ends and tuck them under the cord so they won't scrape your skin (see Figure 4). Dot the glue on the back of the rock where the edges of the cord and wrapped wire touch the rock.

8 Set the necklace on a flat surface and let the glue dry completely.

9 Wrap the cord around your neck and tie the ends together with a square knot (see page 102). (You may need someone else's help for this.)

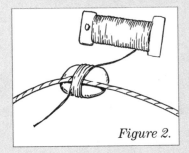

Figure 2.

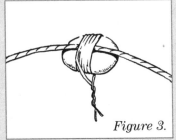

Figure 3.

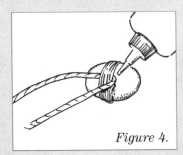

Figure 4.

Groovy Grass Bracelet

What You Need

A small, 3-foot-long bunch of tall grasses (about pinky-finger-width)

A pot of water

Paper towels

Twisted together, the golds, greens, and tans of dried grasses make an awesome ornament for your wrist. Soak the grasses in the evening, and they'll be ready for braiding by morning.

What You Do

1 Soak the grasses in the pot of water overnight; this will make them supple and easy to work with.

2 The next day, retrieve the grasses from the pot and let them drain on paper towels. Gather the grasses together in a bunch, making sure one end of the bunch is even.

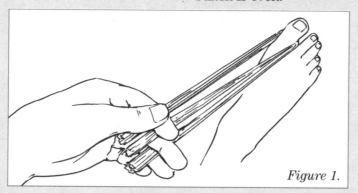

Figure 1.

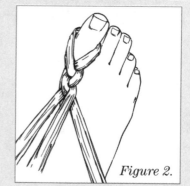

Figure 2.

3 Find the midpoint and fold the whole bunch in half.

4 Hook the loop you've just made around your big toe (Figure 1) and separate the grasses into 3 equal groups (as you would when braiding hair).

5 Start to braid by placing the right bunch over the center bunch, then wrapping the left bunch over the new center bunch (see Figure 2). Alternate wrapping left over center and right over center until you get a braid long enough to wrap around your wrist loosely. Make sure at least 2 inches of unbraided grasses remain at the end.

6 Take the loop off your toe—it will help secure the bracelet to your wrist. With a buddy's help, wrap the bracelet around your wrist and thread the unbraided ends of grass through the loop (Figure 3). Pull these ends back toward the braid to tighten the bracelet a bit, and then tie them to the braid to secure the bracelet (Figure 4).

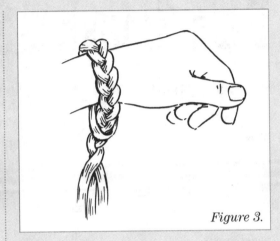

Figure 3.

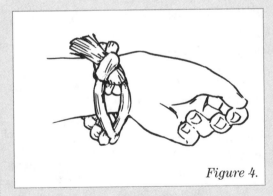

Figure 4.

Camping Activity

Fern Smash T-Shirt

What You Need

Newspaper

A white T-shirt

Cardboard (roughly the width and length of the "body" part of the T-shirt)

Fern leaves (see Note)

Paper towels

A hammer

A plastic shopping bag

A clothes dryer (when you get home)

Note: *This works best with fresh leaves, so to be mindful of the environment, only gather a few and be sure to take them from different plants, each of which has many more leaves.*

Chlorophyll, the chemical that makes grass and other plants green, is a great stain-maker—so why not go with the flow? Smash some ferns, and the chlorophyll they ooze will dye your T-shirt with cool leafy shapes.

What You Do

1. Spread a layer of newspaper on a flat surface. Place the T-shirt on the newspaper.

2. Slide the cardboard inside the T-shirt; it will prevent the fern stains from soaking through to the back of the shirt.

3. Place the fern leaves facedown on your shirt in whatever design you like.

4. Place a couple of paper towels over the ferns.

5. Carefully hammer on top of the paper towels and ferns. Make sure you hit every part of your design, or the whole thing won't show up on the T-shirt.

6 Remove the paper towels slowly and gently lift the ferns off the T-shirt.

7 Lift the newspaper with the T-shirt on top, move it to a shady spot (sunlight will fade the design), and let the shirt dry. Wrap it loosely in the plastic bag.

8 When you get home, toss the shirt in the dryer for 10 minutes to set the design.

Try this: *Many types of plants will stain a white shirt when you smash them. Look for interesting leaves and flowers and create your own designs, following the steps above.*

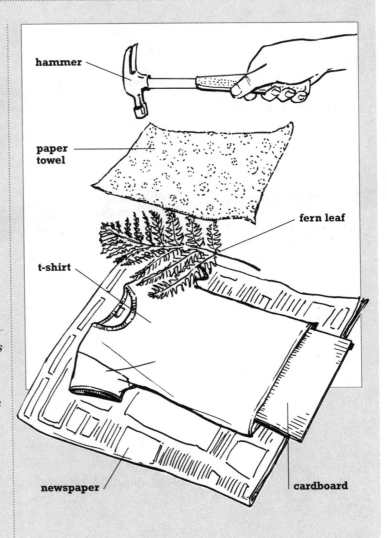

hammer

paper towel

fern leaf

t-shirt

newspaper

cardboard

Leaf Printing

What You Need

Paper in different sizes

An assortment of leaves

A paintbrush

Paint (tempera or acrylic works well)

A cup of water, to wash the brush

Your Field Journal (page 200), pen or pencil

Make nifty nature-inspired note cards, wrapping paper, and T-shirts for your friends back home, or cut out leafy shapes and paste them into your Field Journal.

What You Do

1 Place the paper on a table or flat surface.

2 Lay the leaves on the paper underside up (so you can see the veins).

3 Use the paintbrush to coat the underside of the leaves with any color or combination of colors you choose. If you're switching colors, swish the brush in the water between colors.

4 Turn the leaves paint-side down and use your finger to press them on the paper. Press over every inch of the leaf.

5 Carefully peel the leaf away from the paper.

6 Let the paint dry, about 30 minutes.

7 Cut the leaf shapes out and glue them into your Field Journal. You can also use the leaves in other ways:

- Make a card by folding the paper in half with the image on the cover.

- Make wrapping paper—use a larger sheet of plain paper and make leaf prints all over.

- Use fabric paint instead of acrylic or tempera and print your leaves on a T-shirt (see page 288 for directions on how to set up the shirt).

Leaf Stencil Tablecloth

What You Need

Flat leaves in various shapes and sizes

A paper tablecloth or large sheet of butcher paper (see Note)

4 medium-size rocks

Tempera or poster paints (see Note)

Paper plates (1 for each color of paint)

A small kitchen sponge, cut up into 2 inch squares

An old toothbrush (optional)

Use leaves to make a beautifully stenciled tablecloth (which you can cut into placemats, if you prefer). By painting around carefully placed leaves, you'll have cool blobs of color all over, with outlines of leafy shapes in the center. This project is best done in the backyard or at a campsite with a picnic table—somewhere you can spread out. It's a little tougher as a backwoods project.

What You Do

1. Open up the tablecloth or spread out the piece of paper, laying it flat on the table or ground. Place the rocks on the corners to hold the tablecloth or paper down.

2. Set out the paints in separate plates. You can use an extra plate for mixing colors together.

3. Decide how you want your tablecloth to look. You can make a border of leaves around the outside, invent a pattern for the entire cloth, mix leaves of different shapes and colors to create a random look, or come up with a design all your own. Try using different colors for each type of leaf.

4 Position a leaf on the paper.

5 Take a sponge square and dip it in the paint. Gently dab all around the outside of the leaf.

6 When you're done, lift up the leaf. You should have a perfect leaf shape.

7 Repeat steps 4 through 6 with different leaves and paints until you have decorated the surface with leafy shapes.

8 If you like, use an old toothbrush to splatter paint across the paper. Dip the brush into paint and rub your thumb quickly across the bristles to splatter the paint all around the leaves.

9 Let the paint dry, about 30 minutes to 1 hour. Your tablecloth is good to go!

Note: *If you want a longer-lasting tablecloth, use fabric paints on a white cotton tablecloth. Follow the directions on the paint package to set the design.*

Spore Prints

What You Need

A fern leaf or store-bought mushroom, such as Portabello, stem removed

A few sheets of paper, both black and white

A plastic tub or large bowl (big enough to fit over the fern or mushroom)

Hairspray (see Note)

Note: *If you want to bring your print home, spray it with hairspray to set the spores. Let the hairspray dry, and wrap the print in newspaper. When you get home, cover the print with another piece of paper and place it at the bottom of a trunk, box, or other flat-bottomed container so that it doesn't get smushed.*

Many plants reproduce by making flowers and seeds, but some—like ferns and mushrooms—don't flower at all. They make tiny cells called spores (for more on spores, see page 229). To see them without a microscope, you can make a spore print, which you can use to dress up your tent or bedroom walls!

In midsummer, many wild ferns have tiny red-brown circles on their undersides that are packed with spores. These leaves are perfect for printing. If you find leaves that *don't* have these dusty rust-colored dots, you can still make a print—but not with that fern. Use a store-bought Portabello mushroom instead.

What You Do

1 Put the fern on a piece of paper bottom-side down; if you're using a mushroom, place it gill-side down. Depending on the type of fern or mushroom, black paper might work better than white. Try both if you like. Place the tub or bowl over the fern or mushroom and paper. (It will seal in the moisture, allowing the leaf or mushroom cap to release its spores.)

2 Leave the fern or mushroom cap in place overnight. It will release its mature spores, and they will fall onto the paper.

3 In the morning, lift up the tub and fern or mushroom. You should have a beautiful print made out of spores!

Spore prints are used in many mushroom handbooks to help readers identify different types of mushrooms.

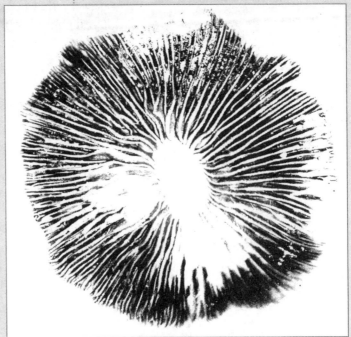

Pinecone Bird Bistro

What You Need

A good strong pinecone, the biggest one that will fit in your hand

Twine or sturdy string

2 cups bird seed

A paper plate

A plastic knife

Smooth peanut butter

What do you get when you combine a pinecone, a little peanut butter, and some bird seed? A feast for your feathered friends. Make this bird feeder and hang it from a high branch, then watch the birds come flocking.

You can try this project in your backyard or at the park, but you should probably skip it at a campsite or in the backwoods (you don't want to invite any curious raccoons or bears to your camp at night).

What You Do

1 Tie one end of the string around the top of the pinecone, about two sections down.

2 Sprinkle the bird seed on the plate.

3 Use the knife to spread a thick coat of peanut butter all over the pinecone. Make sure to stuff peanut butter into all the cracks and crevices. It won't be pretty, but the birds will think it's very tasty.

4 Roll the peanut-buttered pinecone in the seeds so they stick to the peanut butter and coat the cone.

5 Tie the free end of the string to a branch to hang your culinary creation. Enjoy watching the birds as they flock to your peanut butter pinecone treat.

Sand Candles

What You Need

A trowel or large spoon

A small shell (optional)

Shells, pebbles, sea glass, and/or driftwood

A candlewick (see Note)

Scissors

A sturdy 1-foot-long stick

A medium-size pebble

2 cups paraffin wax chunks (see Note) or old candle chunks

A camp stove

A saucepan

A tin soup can, label removed

Oven mitts

Note: *Candlewicks and paraffin wax are available at crafts stores.*

Misty, cool summer days on the beach when the fog rolls in are the best days to wander the shore exploring tide pools, collecting shells, and making sand candles. You can use your candles at camp, or save them to light up a wintry night with summer camping memories.

What You Do

Prepare the sand:

1 Select a spot on the beach that's away from foot traffic. The sand should be damp but not drenched. Avoid areas right near the shore where the tide could swamp you and your project.

2 Use the trowel or spoon to dig a hole approximately the size and shape of the soup can (or smaller).

3 Use the shell or your fingers to scrape down and flatten the bottom of the hole. (This is the part of the finished candle that will sit on the table surface.)

4 If you like, line the sides of the hole with a layer or scattering of shells, pebbles, sea glass, and/or driftwood. Press the objects into the sand so they stick.

5 Measure the candle-wick from the bottom of the hole to the top. Add about 6 inches to the length and cut the wick with the scissors.

6 Tie one end of the wick to the stick and dangle the other end down into the hole. Lay the stick across the hole so the wick is centered in the hole. Pin the end of the wick to the bottom of the hole with the medium-size pebble, pressing the pebble into the sand to keep the wick taut.

Prepare the wax:

7 Set up the camp stove near the hole. Put the saucepan on the stove. Place the wax in the tin can and put the can in the saucepan. Pour water into the saucepan to come halfway up the side of the can (the can shouldn't be submerged).

8 Turn the stove on medium and bring the water to a gentle boil. As the water boils, the wax will melt.

tell your folks!

Sand candles are made with hot wax. Have an adult heat and pour the wax for you and keep an eye on the candles as they cool.

(Wax can catch fire pretty easily, so never put it directly over a flame— always use the boiling water method and keep an eye on it.)

9 Once the wax has melted, carefully remove the saucepan from the heat with the oven mitts.

Make the candle:

10 Have a grown-up gently pour the wax into the hole using oven mitts. Stop pouring when the wax reaches the brim of the hole or runs out.

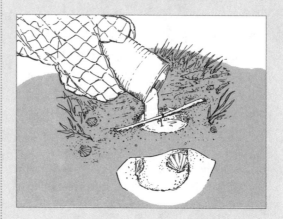

Sand Candles, contd.

11 Let the candle cool for at least 1 hour. Don't leave it alone, because something might disturb it or a curious animal may check it out and burn its nose. The candle is cool enough when the top is hard in the center.

12 Gently dig up the candle with your hands and carefully brush off the loose sand. You want to keep some sand intact along with the shells and other decorations you used.

13 Snip the wick about a quarter inch from the top of the candle. Enjoy! (But remember—never burn a candle without a grown-up around.)

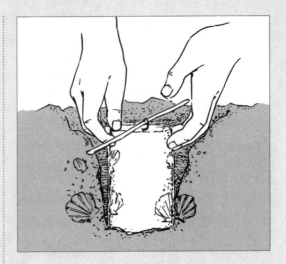

Sand Candles at Home: If it's too rainy or crowded to make a sand candle at the beach or campsite, bring home some decorations (shells, pebbles, wood, etc.) and sand (or buy sand at a hardware store), and make the candles at home.

Spread out some newspaper on a table, place the sand in a bucket, moisten the sand with a water mister, and follow the instructions from Step 2 on.

CHAPTER 9

LETTING LOOSE

Campout Fun and Games

O nce you're all hiked and biked and canoed out, it's time to cut loose. In this chapter you'll find all sorts of games to help you liven things up: active games and quiet games, games for groups and games for two, car games and camp games, silly games and serious games, games for day and games for night, brain games and brawn games. But enough about games already! There are cool shadow

animals and creepy ghost stories, too. So read on and prepare yourself—you're about to have some serious fun.

GREAT GAMES FOR THE CAR

You're in the backseat, on the way to the campsite, but the ride goes on and on and on. Mile after mile, the minutes drag. You twitch. You fidget. You ask "How much longer?" in the most nasal whine you can muster. And still only five minutes pass. Well, fidget no more! These games will make even the longest car trips zip along.

They are designed with everyone in mind. You can involve the whole car (though you might want to leave the driver alone), or just enlist your backseat pal. With some minor tweaks, you can even play the games on your own. Keep score if you want, and eliminate players or assign penalties. Set time limits, or check the odometer to use distance—a number of miles—to signal the end of a game.

The ABC Game

Look for something that begins with the letter A. You can look at the scenery, or use signs, billboards, and even license plates. Once you get something with the letter A (such as automobile, antenna, or apple tree) move on to B, and so forth—until you make your way through the alphabet. You can all play at the same time or take turns.

Going on Safari

In this game, a player starts with the letter A and says: "I'm going on safari and I'm taking an . . ." The player says something that starts with the letter A (let's say apple). The next player repeats the line with the first player's object and then adds one beginning with B. "I'm going on safari and I'm taking an apple and a bench." The third player repeats the previous two items and adds a C item. The game goes on as all players recite the entire list alphabetically, adding an item beginning with the next letter. Anyone who makes a mistake or can't come up with the name of a new object is out. The surviving player wins.

Destination

This game is a bit harder. Players start with the letter A and then make up sentences that have a destination, a mode of transportation, and an activity that all begin with that letter. For example:

I'm going to **Alabama** on an **Alligator** to **Anchor** a boat.

The next player has B—I'm going to **Bavaria** on a **Bus** to **Buy** a hat—and it goes on from there through the alphabet. If you can't think of three things for each letter, you're out. The game ends when everyone's stumped.

Want to make it harder? Add a time limit for each sentence. If you can't do it when the time runs out, you're out.

The Minister's Cat

This is an oldie but goodie. Players take turns coming up with adjectives to describe the minister's cat, starting with A. "The minister's cat is an (angry) cat." The next player repeats the sentence with a B word, and the play progresses through the alphabet. Want to make it harder? Set a time limit. Everyone claps as they chant, and you have to come up with your word in time or you're out.

For a variation, all players can come up with A words until one is repeated or a player can't come up with a new word. Then the game goes to B.

A, My Name Is Annie

Starting with A, players describe a person, that person's friend, where they are both from, and what they're selling. For example:

A, my name is Annie, my friend's name is Alex, we come from Alaska, and we're here to sell you apples.

The next player starts with B. If you can't come up with a sentence, you're out.

Want to make it harder? Play in rounds where all players first have to come up with an A sentence before going on to B. No repeating!

License Plate Bingo

You'll need paper and pencils for this game. Make a bingo card by drawing a grid of five boxes across and five boxes down. Fill the boxes with letters from the alphabet—either in order or at random. Put the Z in the center box along with whatever letter is already there (there are only 25 boxes, so you have to double up in one in order to fit all 26 letters).

Now look at the license plates around you and check off the letters that you see. When

CAMPGROUND

you get a straight line up, down, across, or diagonal, you win!

Want to make it harder? To win you have to check off all the letters in your bingo card grid!

Guess the Number

One player thinks of a number (between 1 and 1,000). The other players must guess what number it is. The person who is thinking of a number can only say "higher" or "lower," narrowing down the choices until one of the players gets it right. The winner gets to think of the next number.

Bizz, Buzz

This is a counting game. Each player takes turns counting—player one says "1"; player two says "2," etc. But every time a player gets to a number with a 3 in it, they must shout "Bizz!" instead of "3." (That's 3, 13, 23, etc.)

Want to make it harder? Every 3 is a bizz and every 7 is a buzz, so 37 is bizz buzz. If you mess up, you're out.

20 Questions

One player thinks of something—anything: a person, place, or thing. The rest of the players can ask up to 20 questions to figure it out. You can only ask yes/no questions.

I Spy

One player spots something and says, "I spy, with my little eye . . ." something that begins with the letter (you choose the letter). The other players must guess what the object is by asking yes/no questions. The player who guesses correctly gets to spy the next object.

Hum that Tune

One person hums a tune, and the rest of the players have to guess what the song is. The player who guesses the right answer gets to hum next.

You can also play "Draw that Tune." One player draws pictures to describe a song's title or lyrics. The other players have to guess what the song is.

DAYTIME CAMP GAMES

The sun is shining, the birds are singing, and you're itching for something to do. It's time to gather your crew and get your game on!

Give Tag a new twist with Camouflage. Make it a matter of life and death with Predator and Prey, or get jumpy in Hungry Frog. Skip over molten rock in Hot Lava, turn sticks into the banks of raging rivers, and race boats you craft out of leaves and twigs. Or compete in the Crazy Olympics—test your mettle to win a medal in seed spitting, eight-legged spider races, pass the orange, pinecone jog, and other wacky events.

Whether you're hanging out in camp, or you're out and about hiking and exploring, *you've* got game!

Camouflage!

A fun game to play on any hike.

What You Need

✔ **3 or more players**

✔ **A wooded area**

What You Do

1. One person gets to be "It."

2. It yells "Camouflage," closes his or her eyes, and counts to 50.

3. Everyone else hides. Each player must find a spot from which they can still see It but are invisible—camouflaged, in other words.

4. It opens his or her eyes and holds up 1 to 5 fingers. The "camouflaged" players must be able to see the number of fingers (otherwise they hid too well).

5. Remaining in place, It shouts out the name of anyone he spots.

6. The last person to be spotted is the winner . . . as long as they can say how many fingers It was holding up.

Pick Up Twigs

H ere's an outdoor twist on the indoor game Pick Up Sticks.

What You Need

✔ **2 or more players**

✔ **About 20 small, straight sticks (they should be about the same size)**

✔ **A flat area to play, like a picnic table or a clear patch of ground**

What You Do

1. Hold all the sticks in your hand, raise it about 2 feet above the playing area, and drop the sticks in a pile.

2. Take turns picking up the twigs. If you pick up a twig without moving any other twigs, you get to put it in your pile and keep going. If you accidentally bump or move another twig, your turn is over, and the next player goes.

3. Whoever has the most twigs at the end of the game is the winner.

Hot Lava

Imagine the ground is covered with hot lava and you only have small, floating pieces of earth to stand on. Fall off, and you're toast!

What You Need

✔ 1 or more players

✔ Your imagination and some paper plates (and don't forget to clean up afterward)

What You Do

The object of the game is to jump from one piece of land to the next *without* falling into the lava. The paper plates represent safe pieces of land and the ground is a stream of lava.

If you're playing with a group

1. Choose a person to be "It."

2. It chases the other players as they jump from spot to spot. (It can't step in the lava either.)

3. If you get tagged or fall off land, you are out.

4. If It falls off land, everyone is back in again.

5. The last surviving player wins.

6. Make the rounds harder by pushing the plates farther apart.

If you're playing by yourself

1. Jump from spot to spot. If you fall off, start over.

2. If you get good at it, push the paper plates farther apart. Count how many times you can jump without falling in the lava.

Guess What?!

Put your keen detective skills to the test with this tricky two-player game.

What You Need

✔ 2 players

✔ 2 objects

What You Do

1. Players sit back to back.

2. Each player chooses a small object from around camp—making sure that the other player doesn't see what it is.

3. Players take turns asking each other yes/no questions about the object.

4. The first person to guess the other's object wins.

Predator and Prey

What do you get when you mix hide-and-seek, tag, and animal sounds? A howlin' good time!

What You Need

✔ **2 or more players**

What You Do

1. One player is the predator. Everyone else is the prey.

2. The predator closes his or her eyes and counts to 50 while the prey scrambles to hide.

3. While growling and snorting, the predator hunts down and "captures" the prey by tagging them.

4. When people get tagged, they are out.

5. The last of the prey remaining gets to be the next predator.

Nature Hunt

Explore the environment you're camping in while collecting enough natural stuff to win.

What You Need

✔ **2 or more players, plus an adult to act as timekeeper and judge**

✔ **Paper and pencil (1 set per team)**

✔ **Bags (1 per team)**

What You Do

1. Make a list of natural objects to look for, such as pinecones, stones, flowers, and shells. See what's near you. Remember not to pick anything from living plants (or animals for that matter—ouch!); instead, look for things that have already fallen. Some ideas:

● Get fancy with your pinecone selection— different sizes, shapes, or types.

● Raise the difficulty level by requiring the teams to find and identify a few different kinds of leaves (e.g., maple, oak, pine needle, grass blade). Search for leaves that resemble other things—a heart, an oval, your Aunt Mary.

● When hunting for rocks, be specific—do you want large smooth rocks or jagged pebbles? Would you rather discover black rocks with white stripes or white rocks with black spots?

● Find shells of different colors, sizes, and shapes.

● Set out to find a specific number of different types of seeds, including maple helicopters, burrs, berries, pods, and nuts.

2. Divide into teams (if there are only 2 players, each person is his own team).

3. Each team gets a bag and a copy of the list.

4. Set a time limit, say 15 minutes, and decide on the boundaries of the searchable area. (Make sure the grown-ups know where you'll be.)

5. Now get going and try to find the stuff on the list! The team that returns with the most listed items wins.

Mix it up: *If you'd like, the players who don't win can reward the team that does. For example, for one night the other players can wash the winning team's dishes or be their personal s'mores makers. Use your imagination to come up with fun prizes.*

Snapshot Nature Hunt

If you have a digital or Polaroid camera, you can go on a nature scavenger hunt and bring home awesome pics to remind you of the game. The items you list in this game can also be bigger than the ones in Nature Hunt (left), since you don't collect them in a bag—you collect them on your camera, as pictures. If you have more than one camera and a number of players, you can split into teams and compete to see who "collects" all the items first.

What You Need

✔ **2 or more players, plus an adult to act as timekeeper and judge**

✔ **Paper and pencil (1 set per team)**

✔ **A digital or Polaroid camera (1 per team)**

What You Do

1. Make a list of objects to find. Remember, the items can be really big and kind of wacky, since you just need to photograph them, not put them in a bag. Some good items to look for:

- A rock or boulder shaped like an animal
- A pine tree
- Animal tracks or poop
- A bird's nest or egg
- 3 different kinds of birds
- An anthill
- A picnic table with food on it
- Boats on a lake
- A chipmunk
- A natural object that appears to have a face
- Deer
- Someone's undies drying on a line

2. With a grown-up's help decide on a time limit, say 15 to 30 minutes, and set boundaries.

3. Go hunting! Take pics of what you find and cross items off your list as you go. The player or team that collects the most in the time allowed wins.

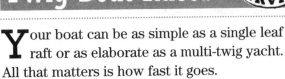

Twig Boat Races

Your boat can be as simple as a single leaf raft or as elaborate as a multi-twig yacht. All that matters is how fast it goes.

What You Need

✔ **2 or more players**

✔ **Leaves, twigs, grass, bark, and/or other found objects**

✔ **A small stream or babbling brook**

What You Do

1. Gather natural materials to create the boats. Stick to objects you find on the ground instead of picking anything off a tree.

Come up with imaginative ways to attach the parts of your boat to each other, make it float, and prevent it from tipping.

You can try:

● Using a flat piece of bark for a base and a leaf and twig for a sail.

● Tying a bunch of sticks together with grass to make a raft.

● Making a frame with 4 sticks tied together at the corners with grass.

● Using a big leaf that floats and placing tiny pebble "sailors" on it.

● Using pebbles to weight the boat and prevent it from tipping over.

2. Get an adult to help make a mark on the bank downstream.

3. Head upstream a few yards and drop your boats in. The race is on!

4. Whoever's boat crosses the finish line first wins.

Hungry Frog

This variation of tag will really get you croaking.

What You Need

✔ **2 or more players**

✔ **A sturdy stick**

What You Do

1. Use the stick to make a big circle in the dirt—about 6 to 7 feet in diameter.

2. Select a person to be the "frog."

3. The frog squats in the middle of the circle.

4. The rest of the players are flies. The flies buzz and run near the frog.

5. If the frog tags a fly—without stepping outside the circle—the fly becomes a frog, enters the circle, and helps to catch other flies.

6. The last fly buzzing becomes the new frog for the next round.

Frog Hop

Prove you have the legs to reign over the frog kingdom by jumping the farthest in this hopping game.

What You Need

✔ **1 or more players**

✔ **2 sticks about the length of your arm**

✔ **Space to jump**

What You Do

1. Place the sticks on the ground, a couple of feet apart.

2. Try to jump from one side to the other.

3. Once all players have jumped, spread the sticks apart a little more.

4. Keep spreading apart the sticks to see how far you can jump. If you don't make it, you're out.

5. The last player left is the Frog Hop champ.

CRAZY OLYMPICS

Come up with a bunch of outdoor "Olympic" events and divide into teams (you can also play with just a few people). Ask a couple of adults to be judges. The events you choose should be safe and practical—but that doesn't mean they can't be totally wack-a-doo silly.

Here are a few suggestions:

Wheelbarrow Races:

In this faster-to-the-finish race, one player is on his hands and knees. The other player grasps the ankles of that player and lifts him up—holding him like a wheelbarrow. The player on the ground walks on his hands as the player behind "pushes" the wheelbarrow.

Count 'em:

Guess the number of pebbles in a pail.

Somersaulting:

Who can somersault across the finish line first?

Leaf Scramble:

Players dash toward the finish line, while balancing a leaf on their head. Whoever crosses first without dropping the leaf wins.

Cheek to Cheek:

In teams of two, place a leaf (make sure it's not poison ivy!) between your cheek and your partner's cheek. Race to the finish without dropping it.

Pinecone Jog:

Players race with a pinecone squeezed between their knees. If they drop it, they have to start over!

Seed Spitting:

Go ahead, play with your food! See who can spit a seed the farthest.

Eight-Legged Spider Races:

Teams of two stand side by side and tie a cord around their waists to connect them, then hurry on all fours to the finish line.

Seashell Grab:

See how many seashells you can pick up from the beach and hold in two hands in a given time limit.

Pebble Stacking:

How high can you go?

Pass the Orange:

Two teams form two straight lines. The first person in each line holds an orange under his chin and passes it to the next person's chin without using his hands. The first team to pass the orange to the end without dropping it wins.

Untie the Human Knot:

One player is "It" and the rest of the players hold hands and tangle themselves. It has to tell people what to do to untangle the human knot.

Awards Ceremony:

Make awards for each event:

● String seeds together for the champion long-distance seed-spitter.

● Tie a pinecone on a string to award the pinecone joggers.

● Make a crown of leaves and dandelions for the winning team.

● Present the winners with bouquets of grass.

NIGHT TIME GAMES

Killer Wink

There's a killer among you, and no one knows who it is. Play this game around a campfire or when it's still a little bit light out.

What You Need

✔ **5 or more players**

✔ **Paper**

✔ **A pen or pencil**

✔ **A hat or container**

As the sun sets and the shadows grow long, crickets, owls, creepers, and peepers fill the air with their songs. Darkness brings a whole new twist to any game, making everything more surprising and suspenseful. Try some of these nighttime favorites and see for yourself!

What You Do

1. Tear a sheet of paper into smaller pieces, one for each player. Draw an ✕ on one piece. Fold up all the pieces and toss them in a cap or a container. Each player selects a piece of paper without letting anyone else see its contents. Whoever selects the ✕ is the "killer."

2. Everyone sits in a circle with their eyes open, carefully looking around. The killer slyly winks at other players to kill them.

3. If you are winked at, you fall over dead (the more drama the better) and are out.

4. While the killer tries to kill off the group, the rest of the players (except the ones who are out) try to avoid getting killed and also try to figure out who the killer is. (This game is tricky because you don't want the killer to look at you and wink, but you need to look around—to see who is looking at whom and who is dying—in order to guess who the killer is.) When you think you know the killer's identity, shout out his name. If you're right, you win. If you're wrong, you're out.

5. Play until the killer is exposed or until everyone is dead.

Ghastly Handshake

This game is like Killer Wink, but you can play it when it's dark, dark, dark. Spooky.

What You Need

✔ **5 or more players**
✔ **Paper**
✔ **A pen or pencil**
✔ **A hat or container**

What You Do

1. Tear a sheet of paper into smaller pieces, one for each player. Draw an ✕ on one piece. Fold up all the pieces and toss them in a cap or a container. Each player selects a piece of paper without letting anyone else see. Whoever selects the ✕ is the "killer."

2. Pick a Ghastly Handshake that only the killer will use, like a tickle on the palm or a pumping squeeze.

3. Wander around, shaking each other's hands.

4. If you get the Ghastly Handshake, shake two more people's hands, and then collapse in a heap—you're out.

5. If you think you know who the killer is, shout out the name. If you're right, you win. If you're wrong, you're out.

6. Play until everyone is either killed or until the killer is discovered.

Bat Tag

Bats are amazing hunters. Many of them use echolocation—or bouncing sound—to find their prey. How well do you think you'd do as a bat? This game is best played while the sun is setting, so it's kind of dark but you can see the ground and avoid tripping over anything.

What You Need

✔ **3 or more players**
✔ **A grassy field**

What You Do

1. Select a player to be the "bat." All other players are "bugs."

2. The bat counts to 50 with eyes closed while the bugs all hide.

3. After 50, the bat opens his or her eyes and emits a peeping sound.

4. When players hear the peep, they peep softly back.

5. The bat runs around trying to find the bugs by peeping and following the echo.

6. When each bug is found it becomes a bat and starts peeping to find other bugs.

7. The game is over when all the bugs are caught.

8. The last bug caught becomes the new bat.

Flashlight Tag 1 and 2

Make sure to set up your playing area before it gets dark. It should be open and free of roots, boulders, and holes—a grassy field is best. A grown-up should set some boundaries, too, so you know how far you can go. This way, when it gets darker, you can play either version of this game and you won't have to worry about the nitty-gritty.

What You Need

✔ **3 or more players**
✔ **A grassy field**
✔ **A flashlight**

What You Do: "It" Version

1. Pick someone to be "It." (If you can't choose, have an adult pick a number—whoever guesses the number gets to be It.)

2. Designate a special jail area for the players who get caught.

3. It counts to 50 with his or her eyes closed. The other players scramble to hide.

4. Using a flashlight, It searches for the others. The flashlight must remain on and uncovered at all times.

5. After spotting someone in hiding, It shines the light on that player and calls out the person's name.

6. When a player is caught he or she goes to jail until everyone else is caught.

7. The last player caught then becomes It.

What You Do: "Pairs" Version

1. Everyone picks a partner.

2. Each team creates a special secret flashlight code (like 1 short and 1 long flash or 2 short flashes). Have a grown-up make sure all the signals are different.

3. Turn off the flashlights and have the grown-up count to 50 while everyone separates and runs away on their own.

4. At the count of 50, all players flash their signals.

5. Team members try to recognize their secret signal and find each other. The first two people to find each other win.

Old-Fashioned Movie Movements

You can use your flashlights to make a cool old-movie look. One person is the performer. Everyone else takes their flashlight and flickers it at the performer. Because of the flashing lights, it looks like the performer is making jerky motions. It's pretty neat. It really looks like an old movie. Try it! You can even do this as part of a game of charades. It's especially fun when you're acting out a movie title.

Talking in Codes

Morse code has been around since the days of the telegraph. ("What's a telegraph?" you ask. It's an old-fashioned machine used to transmit messages over long distances —very popular before telephones were common; today, not so much.) Morse code is a great way to communicate messages through either sound or light. If you and a partner memorize the code, you can talk to each other with your flashlights.

The chart on the right shows you how to "say" letters and words in code. Each dash rep-

resents a long flash (shining the flashlight for two seconds) and each dot is a short flash (quickly turning it on then off).

Leave a short pause (1 second) between letters and a longer one (3 seconds) between words. You might want to have paper and pencils to write down your messages and their codes until you know Morse code by heart.

Here are some sample words and phrases to flash at your friend's tent:

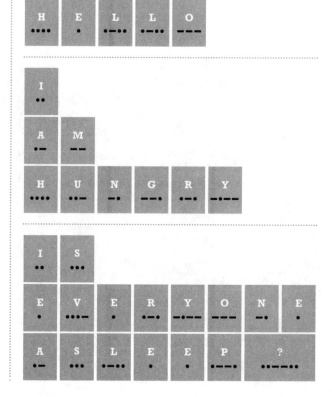

Morse Code

A ●—	**B** —●●●	**C** —●—●
D —●●	**E** ●	**F** ●●—●	**G** ——●	**H** ●●●●	**I** ●●
J ●———	**K** —●—	**L** ●—●●	**M** ——	**N** —●	**O** ———
P ●——●	**Q** ——●—	**R** ●—●	**S** ●●●	**T** —	**U** ●●—
V ●●●—	**W** ●——	**X** —●●—	**Y** —●——	**Z** ——●●	**0** —————
1 ●————	**2** ●●———	**3** ●●●——	**4** ●●●●—	**5** ●●●●●	**6** —●●●●
7 ——●●●	**8** ———●●	**9** ————●	**Period** ●—●—●—	**Comma** ——●●——	**?** ●●——●●

Dog

1. Bring your hands together palm-to-palm, and stretch them out in front of the light so they look like a single hand.

2. Curl your left hand into a fist that sits against your open right hand.

3. To make the eyes/forehead, bend the index finger on your right hand in half.

4. Cross your thumbs, making a V for the dog's ears.

5. Wiggle your right pinky up and down. This is the dog's mouth. Try to move only your pinky! If you can't stop moving your other fingers, too, use a hair elastic to hold them together. Is this cheating? Maybe, but it works!

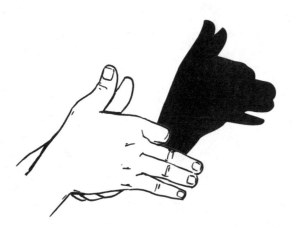

SHADOW

Use your hands to create your very own puppet show. With a tent, sheet, or boulder as your screen, have an assistant point a flashlight at your hands from about five feet away. Put your hands about a foot in front of the flashlight's beam. It'll take

Ostrich/Dinosaur

1. Lift your right arm up to shoulder height and bend the elbow so your hand is eyebrow height. This is your ostrich.

2. Tuck your thumb behind your palm to make the eye. Curve the tips of your index and middle fingers so they're squeezed behind your ring finger.

3. Move your pinky for the mouth.

ANIMALS

some experimenting to find the perfect distance away from the light and the screen; your shadow should be large and sharp.

Once you get the hang of it, try making the animals move. Add silly voices, and you'll have your own little movie.

Flying Bird

1. Hold both hands in front of you with your palms facing up.

2. Cross your right wrist over your left, and link your thumbs.

3. Keep your fingers tightly closed and flap your hands as wings.

4. Adjust your hands in front of the flashlight beam so the shadow of the bird can be seen flying.

Rabbit

1. Hold one hand out in front of you, fingers up. Turn the palm facing you.

2. Curl in your pinky and ring finger and hold them down with your thumb. Push up your ring finger slightly to create a hole—this will be the rabbit's eye.

3. Your index finger and middle finger are the ears. Point them both up in a V shape, then tilt your middle finger down a bit.

4. Turn your wrist away from you slightly, and you should be able to see the rabbit's eye on the wall. You can wiggle the rabbit's ears if you like, or give him front paws by twisting your other hand, tucking it behind the wrist of the first hand, and bending the forefinger and middle finger of the second hand so they poke out slightly.

GHOST STORIES

Darkness has blanketed the sky, dinner is winding down, and people begin to huddle around the campfire. The shadows dance across everyone's face, and the fire flickers and pops. Faces look different. Distant sounds take on a distinctly unnerving tone. It's the perfect time for telling ghost stories!

Here are some classic examples of campfire tales that have been told over the years. You can also make up your own, or you might even do some research at the library before you leave home to find ghost stories set in the area where you're camping.

People hear (or tell) a version of this story on almost every camping trip. Add your own details to make it really convincing.

One night last spring, my Aunt Ellen and Uncle Jim were heading home after visiting my cousin Bill at college. It was a dark and moonless night. Aunt Ellen and Uncle Jim were laughing and talking about the great time they'd had at dinner with Bill and a few of his college pals. Then, suddenly, they saw a young girl in the road! She was all alone and soaking wet.

Ellen grew worried, and she made Jim stop. "She must be lost, Jim!" she said. "Young girls shouldn't be out at this time of night. And look! She's soaked to the skin!"

Jim stopped the car. They backed up to where the girl was standing—she hadn't even budged—rolled down the window, and asked if she needed any help. The girl was shivering. All she wore was a thin little dress, which was soaked through.

She didn't say a word.

"What's your name, honey?" said Ellen.

The girl didn't reply. She just looked straight ahead and shivered.

My aunt asked if she needed a ride home, and the girl nodded. My uncle got out of the car and directed her to the backseat. The girl was shaking, so my uncle gave her his fleece jacket, which she put on silently. Uncle Jim, feeling cold himself, put on the heat, too.

My aunt and uncle wondered if anything bad had happened to this girl, but they didn't want to scare her, so they just quietly drove her home. She pointed the way to her house.

My aunt asked her if she should call 911 or bring her to the police, but the girl just shivered and shook her head no.

Eventually they drove down a winding gravel lane just off Bowery Beach Road. The lights were on. The name on the porch said Griffin. Before my aunt and uncle could even get out of the car, the girl opened the door and ran into the house.

Jim and Ellen looked at each other. Ellen wanted to ring the bell and ask if they could help—or at least talk to the parents. But Jim thought the whole thing was too weird. They sat in the car and talked about what to do. The car was still freezing cold even though the heat was on full blast.

My aunt finally just got out of the car and walked up to the porch. Jim didn't want her to go alone, so he went, too.

They rang the bell. Eventually an old man came to the door.

"Do you folks have a granddaughter who may have been lost tonight?" my aunt asked. "We picked up a beautiful young girl in a dress who was soaked to the bone, freezing cold, and looked very, very lost," she continued.

The man's face went white as a sheet. His wife had come up behind him. She shared her husband's tortured expression.

"Lily," she whispered. And both of them looked as if they would cry.

"We just dropped Lily off and she ran inside. I think she may need some help. I wonder if something awful happened to her tonight," said Ellen.

The Hitchhiker

The older woman screamed and sank to the floor in a faint.

Ellen and Jim were dumbfounded.

The older man cradled his wife and wept.

"You've made a mistake," the man said. "Our daughter, Lily, was killed 40 years ago this very night. She was killed in a car accident on prom night."

"But who was that girl we dropped off?" asked Jim.

"It's NOT our girl! She's buried in the cemetery near the town center. Now please leave!" cried the old man and slammed the door.

Now my aunt and uncle were really freaked

out. They didn't say a word to each other as they went back to the car.

They had driven only a mile or so when—suddenly—they came upon a sign for a cemetery along the road. They looked at each other, wide-eyed. Jim stopped the car.

"What in the world are you doing?" asked Ellen.

"I don't know . . . I . . . I just want to see something," Jim replied.

They got out of the car and held hands tightly as they wandered into the cemetery. Suddenly Jim's grip tightened. Ellen turned to see what had stopped Jim in his tracks.

It was a gravestone. It read "Lily Griffin 1950–1967."

The earth over the grave was fresh.

And lying on top—still wet, still cold—was Jim's fleece jacket.

The Golden Arm

This classic tale scares folks silly. Read it through silently once before telling it to the crowd. Before the last line, get ready to reach out and grab your neighbor. And try to sit next to the bravest person in the group; it will add a thrill to the climax.

Once there was a man with a golden arm. Though he had lost his real arm in an accident years before, the golden arm was comfortable, and he was proud to show it off. One day he told his wife that when he died, she must bury him with the golden arm. The wife found his request strange, but promised to carry out his wish. When the man eventually died, the woman buried him with his golden arm just as she had promised.

Years passed, and the wife began to run low on finances. She had to sell her house to pay off her debts, and moved to a small apartment on the edge of town. She ate very little, and just managed to squeak by on a meager allowance. Life was tough. And she began thinking about how much that old golden arm might've been worth. At first she dismissed the thought outright. She felt guilty and awful even thinking of it. But after a few more months of stale bread for breakfast, lunch, and dinner, the woman could not put those thoughts to rest. At first she told herself that her husband wouldn't have wanted her to suffer; he would've wanted her to have the arm. She reasoned that she did, in fact, fulfill her promise, as she had buried him with the arm. It wasn't worth anything to him now, which seemed like such a waste. Finally, one dark night, she gathered her courage and a shovel, and went to the cemetery to dig up the golden arm.

She dug and dug until she finally unearthed the arm. It was beautiful, glowing in the moonlight. She tucked the arm under her coat and made her way home. "No more stale bread!" the woman thought as a storm gathered in the night sky. The rain poured down, and the wind blew.

The woman finally made it home, cold, wet, and tired. She didn't know what to do with the arm, so she brought it to bed with her. All night she shivered, unable to get warm.

The wind raged outside. Its howling almost sounded like a whispering voice.

"Briiiiiiing baaaaack my goooooolden aaaaaaarm!"

The voice sounded far away, and the woman thought she must be imagining it. She put a pillow over her head, but the voice only grew louder. From the other side of her front door, she heard:

"Briiiiiiing baaaaack my goooooolden aaaaaaarm!"

She shook her head, trying to convince herself that she was just imagining it. She buried her head under the pillow again.

Then the voice seemed even closer, and it sounded clearer now!

"Briiiiiiing baaaaack my gooolden aaaaarm!"

The woman screamed at the top of her lungs, but she couldn't be heard as the screaming wind burst the window open. Terrified, she shivered uncontrollably under her blankets.

The woman knew something was in the room with her. She could sense it. She was terrified, but she had to peek. She drew the blanket back ever so slightly, and there it was— a tall figure, white and ghostly.

It said, "I'mmmmmm here!"

The woman was petrified. She couldn't even scream as the thing slowly glided toward the bed.

"I'mmmm staaaanding by your beeeeeed!

"I'MMMMM PULLLLLING DOWWWWWN THE BLANKET!

"I'MMMMMMM GETTTTTING INNNNNN YOURRRRRR BEDDDDD!"

The woman was so scared she couldn't even breathe.

And then . . .

[Get ready to grab your neighbor] It GRABBED her!

There are a few versions of this next story, some scary and some funny. This is the creepy and suspenseful version, with a surprise ending.

One sunny, hot afternoon, four young friends said good-bye to their parents and headed out for a camping sleepover. Brothers Kai and Leo, and their friends Cort and Trenton had all been camping quite a bit with their families, but this was their first adventure on their own. They were all very excited.

They spent the afternoon swimming, hiking, and laughing. As the sun set, they made a campfire and cooked dinner. Darkness fell, and the owls started hooting. The crickets chirped, and the night became louder. Though they didn't say anything to each other, the boys were a little on edge, and they huddled closer to the campfire.

The heat of the day had left now, and a low cloud of fog from the nearby lake hovered around the boys, making it difficult to see anything in the woods.

Leo began telling a story that he had heard from his friend Hazel.

"Did you guys know there was an old prison near here years ago?" Leo started.

"It was on a foggy summer night, like this one, about 50 years ago, that something strange happened. A bus was winding along the road just over there, carrying a single convict to the prison. The man was criminally insane, according to the tag on his prison uniform. On either side of him in the back of the bus, there was a prison guard who never doubted for a minute that this criminal was crazy. The prisoner was very tall and had huge broad shoulders and strong arms. His thick wrists were handcuffed and his muscular legs were chained together. To make sure he wouldn't run or kick at anyone, the warden had added an old-fashioned ball and chain, which he had found in a prison storeroom. The thick chain was clamped to the

prisoner's right ankle, and on the end of it was a 25-pound iron ball that had become rusted bright red.

"The prisoner sat quietly as the bus rolled along. His eyes were closed, and he had a smirk on his face. The guards thought the prisoner was asleep, so they let their attention wander. They gazed out the window at the foggy night. Then suddenly, the bus lurched—the driver had swerved to avoid hitting a deer that had wandered into the road. One of the guards lost his balance and fell into the prisoner, who wasn't sleeping at all. As soon as the guard fell, the convict knocked him out cold with one punch.

The other guard leapt up to subdue the prisoner, but the prisoner elbowed him in the face, and—as the guard struggled to get up—the convict hit him with the iron ball before he had so much as a chance to cry out.

"The maniac searched both guards for the keys to his shackles. He found ones to remove the cuffs and the leg irons, but he could not find a key for the ball and chain. Meanwhile, the bus was still moving along, as the driver had no idea what was going on behind the screen in the back of the bus.

"The convict picked up the iron ball again, smashed the wire-glass window to the cab of the prison bus, and grabbed the driver. The bus swerved all over the road and finally ran into the deep ditch beside the road, crashing into a large tree. You know that huge stump at the entrance of this place? That's the tree! Well, no one could have survived that crash because the whole bus went up in flames. The thing is—they found the bodies of the guards and the driver, but they never did find the body of the convict. They say he still haunts these woods to this day."

Leo finished his story and looked around at the three boys who were staring at him wide-eyed.

"GOTCHA!!" he yelled. "You guys look so spooked!"

The boys dissolved into laughter, and Kai, Cort, and Trenton tackled Leo and began wrestling.

Then a faint noise came from the woods. A pair of headlights shimmered in the fog and stopped right at the big stump. The lights went out.

All the boys stopped playing and stared out at the fog. The crickets had stopped chirping, and only the crackle of the fire could be heard.

They heard a faint sound. Step . . . draaaag, step . . . draaaag, step . . . draaaag.

It got louder and closer. The boys looked at one another in disbelief.

"I thought you made it up!" said Trenton frantically.

"I did!" said Leo.

"Ssshhh!" whispered Kai. They all strained to listen. In the trees, somewhere nearby, they heard it again, this time faster:

Step . . . drag . . . step . . . drag . . . step . . . drag . . .

A deathly silence followed. The boys hardly dared to take a breath. The fog was so thick they couldn't see a thing.

Everything was quiet as a graveyard.

Then they heard a sound. Someone was coming close to their fire: slow footsteps along with the sound of something dragging along the ground.

The sound came closer.

Closer.

Suddenly it stopped, right there in front of the fire.

The boys couldn't stand it anymore.

A tall, muscular form stepped into the firelight. The boys screamed!

"Easy, guys!" said Kai and Leo's dad, pulling four big sacks into the firelight. "You forgot your sleeping bags!"

A Final Note: *There's nothing like camping out. Be it in your backyard or the backwoods, camping is all about spending time together, having fun, adventuring, and exploring the amazing outdoors. We're so lucky to live on such a beautiful planet and to share it with such awe-inspiring creatures and natural features.*

Keep your eyes open. Wonder. Wander. And explore with respect and thoughtfulness.

Happy Camping!

EXTRAS

Who Goes There?, the Singing Camper's Book of Silly Songs, and Index

Who Goes

Sometimes you can tell an animal has been around not by seeing it, but by seeing what it left behind. Just like people, animals leave behind tracks when they walk. Unlike people (hopefully), they also leave behind poop, which is known as scat. To see which critters have crept over your park, you can do some scat-and-

There?

track sleuthing. The tracks on the following pages are pictured at their actual size (or close to it) to help you on your search. (The poop is not at actual size—do you really want a big pile of poop staring you in the face?—but most photographs include references to show you how big or small it is.)

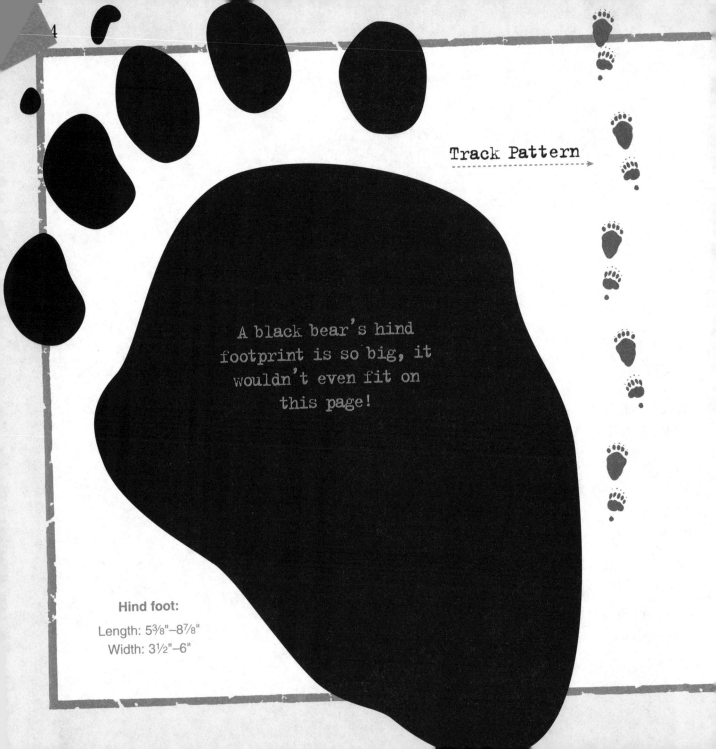

Track Pattern →

A black bear's hind footprint is so big, it wouldn't even fit on this page!

Hind foot:

Length: 5⅜"–8⅞"
Width: 3½"–6"

Black Bear

Black bears are large and furry forest dwellers. They can measure five feet at the shoulder, with the largest males weighing in at a hefty 500 pounds. In the summer and fall, black bears love places near the water where juicy berries, grasses, insects, and fresh water are plentiful. Bears are magnificent foragers— they'll eat anything they come across—including garbage, dead animals, and camp food. Black bears have nonretractable claws they use for climbing, digging, and hunting.

Scat

Front foot:

Length: 3¾"–8"

Width: 3¼"–6"

Grizzly Bear

The largest of the brown bears, the grizzly gets its name from the look of its fur, not from being cranky. Grizzlies mainly dine on berries, roots, insects, fish, and mammals, but they will eat just about anything if need be.

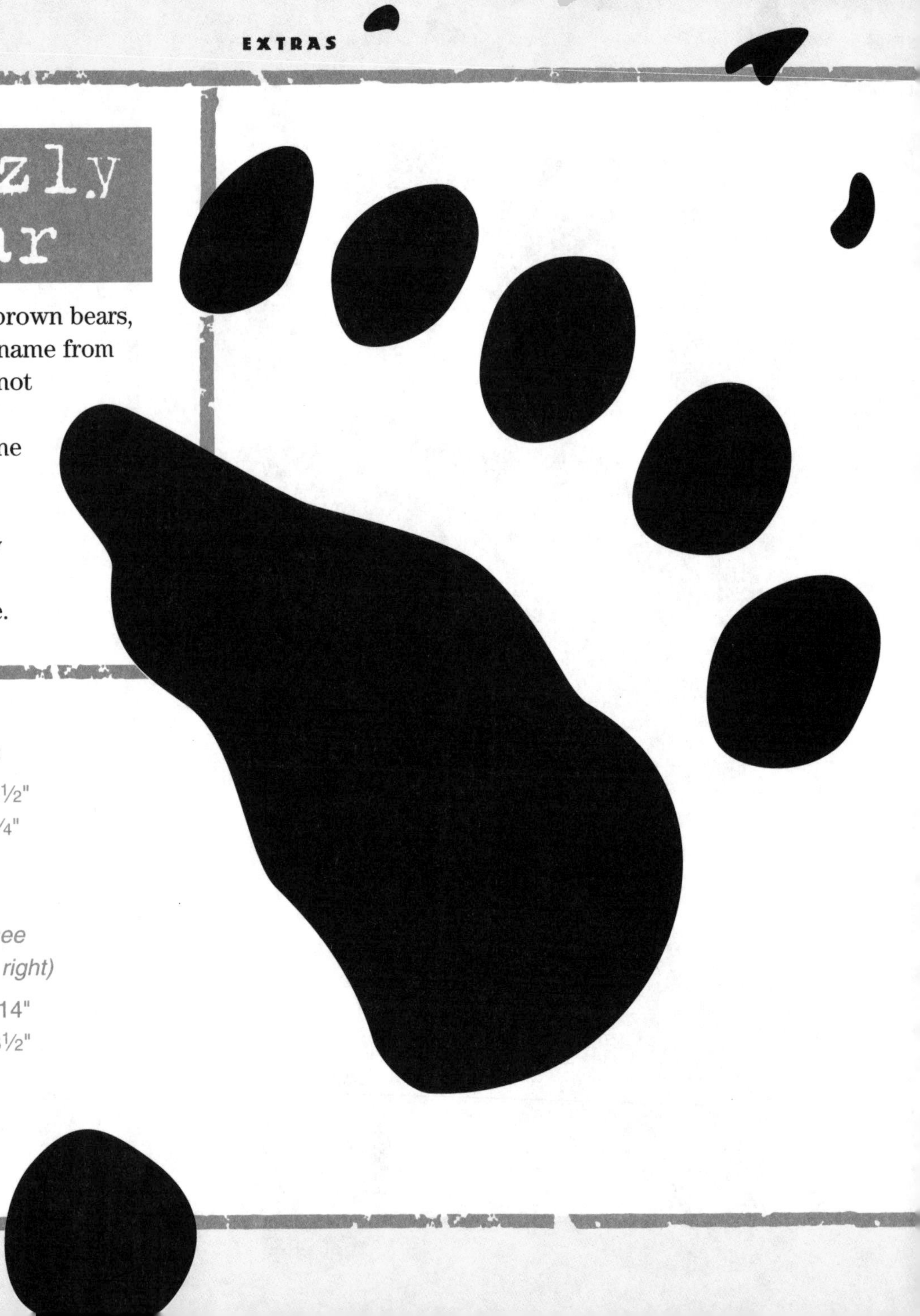

Front foot:

Length: 7"–13½"
Width: 5"–5¾"

Hind foot:

(not shown, see track pattern on right)

Length: 8¼"–14"
Width: 4⅝"–8½"

Track Pattern

Grizzly Bears have long, curved claws that they use to dig, pry off tree bark, and hunt.

Front foot:
Length: ¾"–1"
Width: ⁷⁄₁₆"–⁷⁄₈"

Hind foot:
Length: ½"–⁷⁄₈"
Width: ⁵⁄₈"–¹⁵⁄₁₆"

The chipmunk is a tawny brown, furry critter with black and white stripes over its eyes and down its sides. It's very small —only about 5 to 6 inches long—and has a 3- to 4-inch-long, slightly bushy tail. Chipmunks tend to hang out in and around trees. You'll hear a sharp "chuck-chuck-chuck!" if a chipmunk notices you before you see it.

Scat

Coyote

Coyotes are among the most adaptable animals in the U.S. and they can be found in a wide range of habitats, from the foothills of forested mountains to southwest deserts to urban areas in between. A close relative of the wolf and dog, coyotes are famous for their yipping howls. Listen after sunset for the high-pitch calls that help the animals keep in touch with one another over long distances. Coyotes are most active early in the morning and at sundown. Most move around in pairs or packs, although some go off on their own.

Front foot:

Length: 2¼"–3¼"
Width: 1½"–2½"

Track Pattern

Hind foot:

Length: 2⅛"–3"
Width: 1⅛"–2"

Scat

Opossum

These animals often play "'possum" with their predators, which is another way of saying they play dead. Like kangaroos, opossums are marsupials—mammals that develop and carry their young in a pouch on their belly.

Front foot:

Length: 1"–2 5/16"
Width: 1 1/4"–2 1/2"

An opossum has long thumbs, and you might see a tail mark with its tracks.

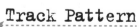

Track Pattern

Hind foot:

Length: 1 3/16"–2 3/4"
Width: 1 1/2"–3"

Scat

Rabbit

Rabbits' teeth never stop growing. They are born without fur (it grows as the babies, called kits, get older), and when rabbits mature, they can jump more than 36 feet.

Like the squirrel and the chipmunk, a rabbit lands with its big back feet in front of its smaller front feet.

Track Pattern

Front foot:

Length: 1"–1⅞"
Width: ¾"–1⅜"

Scat

Hind foot:

Length: 1¼"–3¼"
Width: ⅞"–1¹³⁄₁₆"

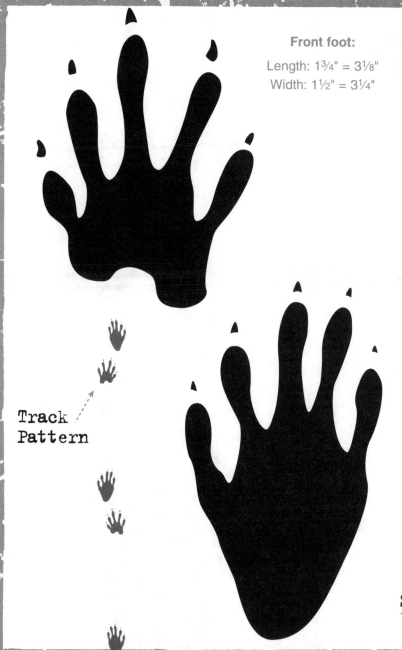

Front foot:
Length: $1\frac{3}{4}$" = $3\frac{1}{8}$"
Width: $1\frac{1}{2}$" = $3\frac{1}{4}$"

Track
Pattern

Hind foot:
Length: $2\frac{1}{8}$" = $3\frac{7}{8}$"
Width: $1\frac{1}{2}$" = $2\frac{5}{8}$"

Raccoon

These black-masked, ring-tailed animals are excellent swimmers and climbers and can adapt to many environments. They've been known to live in dens made out of old logs, piles of brush or rubble, caves, and even under houses. In the wild, raccoons eat berries, nuts, leaves, grasses, mice, fish, frogs, and crustaceans. In more urban areas, they are amazing scavengers adept at opening garbage cans, bags, and boxes.

Scat

Porcupine

This cat-size creature is covered from head to tail in long, hairlike quills. The porcupine defends itself with its quills, slapping at a predator with its tail and releasing the barbed spikes into the other animal's skin. Ouch! A slow-moving rodent, porcupines live in hollow trees or piles of rock or brush, and they eat leaves and bark.

Front foot:
Length: 2¼"–3⅜"
Width: 1¼"–1⅞"

A porcupine's tail, with its quills, will leave a line of marks with its tracks.

Track Pattern ----→

Hind foot:
Length: 2¾"–4"
Width: 1¼"–2"

Scat ←-----

Skunk

Although skunks can make a big stink (they spray nasty-smelling stuff from beneath their tail to ward off predators), they're actually very shy. Skunks eat insects, fruit, berries, birds, and small rodents.

Front foot:

Length: 1⅝"–2¹⁄₁₆"
Width: 1"–1³⁄₁₆"

A skunk's back feet have two rounded pads, or lobes, and the front feet have longer claws for digging.

Track Pattern

Hind foot:

Length: 1¹⁵⁄₁₆"–2"
Width: ¹⁵⁄₁₆"–1³⁄₁₆"

Scat

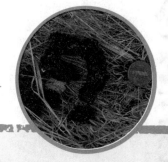

Beaver

Beavers cannot breathe underwater, but they can hold their breath for up to 15 minutes. This is great news for the animal, since it spends so much time in the water, building and tending its home. Beavers are the largest rodents in North America, and the second largest in the world (the biggest rodent in the world is the capybara).

Front foot:

Length: 2½"–3⅞"
Width: 1½"–3½"

Scat

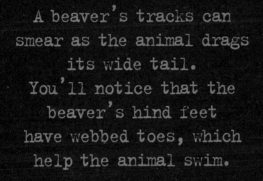

A beaver's tracks can smear as the animal drags its wide tail. You'll notice that the beaver's hind feet have webbed toes, which help the animal swim.

Track Pattern ---------->

Hind foot:

Length: 4¾"–7"

Width: 3¾"–5¼"

Red Fox

These small relatives of dogs and wolves have black-tipped ears and a white-tipped tail. Foxes are fast, alert, and adaptable, and have keen senses. They are omnivores, which means they will eat just about anything, including leaves, grasses, berries, small animals, insects, and garbage. The best times to spot a fox are dawn and dusk. Foxes don't hibernate, so you should be able to see them year-round.

Keep an eye out for animal fur in fox scat.

Scat

Track Pattern

Front foot:

Length: $1\frac{7}{8}$"–$2\frac{7}{8}$"
Width: $1\frac{3}{8}$"–$2\frac{1}{2}$"

Hind foot:

Length: $1\frac{5}{8}$"–$2\frac{1}{2}$"
Width: $1\frac{1}{4}$"–$1\frac{7}{8}$"

Front foot:

Length: 1⅝"–2½"
Width: 1⅜"–2⅝"

Bobcat

Bobcats take their name from their short, bobbed tail. Their fur is tan or brown with dark brown spots or stripes. Bobcats are generally not interested in humans (they eat rabbits, rodents, and occasionally deer), but if you see one or its tracks, make loud noises to alert the cat and scare it away.

A bobcat's claws retract, so they don't leave marks when the bobcat walks.

← **Track Pattern**

Hind foot:

Length: 1⁹⁄₁₆"–2½"
Width: 1³⁄₁₆"–2⅝"

Scat ┈┈┈┈>

White-tailed Deer

The white-tailed deer has a patch of pure white hair on the underside of its tail. When threatened, the deer flips its tail, flashes the white, and flags danger for other deer as it runs away. The white-tailed is a graceful animal, with a body length of up to 6 feet, a height of about 4 feet at the shoulder, and a tail up to 11 inches long. It feeds on fruit, nuts, leaves, and grasses, and likes to chew on the bark, buds, and twigs of woody plants.

Track Pattern

Front foot:

Length: 1⅜"–4"
Width: ⅞"–2⅞"

Hind foot:

Length: 1¼"–3½"
Width: ¾"–2⅜"

Scat

Track Pattern

Wild Turkey

Weighing up to 25 pounds and measuring up to 3 feet high, the wild turkey is the largest North American ground bird. Surviving on insects, nuts, berries, and seeds, they roost in low tree branches. Wild turkeys can fly for short distances and run in short spurts at speeds of up to 35 miles per hour.

Both feet:

Length: 3½"–4½"
Width: 3¾"–4¼"

Scat

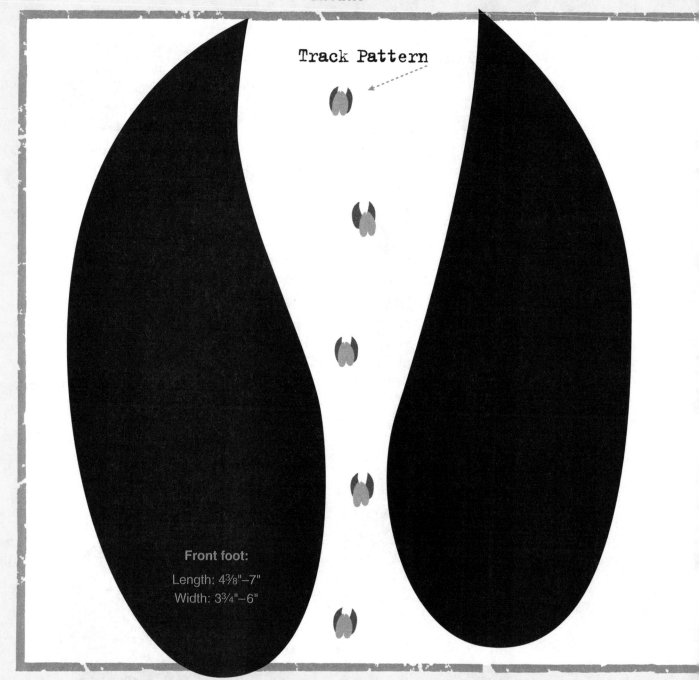

Track Pattern

Front foot:
Length: 4⅜"–7"
Width: 3¾"–6"

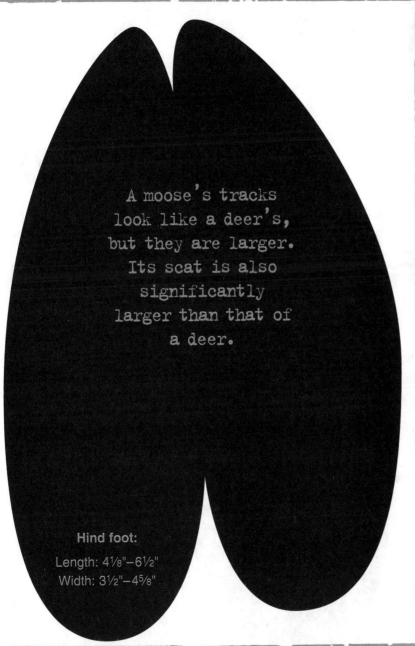

A moose's tracks look like a deer's, but they are larger. Its scat is also significantly larger than that of a deer.

Hind foot:
Length: 4⅛"–6½"
Width: 3½"–4⅝"

Moose

Moose are the largest members of the deer family. These gentle giants can stand up to 7 feet tall at the shoulder, and a male moose can weigh half a ton. The males have a set of antlers that can span an amazing 6 feet! Moose shed and regrow their antlers each year. They are fast moving but surprisingly quiet. They spend much of their time knee-deep in water, munching on floating plants. Try looking for moose in the early morning on the shores of lakes and ponds.

Scat
- - - - - - - ->

Snapping Turtle

You don't want to make a snapping turtle angry. The freshwater reptile gets its name from its fearsome, beaklike jaw. Though the snapping turtle typically avoids confrontation while in the water, it is known to strike rapidly and aggressively if disturbed on land.

You can find the snapping turtle as far south as Ecuador, and as far north as Canada. It hangs out mostly underwater, feeding on small animals and water plants.

It is distinguished from other turtles by its muscular legs, long tail, and sawlike edges on the back of its shell.

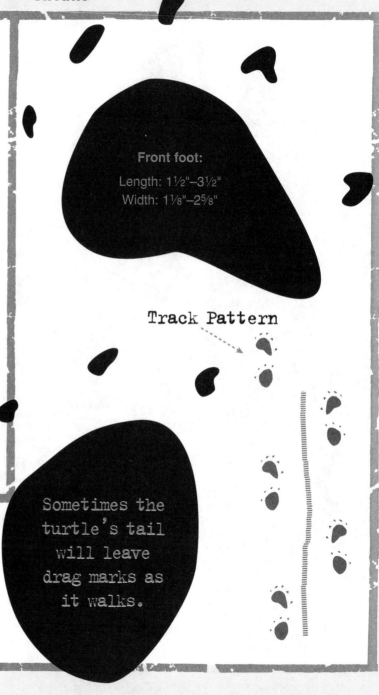

Front foot:

Length: 1½"–3½"
Width: 1⅛"–2⅝"

Track Pattern

Sometimes the turtle's tail will leave drag marks as it walks.

Hind foot:

Length: 1½"–3½"
Width: 1⅛"–2⅝"

Scat

Both feet:

Length: 2⅜"–2¹⁵⁄₁₆"
Width: 3¾"–7½"

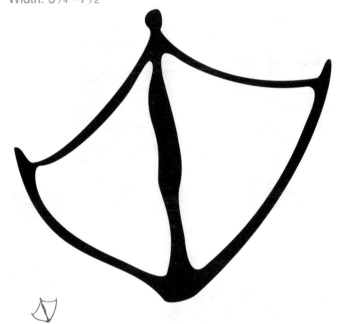

A duck's three toes
are webbed.

Wood Duck

Wood ducks nest in trees near the water. The male has a very distinctive look: a long tail, a green head with a crest, and iridescent blue-green and chestnut feathers on its back and breast. Golden feathers cover its belly, and white stripes appear on its head. The female is more gray-brown without the crest. You won't hear a wood duck quack. The male makes a whistling "zeet" that rises and falls, and the female makes a loud "oo-eek, oo-eek" while taking flight.

Track Pattern ←- - - - - - - - - -

Scat - - - - - - →

Wolf

Wolves live, travel, and hunt in packs. A wolf's sense of smell is more than 100 times greater than that of a human.

Front foot:
Length: 3¾"–5¾"
Width: 2⅞"–5"

Wolves often have hair in their scat.

Scat

A wolf's tracks are not much different than a large dog's. You can distinguish them by habitat, as wolves live farther away from humans, mostly in the northern United States, Canada, and Alaska.

Track Pattern

Hind foot:
Length: $3\frac{3}{4}"$–$5\frac{1}{4}"$
Width: $2\frac{5}{8}"$–$4\frac{1}{2}"$

Garter Snake

Garter snakes give birth to live babies, unlike other snakes, which lay eggs. Typically 20 to 40 babies are born at a time. And some people think having triplets is a big deal!

A snake's tracks look like wavy lines, because it uses its whole body to move.

Front foot:

Length: 1¼"–1¾"
Width: ⅝"–1⅛"

Hind foot:

Length: 1¼"–3¼"
Width: 1"–1½"

Track Pattern

You may come across old snake skin more frequently than snake scat.

Scat

Snakes molt, or shed, several times a year, often shedding their skin in one whole piece.

A squirrel has tiny tracks with short curved claws. When running, a squirrel's hind legs land ahead of its front legs.

Gray Squirrel

Gray squirrels actually come in many colors. Shades of gray are most common, obviously, but you'll also find ones that are brown, white, or black. Squirrels are foragers, which means they gather their food and store it for later. You'll often see squirrels collecting acorns and other nuts in the fall—they stash these goodies for eating in the wintertime, when food is scarce.

Scat

The Singing Camper's
Coming of the Frogs

This silly lil' ditty is sung to the tune of "Battle Hymn of the Republic."

1st VERSE:
Mine eyes have seen the horror
of the coming of the frogs.
They are sneaking through the swamps,
they are lurking under logs.
You can hear their mournful croaking
through the early morning fog.
The frogs keep hopping on.

CHORUS:
Ribbit, ribbit, ribbit, croak, croak
[Repeat three times]
The frogs keep hopping on.

2nd VERSE:
The frogs have grown in numbers,
and their croaking fills the air.
There's no place to escape to

Book of Silly Songs

'cause the frogs are everywhere.
They've eaten all the flies
and now they're hungry as a bear.
The frogs keep hopping on.

REPEAT CHORUS

3rd VERSE:
I used to like the bullfrogs,
liked to feel their slimy skin.
Liked to put them in my teacher's desk
and take them home again.
Now they're knocking at the front door,
I can't let those frogs come in.
The frogs keep hopping on.

REPEAT CHORUS

4th VERSE:
They have hopped into the living room
and headed down the hall.
They have trapped me in the corner
and my back's against the wall.
And when I open up my mouth
to give a desperate call,
This is all that's heard:

REPEAT CHORUS

Clementine

This is a classic campfire song, and a sad one at that.
Sing it with gusto.

1st VERSE:
In a cavern, in a canyon,
Excavating for a mine,
Lived a miner, forty-niner,
And his daughter, Clementine.

CHORUS:
Oh my darling, oh my darling,
Oh my darling, Clementine
You are lost and gone forever,
Oh my darling, Clementine.

2nd VERSE:
Light she was, and like a feather,
And her shoes were number nine,
Herring boxes without topses,
Sandals were for Clementine.

REPEAT CHORUS

3rd VERSE:
Drove her ducklings to the water
Ev'ry morning just at nine,
Hit her foot against a splinter,
Fell into the foaming brine.

REPEAT CHORUS

4th VERSE:
Ruby lips above the water,
Blowing bubbles soft and fine,
But, alas, I was no swimmer,
So I lost my Clementine.

REPEAT CHORUS

5th VERSE:
In a churchyard near the canyon,
Where the myrtle doth entwine,
There grow roses and other posies,
Fertilized by Clementine.

REPEAT CHORUS

6th VERSE:
Then the miner, forty-niner,
Soon began to peak and pine,

Thought he oughter join his daughter,
Now he's with his Clementine.

REPEAT CHORUS

7th VERSE:
In my dreams she still doth haunt me,
Robed in garments soaked with brine,
Though in life I used to hug her,
Now she's dead I draw the line.

REPEAT CHORUS

8th VERSE:
Listen fellers, head the warning
Of this tragic tale of mine,
Artificial respiration
Could have saved my Clementine.

REPEAT CHORUS

Found a Peanut

Sing this song to the tune of "Clementine" on page 360.

1st VERSE:
Found a peanut, found a peanut,
Found a peanut just now,
Just now I found a peanut,
Found a peanut just now.

2nd VERSE:
Broke it open, broke it open,
Broke it open just now,
Just now I broke it open,
Broke it open just now.

3rd VERSE:
It was rotten, it was rotten,
It was rotten just now,
Just now it was rotten,
It was rotten just now.

4th VERSE:
Ate it anyway, ate it anyway,
Ate it anyway just now,
Just now I ate it anyway,
Ate it anyway just now.

5th VERSE:
Got a bellyache, got a bellyache,
Got a bellyache just now,
Just now I got a bellyache,
Got a bellyache just now.

6th VERSE:
Called the doctor, called the doctor,
Called the doctor just now,
Just now I called the doctor,
Called the doctor just now.

7th VERSE:
Cut me open, cut me open,
Cut me open just now,
Just now he cut me open,
Cut me open just now.

8th VERSE:
Found a peanut, found a peanut,
Found a peanut just now,
Just now he found a peanut,
Found a peanut just now.

The Littlest Worm

Since this song is an echo song, it is best to sing it in two groups.
One group leads the song, with the second group singing the echo
everytime the (echo) signal appears. When there is no echo signal,
the lead can sing alone or everyone can sing together.
Your groups can be divided equally or one person can
sing the lead and the rest can follow.

1st VERSE:
The littlest worm (echo)
I ever saw (echo)
Got stuck inside (echo)
My soda straw (echo)
The littlest worm I ever saw
Got stuck inside my soda straw.

2nd VERSE:
He said to me (echo)
"Don't take a sip (echo)
'Cause if you do (echo)
Down I will slip." (echo)
He said to me, "Don't take a sip,
'Cause if you do, down I will slip."

3rd VERSE:
I took a sip (echo)
And he went down (echo)
Right through my pipe (echo)
He must have drowned (echo)
I took a sip and he went down
Right through my pipe, he must have drowned.

4th VERSE:
He was my pal (echo)
He was my friend (echo)
There is no more (echo)
He met his end (echo)
He was my pal, he was my friend
There is no more, he met his end.

5th VERSE:
Now don't you fret (echo)
Now don't you fear (echo)
That little worm (echo)
Had scuba gear (echo)
Now don't you fret, now don't you fear,
That little worm had scuba gear.

Do Your Ears Hang Low?

Feel like livening up your hike? Watch your step, because this song is guaranteed to cause a fit of giggles.

1st VERSE:
Do your ears hang low, do they waggle to
and fro?
Can you tie them in a knot,
can you tie them in a bow?
Can you throw them o'er your shoulder
like a continental soldier?
Do your ears hang low?

2nd VERSE:
Do your ears stick out, can you waggle
them about?
Can you flap them up and down
as you fly around the town?
Can you shut them up for sure
when you hear an awful bore?
Do your ears stick out?

3rd VERSE:
Do your ears stand high, do they reach up
to the sky?
Do they hang down when they're wet,
do they stand up when they're dry?
Can you semaphore your neighbor
with a minimum of labor?
Do your ears stand high?

Index